Spiritual Vagabondry and the making of a Rabbi

Jeremy Gordon

Spiritual Vagabondry and the making of a Rabbi

Jeremy Gordon

new london
synagogue

Masorti
Judaism

First published in 2015
A Masorti Publications book

ISBN 978-0-9518002-3-2

© 2015 Jeremy Gordon

Designed by Martin Colyer.

Genizah A store of used items of sacred significance in Judaism. As a matter of Jewish law such items shouldn't just be discarded even as they fade and are no longer fit for their original use.

Cairo Geniza A store of over 300,000 documents built up over a thousand years recovered from the attic of the Ben Ezra Synagogue, Egypt. It contains much that is mundane, but also some extraordinary gems still capable of moving and shaping what we, as Jews, thought we knew of ourselves, our tradition and our faith.

Spiritual Vagabondry A selected tour of my personal Genizah.

CONTENTS

Introduction

On Hubris, the Making of a Rabbi, and the Making of This Book

The ancient collection Pirkei Avot has a teaching my rabbinic colleagues and I understand quite differently from other, more sensible souls. The instruction *aseh lecha rav* clearly means 'seek out those wiser' or, literally, 'greater,' than yourself. My own interpretation cum translation – and there is no escaping the hubris involved – is 'make yourself a rabbi.'

The hubris of becoming a rabbi isn't one of confusing personal opinions with those of the Divine. I know perfectly well ordination involves no magic; there is no theological difference between a rabbi and any other human being. The real hubris lies in believing, somehow, that ordination is a required response. I became a rabbi because I couldn't escape the belief that there was a particular voice only I could bring to the millennial unfolding of a Jewish narrative; a voice that would go forever unheard if I didn't pack myself off to yeshiva and seminary.

I began my own rabbinic journey sixteen years ago, and ever since then an irregular stream of other potential rabbinic students have come to share their own hopes and fears as they reach, or escape, the same interpretation of the phrase *aseh lecha rav* as I felt. I've told each that there is only one reason to become a rabbi – the impossibility of doing anything else that will let you feel fulfilled. That's been true for me, but I'm not sure it's enough. You also have to believe in your rabbinic possibility, the importance of your being a rabbi. Certainly as a rabbi giving weekly sermons you have to believe that in twelve minutes, on an ongoing basis, you can share something with your community that they can't get from reading the papers, chatting with friends, or even reading a book written by rabbinic scholars who know far more than you ever will. If there is hubris in offering a collection of sermons and other writings, it's only an aspect of the necessary hubris of seeking ordination in the first place.

The school newspaper at my wonderful primary school was called *Chip Wrappings* – today's newspaper being tomorrow's chip wrapper. It's a salutary – and entirely accurate – way to consider much of what I do. Nothing is as out of date as yesterday's sermon. The Torah scroll rolls on, the congregation move on. Often it feels as though they have moved on before they even get to Kiddush, and usually I'm at peace with the fleeting nature of rabbinic engagement. But not in every case. In May 2014 I marked a decade in the rabbinate. I've looked back at – gevalt – 500-plus sermons clogging up my hard drive, and lectures and articles shared in the most diverse places. I felt, and again there is no escaping the hubris, some deserve a fate better than an eternity spent as a silicon chip wrapper.

The works shared here are an imbalanced lot. This volume is not an accurate reflection of the subjects on which I speak most often, and there's plenty of good stuff left out. I've chosen talks and pieces that sit together across a series of themes, some chosen because of their importance, others because of the way they read (not everything that sounds meaningful from the bimah reads well). I've also included a number of pieces that chart my journey over the last ten years, both professionally and personally. I hope they are of interest. The articles and sermons included have had the occasional edit since they were first aired, and each is introduced briefly by a passage in which I share a thought on how and why it came to be.

RABBIS ALONG THE WAY

This is also an opportunity to consider those who have helped make me a rabbi: my own rabbis, some ordained, others not yet ordained, and some never to be ordained. At every turn I've been taught and inspired by so many remarkable teachers in ways I could never have imagined as I embarked on this path. This is the story of their impact on me. I am more grateful to them all – and many others – than I could ever express.

I grew up at New London Synagogue when Rabbi Louis Jacobs z"tl was in his prime. I never had a personal relationship with Louis as a child, and as I began to prepare for serious rabbinic study I felt sadness that I had never discovered the worlds of mishnah, midrash, or parshanut from one of their greatest scholars. But as my journey unfolded I realised how much 'Louis Torah' I had imbibed, eavesdropping on sermons and just being a part of the community at New London. My serious Jewish journey began when Claire Strauss suggested I would enjoy Limmud – she was right. Michael Kagan, Aviva Zornberg, and Laurence Kushner blew open my mind and fired a desire to explore my Jewish tradition, a tradition, I realised at the age of 25, I had never even remotely understood.

I began to spend time with Jonathan Wittenberg, who remains a wonderfully supportive mentor and colleague; Yehoshua Engleman; and Rafi and Jaq Zarum, who hosted me for my first ever Shabbat lunch. Back at Limmud, the following year, I remember squeezing into a packed room to hear Neil Gillman share extracts from Abraham Joshua Heschel's *The Sabbath*. I was already thinking of training for the rabbinate, but was torn between studying in Israel or London. I arranged to meet Neil, who advised me to consider New York's Jewish Theological Seminary. My excitement about studying at JTS took off over three days spent in New York sitting in on classes and talking with students and faculty. Sarah Graff, in particular, helped me wrap my head around the terrifying notion of scrambling up the mountain that stood between my ignorance of rabbinics and my dream of becoming a rabbi.

To prepare for formal seminary studies I headed to Jerusalem, where I had an extraordinary year at the Conservative Yeshiva. I felt the Yeshiva would be a perfect home for this first year of full-time rabbinic study from the moment I first walked through the gates. There I found the breathtaking inspiration of Steve Wald, the discipline of Josh Kulp and the gentle decency of Mordechai Silverstein, my *Maggid Shiur* (regular Talmud teacher). It was also at the Yeshiva that I met Ari Vernon, who would be my closest study partner for six years. How Ari put up with my dyslexia and Aramaic illiteracy I don't know. Jerusalem also gave me the opportunity to begin a relationship with Chaim Weiner, whose deep knowledge and gentle guidance has shaped me in so many ways.

On my scoping trip to New York I asked as many students as would listen who their favourite teachers were. Their recommendations as to the faculty members I would, in turn, find most inspirational were excellent. But I remember one student sharing a list of names I didn't recognise. 'What do they teach?' I asked. 'Oh,' came the response, 'they aren't on faculty, they're my fellow students.' So many of the students at JTS were inspirational. Certainly it was through the women amongst them that I began to understand what a female voice could bring to a Jewish tradition that had been deaf to the insights of half its members for two thousand years. Joanna Samuels, Paula Mack-Drill, and Melissa Wientraub changed my sense of the need to open up rabbinic Judaism for all, and Joanna, along with Paula and her family, offered in different ways a home away from home in a country that, for all its familiarity and linguistic similarity, remained inalienably foreign. Menachem Creditor, Brett Spodek, and Kenny Richmond were also hugely important colleagues on my student journey. Beyond JTS, Daniel Bush was an extraordinary friend and fellow 'spiritual vagabond' (a term inspired Avivah Zornberg's *The Beginning of Desire*).

None of this belittles the impact of JTS's extraordinary faculty on my learning. I loved discovering midrash with Burt Visotzky and Talmud with Joel Roth. I've never met a deeper reader of the Bible than Stephen Geller. David Roskies finally taught me how to read – at the age of 30. Mychal Springer reminded me of the importance of learning with the heart and not just the head. Steve Brown helped me understand more about what it means to teach than I could have guessed. I could go on. The classes and the student body were tremendous, but negotiating the strange American academic-cum-religious environment of JTS was tough. Without the support of Bill Lebeau and Allan Kensky in the Dean's Office I'm not sure I would have made it.

New York was a wonderful city in which to think about becoming a rabbi, and I drew huge inspiration from the synagogue that is my model for a passionate and committed Jewish life – B'nai Jeshurun. Roly Matalon inspired me, and Anne Ebersman – for whom I worked as BJ's teen director – was incredibly supportive. I returned to England an ordained rabbi! My first position was at St Albans Masorti Synagogue. I couldn't have wished for or imagined a more supportive, or responsive, community. So many families and individuals hosted and fed me and helped me understand how to be a rabbi. I owe more than I can fully express to Liz Oppedijk, and her family, who paved the way for me at SAMS and much else; to Nick and Sarah Grant, whose hospitality could serve as a model for *avraham avinu*; to Laurence Harris and Claudia McQuillan, who supported me as chairs; and to all the families who took such care of me: the Bakers, Barnetts, Freedmans, Osters, Phillips, Rabins, and others – with particular apologies to those I have left out. I also owe a great debt to Rafi Kaiserblueth for taking up the rabbinic reins at SAMS after I moved on.

In 2008 I joined New London Synagogue, in so many ways coming home, ordained and now a family man. My children run along the same corridors and hide in the same nooks and crannies I did as a child. I still can't quite get over the notion that this is the place that has me as its rabbi. There are too many people to whom I owe such success as I have had at New London. But I want to express particular appreciation to Milton Woolf, who led the search committee that resulted in my appointment; my chairs, Adrian Marks, Julian Dawes, and Stephen Greene; my colleagues on the bimah, Stephen Cotsen and Jason Green; and all the office staff, in particular Ronnie Cohen and Jo Velleman and Kala Jerzy and Frances Goldberg, who have had the unenviable task of managing my diary and much else. I also owe a great debt to my rabbinic predecessors: Reuven Hammer, Chaim Weiner, and, of course, Louis – which brings me back to where my Jewish journey began.

THANK YOU

I'm grateful to Meira Ben-Gad for proofreading this manuscript – any remaining failures are entirely mine – and Martin Colyer for shepherding the manuscript into publishable form, and for the cover design. Thank you also to the angels whose financial support have allowed this book to come to fruition. They include an anonymous donor and the family of Woolfe and Fay Popeck. I am particularly honoured the family chose to honour their parents' memory by helping with this endeavour. I'm also grateful to New London Synagogue and Masorti Judaism for their assistance.

AND MORE IMPORTANTLY

The story is told of the rabbi with ten years' experience who finds a box he doesn't recognise at home. He asks his wife about it, and she tells him it's her secret box and he shouldn't open it. The temptation, however, is too great. One day, when the wife is out, the rabbi opens the box. Inside he finds three apples and £100. He puts the box away, but can't handle the mystery. He admits everything to his wife, asks to be forgiven for opening the box, and pleads to know why she is keeping apples as a secret. 'Well,' responds the wife, 'whenever you give a bad sermon I put an apple in the box.' 'Hmmm,' thinks the rabbi, 'ten years and only three apples – not too bad.' 'And then,' continues the wife, 'when there are a dozen apples I sell them for a couple of pounds.'

Becoming a rabbi is the second best thing I have done these past ten years. I was married less than three weeks after being ordained, and I fall in love again every day with Josephine and our children. I've had the honour of celebrating over 150 marriages this past decade. What I feel, regardless of whatever I say under the *chuppah*, is that if they find in each other a fraction of the love and support I've received from my wife they should count themselves truly blessed. My children, Carmi, Harry and Eliana are my greatest inspirations and also serve to remind me that cuddles are more important than even Talmudic passages. The love of both my parents, Martin and Angela, remains hugely important to me, and the incredible support I get week in, week out from my mother and Bob is an incredible gift.

To God, creator and source of all, *modeh ani lifanecha* – I am grateful for everything received from You.

CHAPTER 1

A Job for a Jewish Boy

*The pieces in this chapter represent a
professional biography cum manifesto –
why am I doing what I am doing?
Each derives from a key stage in my rabbinic
journey; my decision to train for the
rabbinate, the induction speech I gave at
St Albans Masorti Synagogue and my
'interview' sermon and then induction speech
at the synagogue I serve today, New London.*

Why Did You Decide to Become a Rabbi?

{2012}

This is my least favourite question, certainly my least favourite question asked on those rare occasions when I get out to a social function, or while I'm waiting to pick up my children from a drama class. It's not just that the decision consumed virtually every moment of three years' waking – and sleeping – thought, and being asked to reduce that journey to an 'on one leg' aphorism reduces the most important decision of my life to a bumper sticker. It's not just that I would rather talk about the richness I find in Jewish life and scholarship and hope that people get how much all this means to me. It's also that the decision is now buried beneath every step I've taken in this process, and that means that when I do try and wheel out a narrative I feel uncomfortable with its own truth. It's as if the process of retelling and the passage of time have resulted in a narrative which isn't false, but is not entirely true either.

That said, the story of deciding to throw a life up in the air to pursue something as crazy as a 21st-century career in the rabbinate makes a party piece of sorts. I'm aware it's a little churlish to complain. This is based on a version I shared as part of BBC Radio 2's *Pause for Thought* slot. At 5:45am, in amongst the pop standards, a religious teacher pops up to share 400 words hopefully worth the attention of the million or so people listening, even at such an early hour. This attempt at a story contains more emphasis on a single moment of epiphany than felt true at the time – but it is, at least, no less true than other versions of the story. It was broadcast in the week of the London Marathon. My London Marathon experience was in 1996.

I decided to become a rabbi at mile 23 of the London Marathon. I had been working at the BBC but I needed a new goal. Run the marathon in under four hours seemed to tick various boxes.

I wasn't especially fit, so I set myself a regime and got on with training. Through the winter I clocked up miles, sometimes in snow and, usually, in darkness – I emerged into the spring fit, fit like I had never been before.

On the day of the marathon I loved the camaraderie of runners making their way to the mass start. Off we went, mile after mile after mile. At mile 23 I knew I was going to do it; I was going to run a marathon in under four hours. Then I saw another competitor, green, crawling along the road, completely spent. I told her I would walk her to the ambulance and she pleaded I didn't. 'They won't let me finish,' she said. She was right. So I put one of her arms over my shoulder and off we went together.

And my mind ticked through these thoughts:

'I'm not going to finish the marathon in four hours anymore.'

'Actually I don't really care about finishing a marathon in four hours.'

'Actually I don't really care about my fancy job at the BBC, what I really want to do is be a rabbi.'

There is something that happens at mile 23 of a marathon. Biologically there is nothing left. Spiritually and emotionally everything is laid bare. Pretences, false hopes and expectations get pounded away, leaving nothing but honesty and heart. Encountering such moments of psychological nakedness is scary, but we should take opportunities to push ourselves out of our comfort zones. And we should muster the courage to listen to the voices that emerge when all the pretences are gone.

To those about to run a marathon, or plotting a journey to the extreme in any other way – good luck. Don't worry – you probably won't become a rabbi – but you might encounter a part of yourself that can give you strength, a sense of purpose and fulfilment. I did.

St Albans Masorti Synagogue
{2004}

My final year at JTS was strange. While my fellow
students were wooed with pulpit positions, in a milk
round similar to that I encountered during my final year
at university, I found myself sitting on the sidelines
a little. I had never planned to stay in the US after
ordination. And then a job became available in St Albans,
just outside London. I remember my first conversation
with Liz, chair of the search committee, wandering
around the balcony outside the JTS library. I was unsure
what I wanted, I couldn't get my head around a position
at a synagogue I had never visited. A trial weekend later
I had fallen for SAMS, its members, and everything
it stands for. I loved my four years as part of the
community and am proud not only of the contribution
I made, but particularly, the way the community has
continued to grow from strength to strength in the years
since I have left.

I made errors and miscalculations aplenty – as every
brand-new rabbi surely does – but SAMS never held my
lack of experience against me. I think they knew that I
was prepared to give my all to support the community
without making the error of confusing my own interests
with their broader interests and needs.

This is the speech I gave at my induction at SAMS. It was
a wonderful day, and I was honoured that so many of the
rabbis and lay leader of the movement came to support
me and the community. I started, as seemed compulsory,
with a joke. Amusingly that very joke was used by a
subsequent chair of SAMS at the induction of my
successor, Rabbi Rafi Kaiserblueth. That, in itself,
encapsulates what I tried to do at SAMS; I shared stuff
with them, they got it and moved on.

What with this being my first rabbinic job, and the first time I have had the opportunity to share with so many members of other Masorti communities my vision for a Masorti rabbinate, I thought I would share some fruits of my research into this question.

What ought a Masorti rabbi do?

Fortunately, it seems someone has already done some research on the perfect rabbi, and I am delighted to report their findings.

THE PERFECT RABBI

The results of an international survey indicate the Perfect Rabbi preaches for exactly fourteen minutes twice a week.

The Perfect Rabbi condemns sins but never upsets anyone.

The Perfect Rabbi works from 8:00 AM until midnight, and is dedicated to spending quality time with their family.

The Perfect Rabbi makes £100 a week, wears good clothes, buys good books, drives a good car, and gives about £100 weekly to the poor.

The Perfect Rabbi is 28 years old and has preached for 30 years.

The Perfect Rabbi has a burning desire to work with teenagers and spends all of his time with senior citizens.

The Perfect Rabbi smiles all the time with a straight face, because the Perfect Rabbi has a sense of humour that keeps them seriously dedicated to his work.

The Perfect Rabbi makes 15 calls daily on congregation families, shut-ins, and the hospitalized, and is always in his office when needed.

The report goes on to suggest that if your rabbi does not measure up, simply send this e-mail to six other synagogues that are tired of their rabbi, too. Then bundle up your rabbi and send him to the synagogue at the top of the list. In one week, you will receive 1,643 rabbis and one of them will be perfect.

Have faith in this procedure. One congregation broke the chain and got its old rabbi back in less than three weeks.

Sadly, as is so often the case, surfing the Internet doesn't produce solutions to complex questions. So I turned to the Talmud.

The single most told story in the Talmud, surely, involves a convert who comes to the great rabbis Hillel and Shammai to ask to be converted on the basis that either rabbi can teach him all of the Torah while standing on one leg. In the version of the story that everyone remembers, Hillel does the right thing and the convert goes away happy, while Shammai is a curmudgeon, vicious and obnoxious – he bashes the poor would-be convert over the head with a wooden plank.

The story ends with the convert telling everyone what a lovely rabbi Hillel is.

We might think the message of this little tale is 'Go Hillel.' Always keep the door open to any passing stranger, and no matter what you are asked, find a way to answer sweetly, kindly, and without scaring anyone away.

It's a daunting charge, to me as a rabbi, because a lot of the time, I side with Shammai. 'Teach me the whole Torah while I stand on one leg.' How absurd. After six years of full-time rabbinic study, all I know is that I have but scratched the surface of the well of knowledge that is Torah.

I know one other thing – that when we always make it simpler, more digestible, when we always boil down the complexities and the nuances, we turn Torah into a bland blob. Not interesting, not powerful, not capable of shifting me, my actions, and the way I view the world.

Torah on one leg is dangerous. You can misrepresent the truth, misrepresent people, misrepresent Torah itself.

In truth, I rarely get asked to explain all of Torah on one leg. But there is a different, and just as difficult, one-legged question I do get asked, a lot.

And I get asked it by Jews.

To tell you what this one-legged question is, I need to share a story. A mother is sitting with her seven-year-old son son in shul on Rosh HaShanah when the person who'll be leading the children's service comes by. He sees the young boy and sidles up to him to explain that in the children's service there will be no sermon. Rather, the rabbi is going to tell a story with questions, and he wants to brief the child on how to answer.

The answer to the first question, he tells the boy, is 'apple with honey.' He wants the boy to shout out the answer at the appropriate time.

'Apple with honey?' replies the kid, 'Fine. But what I really want to know is it possible to be traditional and modern at the same time?'

This is the one-legged question of my Masorti rabbinate. It comes in various forms and sometimes it is assumed rather than asked, but the underlying question is always about tradition and modernity.

'Rabbi – you're not going to give me a hard time about driving to shul on Shabbat, you're a modern kind of person, right?'

'Rabbi – we couldn't possibly move to a service which doesn't read all the Torah portion every week, that just wouldn't be right.'

'Rabbi – do you think women ought to be allowed to wear trousers to shul?'

'Rabbi – do you think women ought to be allowed to lead prayer services?'

Sometimes the questioner is looking for a traditional answer, sometimes a modern one, but there is always an expectation of receiving one answer or the other.

I am always being asked to stand on one leg or the other.

I once heard a commentator explain why Shammai couldn't answer the convert's one-legged question. Shammai knew that if you only have one leg to your Judaism, you will fall over. I think this is a brilliant insight.

One-legged Judaism is inherently unstable. It doesn't matter how brilliant an aphorism Hillel can manage, how witty an aperçu. If there is the only one pillar to a person's Judaism, they will never get it. They will never get what is so essential to being Jewish.

You have to have two legs, two poles, two answers to understand what it is to be Jewish.

Rabbi – are you traditional or are you modern?

I reject the choice. I need both, I am both.

I don't want to live my Judaism on one leg. God gave me two legs. God gave me two hands. One the one hand... On the other hand... Two legs, two hands, two opinions, sometimes working together, sometimes complimentary, sometimes contradictory.

That is exactly how I live my Jewish life, and exactly as I hope to function as a Masorti rabbi.

It's very easy to take potshots at Masorti rabbis. It's easy to take potshots at the Masorti movement. Where is the clarity? Where is the consistency? How come we can't make up our minds to be one thing or the other?

We get attacked from outside the movement, and I think we feel insecure ourselves, of our own bona fides. We don't trust our own hearts and souls.

We crick our necks over to see whether the less observant think we have gone too crazy frum.

We crick our necks over to see whether the Orthodox think we have finally, truly stepped beyond the pale.

Let 'em go, all those insecurities, all those worries – because Shammai was right. You can't do this Jewish thing on one leg. You need both legs to stand strong, and we, Masorti Jews, are uniquely placed to stand on both these legs. We are both traditional and modern.

In the one-legged version of Judaism you, I, all of us are forced into a monochromatic version of our faith. We are forced to choose between white and black. And I think we all instinctively shy away from such a stark choice.

But then we think of ourselves and our Judaism as grey, as wishy-washy, as neither one thing nor the other. And this is the greatest failing of our Masorti community – to believe that between the black and white lies only grey.

For the truth is that between white and black there lies an entire spectrum of colour: crimson, ochre, primrose, turquoise, cyan, magenta, and violet.

I'm a multi-coloured kind of a Jew.

That's why I'm a Masorti kind of a Rabbi.

I reject the choice between *either* tradition *or* modernity. I reject the one-legged choice between either black or white. But I also reject the notion that my Judaism is grey or wishy-washy. My Judaism contains all the colours of the rainbow.

I think, I hope, I pray that this rainbow Judaism will serve me well in my community, here in St Albans. I think, I hope, I pray that this rainbow Judaism will serve me well in the broader Masorti community.

Indeed, it turns out that that 'international survey' might actually have it right.

> The perfect Rabbi has to be on both sides of the table...
> ...Speaking out against sins but upsetting no-one.
> ...Making £100 a week and giving £100 weekly to the poor.
> ...Being 28 years old and having preached for 30 years.
> It doesn't look so easy, from here, even today.

But with the help of all of you here, *bsiata dshmaya* – with the assistance of the heavens – I'm hopeful.

I'm hopeful for my time at St Albans, and I'm hopeful for the Masorti movement in this country.

Thank you all, again, for all your support, both today, in the past, and especially into the future.

I look forward to a long, happy, and successful partnership.

Applying to New London – Here I Am
{2007}

This is the sermon I gave at my official interview
Shabbat at New London. I had had all kinds of
conversations with members of the search committee,
the trustees, and other groups, but this was my one
opportunity to address the community and set out a stall.
The struggle with sermons is always narrowing them
down to a single issue; especially on those occasions
when there is so much that could be said. On this
occasion I think I got it right.
Certainly, I got the job.

Thank this is, I think, the sixth time I have had the honour of addressing this community from this pulpit.

And it always feels a bit strange.

I still think of myself sitting over there somewhere, with my father.

I still think of myself, as a small child, hiding in the velvet curtains and pretending I had understood the sermon so I could join in the conversation between my parents as we walked home from shul.

And it feels particularly strange today, for me, to be applying to become the next rabbi at Louis' shul.

I'm reminded of a previous American presidential campaign where Dan Quayle, a man who couldn't spell the word 'tomato', tried to pass himself off as an inheritor of the legacy of JFK.

'Senator Quayle,' responded Lloyd Benson, 'I knew Jack Kennedy, I worked with Jack Kennedy. Senator Quayle, you are no Jack Kennedy.'

Other faith traditions have tales about the glory of having an occasionally errant child of a community wander away and look to return. Other faith traditions have tales of welcoming back the returning child with extraordinary delight.

But I don't think those stories reflect us, you and I, today.

I've spent almost five hours in interviews this past week facing questions and concerns. And there's been a lot of fear, a lot of anxiety. I am too much this, not enough that, what about the legacy of Louis?

I want, today, to explore what I understand by the burden of inheriting a fearsome and glorious spiritual inheritance, and what I understand by the command to carry a fearsome and glorious inheritance forward.

Today's Torah portion is the perfect *parasha* to explore these ideas; *Ve'eleh toledot*: 'And these are the generations'.

This week's *parasha* is the story of Isaac, an inheritor of a fearsome and glorious spiritual inheritance: a man who 'dug again the wells of water, which they had dug in the days of Abraham his father; and he called their names after the names by which his father had called them.'

Ve'eleh toledot: 'And these are the generations'.

This week's *parasha* is also the story of Isaac the ancestor: a man who bequeathed a legacy to the generation to come – to Jacob, Israel, to all of us sitting here today, some four thousand years later.

The unfolding of generations.
From one to another.

A story, about the unfolding of generations. It comes from Rabbi Jacob's charming autobiography.

Rabbi Jacobs has just been appointed to Anglo-Jewry's flagship congregation, the New West End, and he is, in his own words, indulging in some namedropping. He's telling of all the Lords and Ladies, the dignitaries and captains of industry, in the shul, and he recalls a moment just before his first Kol Nidrei service at the synagogue. He's standing in the vestry with the Third Lord So-and-So, whom he had only recently met.These are Rabbi Jacobs' words:

> Time was pressing and I suggested that we go into the synagogue for Kol Nidrei. The Lord replied that he did not want to enter the synagogue for a while and that he would explain why after the service. His explanation was that his grandfather, the first Lord, although a very observant Jew, did not hold with the Kol Nidrei formula and used to wait patiently in the foyer until this part of the service was over. His son, the second Lord, less observant and a little indifferent to the whole question would still wait outside

because his father had done so. The third Lord explained he personally didn't understand what it was all about, but felt obliged to carry on the family tradition.

I find this a sad tale; a tale of an emptying, a tale about the survival of the husk at the expense of the kernel.

A meaningless ritual followed for no particular reason other than the fact that his father had done it that way.

It's the kind of story that makes me fear for the future of our glorious spiritual inheritance.

It's a story that makes me fear, just a little, about this glorious synagogue.

I'm sure that as Rabbi Jacobs was writing this tale of his Lordship, he had in mind the famous story that closes Gershon Scholem's magisterial *Major Trends in Jewish Mysticism*. Scholem, of course, was much admired by Rabbi Jacobs, who chaired one of Scholem's lectures in London. The story of their Lordships certainly reminded me of this tale.

When [the founder of Hasidism] the Baal Shem had a difficult task before him, he would go to a certain place in the woods, light a fire and meditate in prayer, and what he had set out to perform was done.

When, a generation later, [his student] the Maggid was faced with the same task, he would go to the same place in the woods and say, 'We can no longer light the fire, but we can still speak the prayer' – and what he wanted done became reality.

Again, a generation later, Rabbi Moshe Leib of Sassov had to perform this task. And he too went into the woods and said, 'We can no longer light a fire, nor do we know the secret meditation belonging to the prayer, but we do know the place in the woods to which it all belongs, and that must be sufficient' – and sufficient it was.

But when another generation had passed and Rabbi Israel of Rishin was called upon to perform the task, he say down on his golden chair in his castle and said, 'We cannot light the fire, we cannot speak the prayer, we do not know the place, but we can tell the story of how it was done.'

Rabbi Israel died some 150 years ago, and most of us have forgotten even the story.

It's very easy to become maudlin at the passing of one generation. We mourn those we love. We mourn those who lit a beacon for us.

Even if we think, in theory, that we have 'got over' the mourning for a lost loved one, our losses prey upon us. Most particularly, when we face the all-too-concrete question of moving on – opening our homes and our heart to someone else – that's when our losses can haunt us most fiercely.

And in the face of this ferocity it is all too possible to cast any potential next partner as a fraud, as a failure, as not really 'my type'. It's all too possible to subject any incomer to a test that will break anyone.

I'm sure we have all done it.

It's a good thing to be scared about, if you are in the business of *ve'ele toledot* – the unfolding of generations.

And I am scared.

I was thinking about this particularly last week, in the context of Eliezer's attempt to find a partner for his master's son Isaac. I couldn't help but read this story from the perspective of a rabbinical search process.

Abraham sets out the brief: no-one from the daughters of Canaan, God forbid. And off Eliezer goes, loaded up with trinkets and baubles to attract some bright young thing for Isaac.

I wonder how Eliezer felt on the return journey, coming back with this stranger, someone to lead his family's future. Leading a search committee is a daunting task – Milton, I suspect you know this better than I. A lot of nerves and a good slice of fear.

I wonder how Rebecca would have felt, shifting a little uncomfortably on her camel at the prospect of spending the rest of her life with a man she had never met.

I wonder how Isaac would have felt, at the prospect of some new woman in his life.

Actually, while we know nothing about Eliezer and virtually nothing about Rebecca's feelings, we do know about Isaac – the suitor.

These are the words of Genesis (Chapter 24 verse 67):

> And Isaac brought Rebecca to the tent of Sarah his mother; and he took Rebecca and she was, for him, a wife, and he loved her; and he

was comforted after the death of his mother.

We know it works.

Oddly, there is virtually no rabbinic commentary on this verse, though a charming midrash[1] tells us that once Rebecca was installed as Isaac's wife a cooling wind – a *ruach*, a spirit, that had been lacking since Sarah passed away – returned.

We know it worked, but we don't know how.

There are no stories about Isaac and Rebecca going on dates in the foyer of the King David Hotel.

No clues as to what I can do, now, to help find a way to have you accept me as the next rabbi of this special community.

The verse is so stark in its simplicity –

He took her as a wife, and then he loved her, and then he was comforted.

Maybe there is wisdom in the order of the verbs. You have to commit before you can love. You have to love before you can be comforted.

Courting seems so much more complex these days. But I'm not sure it is possible to feel comforted until you fall in love again. And I'm not sure it is possible to fall in love without commitment.

It's easy to feel maudlin at the passing of a generation.

This is the very last Mishnah in Tractate Sotah. It is describing the end of a generation some 1800 years ago.

When Rebbi Meir passed away, there were no more great tellers of tales.
When Ben Azzai passed away, there were no more keen scholars.
When Ben Zoma passed away, there were no more great sermons.
When Rabbi Akiva passed away, there was no more honour for the Torah.

It goes on:

When Rebbe died, there was no more humility and there was no more fear of sin.

It's an almost terminally despairing view of Jewish life. Admit-

---

[1] Bereishit Rabba 60:16.

tedly, it was written at a time when it was hard to believe in a Jewish future. But we Jews are forbidden from *yeush*, despair – and by the time of the completion of the Gemarah this Mishnah has a different ending:

> Rabbi Yoseph turned to the teacher of the text and he told him,
> 'Don't include the piece about there being no more humility –
> *d'ika ana*: for here I am'.
> Rabbi Nahman turned to the teacher of the text and he told him,
> 'Don't include the piece about there being no more fear of sin –
> *d'ika ana*: for here I am'.[2]

Who did these fools think they were? Rabbi Yoseph, I knew Jack Kennedy, I worked with Jack Kennedy...

Actually I suspect they knew exactly what they were doing.

I love the idea that Rabbi Yoseph waits, while this whole litany of what is no more unfolds, until someone says there is no more humility. And this is the point he challenges. What holy chutzpah does that take!

The Mishnah can't be allowed to stand because it's too maudlin, and we are forbidden to despair.

I love the idea that the only possible response to what has passed, as one generation unfolds into another, is to say *'Ika ana'*. Here I am.

And so, *Ika ana*. Here I am.

And I don't know how to light the fire, I don't know the words of the Baal Shem's magical prayer, I don't know where to go in the forest.

But I do know the story.

I know Scholem's story, the story as it appears in *Major Trends*.

I know a whole bunch of Talmud and philosophy and theology and all that good stuff.

I know the story of this place, of New London Synagogue.

But more important even than all that, I know something else that the Baal Shem and the Maggid and the rest of them knew.

I know that there is something that needs to be done. A task which summons our attention and our best efforts.

And what is that task?

---

[2] Sotah 49b.

The same as it has always been.

We live in a world where the unfettered call of materialism spreads misery and threatens to rip the soul out of human beings, turning us into productive units, overpaid hamsters spinning our way round and round and round and not really getting anywhere.

We live in a world where religious idolatry – fundamentalism – has succeeded in destroying the World Trade Centres and threatens so much more horror.

Ve'ele toldot. Some things change and some just stay the same.

We are still the inheritors of Avraham Avinu, who broke the false idols of faux religious piety and struck out on a journey towards a life with decency, integrity and kindness.

The task is still not done.

The story is not at an end.

D'ika ana. I know this story. I know its past and I think I know its future. It's a future I want to share with you all, if you will do me that honour.

Shabbat shalom.

New London Synagogue
{2008}

There's a line in the TV series 'The West Wing' that struck me when I first heard it. One of the characters – a veritable powerhouse – is looking a little vague and tender. Another character inquires after her state of mind and she responds, 'I feel I am living the first line of my obituary.' I suppose if New London and its current rabbi start to find each other no longer a good *shidduch* I'll have to find a plan B, but I'm not planning on going anywhere. I'm living the first line of my obituary.

The shul I joined was in decline and suffering existentially. Many had lost a sense of what the community stood for. The demographic and financial data were gloomy. Numbers attending prayer services were down and the average age was up. We've come a long way. In the space of five years I've gone from bringing the average age of the community down to bringing it up. At every level, I believe, we are stronger now than we were when I arrived – testament to the huge efforts of so many members of the lay leadership and professional team.

This is the speech I gave at my induction at New London, a wonderful occasion for me and my family – now including two children. I began with thanks, and excavated the tale of the Perfect Rabbi I had used five years previously, at my induction at St Albans – I don't intend being inducted anywhere else for the foreseeable future and it's a good enough joke to warrant at least two outings in a career. Then I got down to the business of teaching Torah and setting out my task as rabbi of New London.

I'm doing something I spent a lot of time doing in my early years at New London – talking about the community, and even the history of the community, not as reportage or history, but as I wanted it to become. In a shul where others who had the temerity to 'follow Louis' were chastised by many longstanding members for their failure to 'get' New London, I refused to cede the definition of what New London had always stood for to anyone else – even if, as I told the story, I gave it gentle tweaks in the direction of where I feel the future of the community lies. It helped that I had joined New London in 1972, admittedly as a one-year-old, and it helped that, fairly quickly after I started as rabbi, new younger members joined and even came regularly.

The very first rabbinic text the small child would learn in the yeshivot of Eastern Europe went like this.

B'tallit ohazin shnaim. Two come before the court holding onto a single tallit, a cloth. One says – it's all mine. The other says – it's all mine.

This is how we begin to train a rabbinic mind. Solving problems, dealing with different tugs in different directions. *B'tallit ohazin shnaim*: Two have hold of a tallit.

I want to suggest what might be thought of as a Hasidic interpretation.

I want to suggest this tallit is us, the New London Synagogue, and that the two forces tugging at this tallit are our past and our future.

On the one hand, we are about our past: our great founding rabbi of blessed memory, the Jacobs Affair, the appalling way that Louis was treated again and again by the United Synagogue. We are the inheritors of all this.

On the other hand, we are about our future. Today, most especially, we are celebrating what it means to look forward and play our part in creating something better.

This presents a challenge, for me and for all of us. How do we stay true to our past, to the passion and the commitment that forged New London, while orientating ourselves towards new challenges that face us as a community, as a people, as citizens of a still-new century?

Im eshkachech... If we forget our heritage as Louis' shul, we abandon a spiritual heirloom almost without price. But we cannot become hidebound, fossilized, atrophied.

I have reread, these past days, Rabbi Louis Jacob's speech on the occasion of his induction at the New West End in 1954. And this is what Rabbi Jacobs had to say about this particular dynamic – the tug between past and the future.

> The analogy of the heirloom must not be pressed too far. An heirloom is set on its pedestal, admired from afar and only taken down and examined at close quarters at certain well-defined periods. This must never be the fate of the living Torah of Israel. It is not sufficient only to admire Judaism, to pay it homage two or three times a year and to feel somewhat uncomfortable in its presence during the rest of the year.

For a while, it has to be said, this shul felt a little like this heirloom on a pedestal, accumulating dust and gradually withering. But in more recent times our gaze has swung round. We believe in our future, we are living our future, and we are working for our future. There is a new lick of paint, we've had a spit and polish. We are ready to play again.

There have been changes, there will be more to come, but we are moving forward tugged by our past, inspired by our past, *inspired* by our founding narrative, inspired by what it means to be members of Louis' shul.

Between our past and our future. *B'tallit ohazin shnaim.*

Yet there is another way of looking at the tallit of that first rabbinic text, and the two forces tugging at us here, today. We stand between tradition and modernity. Between faith and reason.

On the one hand we are a traditional shul, committed to the liturgical foundation of our ancestors, committed to the traditional observance of Shabbat, of kashrut, of Torah and mitzvot. On the other hand we are a progressive shul, committed to modernity and engagement with the real world. We want to integrate what we know from the world of the academy into our commitment to our Jewish faith.

God created the world in six days... Of course we believe in the creation story as a foundational part of our Jewish experience, but we also know about quantum mechanics, about astral physics, evolution, genetics. *God gave the Torah to Moses...* Of course we believe in the revelation at Sinai as a foundational part of our Jewish experience, but we also know about higher biblical criticism, lower biblical criticism, biblical archaeology. We know about anthropology and the Ancient Near East.

If, God forbid, we let go of our commitment to understanding science – we let go of our commitment to understand how the world works – we can quickly look foolish, like a pathetic King Canute railing against the incoming tide. But if, God forbid, we let go of our commitment to faith – then we let go of what it means to treat every human being as a creation in the image of the Divine, we let go of the power and beauty of the Shabbat. If we do that we can quickly forget why we are here, we can forget the purpose of existence, we can lose our souls.

So we must hold onto both. Between tradition and modernity. Between faith and reason. *B'tallit ohazin shnaim.*

So we are here today, a tallit tugged between the past and the future, between faith and reason, between tradition and modernity.

Let me do one more tug: Inward looking and externally focused.

Being Jewish takes up a lot of time. It consumes a lot of our attention. We are called to rise up early in the morning, to run around like crazy people on a Friday afternoon, to schlep our pots and pans around every Pesach... the list goes on. On the one hand, being a Jew is about our own journey as Jews, proud of what we have, perfectly content to see other people pursue other paths while we tend to our needs. On the one hand we are internally focused.

But on the other hand, we believe we have a role in the world out there – in contemporary society. *L'taken olam b'malchut Shadai* – to heal the world under the kingdom of heaven.

This is the shul where the Dalai Lama spoke, back in 1972, fresh from his own experience of exile. This is the shul that founded the Newlon Housing Trust, a charity set up to provide reasonably priced housing for those living in what its founder, Philip Blairman, called situations 'reminiscent of the worst aspects of nineteenth-century slumdom'. The Newlon Housing Trust now provides housing in 7,000 properties.

That is our heritage.

The world is desperately in need of voices able to articulate a compassionate, contemporary religious message, able to engage with the most dangerous and important issues of our day: from how we treat this planet to how we treat the people who live on it, from matters of ecology to asylum seekers, from Darfur to the Middle East.

Internally focused and externally focused.

Hillel hayah omer im ain ani li mi li – uch'she'ani l'atzmi mah ani. Hillel would say, if I am not for myself who will be for me? But when I am only for myself, what am I?

My inclination, for what it is worth, is to be a little more externally focused. We should, as a shul, look to develop a voice that speaks to the most important issues of our day from a place grounded in faith and a commitment to *chesed v'tzedek*, loving kindness and justice.

B'tallit ohazin shnaim. There is a tension here, as we are held by the various tugs.

Some people don't like this kind of tension. Some seem to find this tugged place a little lacking in clarity perhaps, a little inconsistent, *nishta hin, nishta hair* – neither one thing nor another. We are easy to mock.

And so instead of holding both sides of the tallit, some of our critics drop one side or the other. They give in to the call of those who say that the tallit should be owned solely by one of the two competing voices.

And these competing voices are loud and attractive. The first voice is the voice of religious fundamentalism. We live in a world where the siren call of fundamentalism beckons both Jew and non-Jew.

But those who fall prey to the appeal of blinkered theological certainty are not doing God's will. They are rather shuffling backwards into self-deception and a self-imposed ghetto. And while it might be more comfortable in such a place, life in a ghetto comes at a cost. Once inside their ideological hidey-hole, these refugees from the real world find themselves under increasing threat from modernity.

The response, and we have seen it time and time again, is to build thicker and thicker walls, to create ever greater distance between their desire for a simple theology and the real, all-too-complex world.

That's when religion hurts people: when rabbis get treated badly, when good simple Jews get treated badly. We've seen it so many times. It is also when prime ministers get shot. And it is when planes get flown into towers.

Yielding to the call of fundamentalism, letting go of one tug on the tallit, might appear superficially attractive, but it is intellectually dishonest – and, worse, it is terribly, terribly dangerous. We must pledge ourselves to disagree with the first claimant who says *sheli cula* – the tallit is all mine.

Then there is the second claimant who also wants us to stop being tugged. The second siren voice is the voice of unbridled consumerism.

We live in a world driven by consumerism. You are what you can purchase. We tend the ticker of the stock market with more care than the ticker which is our heart. We monitor the ebb and flow of our bank balance with greater diligence than the ebb and flow of our relationships to our creator and our fellow human beings.

Yielding to this claimant on our tallit gives us something to measure, but we lose our souls.

We must pledge ourselves to resist those voices that claim, each in its own way, *sheli cula* – the tallit is all mine.

Standing at this pulpit is a bit like trying to stand on a tugged tallit, walking across a narrow bridge. But I am emboldened by this self-evident truth; there is no better way to live.

More than that, this life – balancing on a tugged tallit, navigating this narrow bridge – has vibrancy, it has nuance. It's beautiful, meaningful, bold, passionate, compassionate. Everything that I would want a life to be.

And this is the shul for this kind of religious life. This is the community who know, in their very bones, what it means to live with this holy tension. That is why I am so excited to be here, to throw my weight behind the sheer importance of this message: *The tallit must always be tugged.*

When I stood just there on the occasion of my bar mitzvah some years ago, Rabbi Jacobs gave me a charge – verses from my portion. 'Stretch out the site of your tent,' he taught me. 'Extend the size of your dwelling. Lengthen the ropes, drive the pegs firm' (Isaiah 54:2).

The guide ropes of our tent, here at New London, and elsewhere in our lives, must be pulled tight, they must be stretched – for in that tug is our greatest strength. We must never sag or droop, never let go.

For my part, I commit myself to this holy work.

We must refuse to let go of either side of this tallit. We must become evangelists for an approach to religious life that is more nuanced, more complex than that.

This is the path.

This is my kind of rabbinate. This is the leadership I hope to provide here, at New London Synagogue, my new congregational home.

This is the path of our past and our future.

I hope you will join me on it.

I want to conclude with words from our founder rabbi's 1954 induction address, because even half a century later I don't think anyone has ever put it better. I don't expect anyone ever will.

Said Rabbi Jacobs then, and say I now:

I hope that the Judaism I preach from this pulpit will be a courageous Judaism. To the best of my ability I shall see to it that no shallow, spineless Judaism, one demanding no challenge and presenting no sacrifice, shall be preached here. But I hope that I shall also see to it that no harsh, unsympathetic, inhuman interpretation of Judaism is voiced here.

'O my Creator, give me understanding that I may transmit your inheritance; Strengthen and uphold me that I may be far from weakness and fear.' [From the *Reshut* of the *sh'liach tzibur* – Rosh HaShanah.]

May You bless all the members of this holy congregation, prosper the work of their hands and bring joy into their lives, and may You always be with us as we continue to labour to do your will in sincerity and in truth.

And let us say,

Amen.

CHAPTER 2

A Rabbinic Family

Being a father while serving as a congregational rabbi isn't always easy (there aren't many jobs where one parents in public in quite the same way), but I know it's easier to be a rabbi/father than to be the child of one. There is (in the States, where else) a psychotherapeutic speciality of 'PKs' – preachers' kids.

I'm uneasy about sharing tales of my family from the bimah – rabbis' children should be able to grow up without having to worry that amusing anecdotes will become sermonic fodder – but I include, in this chapter, three sermons driven by my experiences as a father of three wonderful children.

We'll Take a Broken Leg
{2009}

This was the sermon I gave the week after Carmi,
our oldest son, broke his leg. It was round the time
of my wedding anniversary, and Josephine and
I had made complicated arrangements to leave Carmi
with various relatives and a nanny so we could escape
to celebrate *a deux*. Instead I spent the night at
the hospital with my firstborn.

A s many of you will know, my son, Carmi, took a shine to a cat playing on the pavement and followed the cat into the road, where he was hit by a passing, and thankfully not a speeding, car.

He's fine, he's broken his leg and is not sleeping so well.

But considering how much worse it could have been – we'll take a broken leg and not sleeping so well.

Language, of course, reveals so much.

What do you say about a three-year-old who chases a cat into the road and breaks his leg? *Baruch HaShem* – Thank God?

Is this good news or bad news? Is it a blessing from God, a curse, or a stark warning? Or just chance?

And how do you handle sitting in a hospital chair at three in the morning looking around the scarily named 'paediatric high-dependency ward', knowing that, in the other three beds and on the other chairs, are three sicker kids and three more desperate parents?

Odd, really, that this community was founded on an alleged blasphemy on the subject of how the Torah came to be written. All the words and all the pages and all the sermons on 'who wrote the Torah' amount to a pimple when you come face-to-face with the alleged blasphemies that threaten a serious engagement with questions of pain, loss, and suffering.

I want to share three reflections today.

The first clear response to pain and loss finds its origins in the

Talmudic tractate Brachot.[1] There is a blessing to be said on hearing bad news, and a different blessing to be said on hearing good news.

How do you bless, asks the Talmud, if a flood sweeps across your land, destroying all in its path? The good news is that the flood will bring increased fertility to the soil in the years to come. The bad news is that right now there has been destruction.

The answer is that you say the blessing on hearing bad news. As Jews, we are not supposed to transcend the sufferings of the moment.

There is, as I understand it, a Buddhist notion that perceived suffering, perceived bad news, should be sublimated into nothingness. That's not Jewish. We are allowed to weep, to cry, to cry out, to be scared, to feel loss. We are allowed – nay, we are commanded – to experience suffering as suffering.

Again, in Talmud Brachot, we are told the rabbis asked, what is suffering?

They said, losing the life of a child during the life of a parent. They agreed this was suffering.

They said, suffering from an illness. They agreed this was suffering.

They said, putting your hand in your pocket expecting to find two coins and only finding one coin. They agreed this was suffering.

This is a provocative idea. How can one possibly equate the loss of a child with putting your hand into a pocket to find less money there than one might expect?

The point, I think, is this: there is no experience of loss that the rabbis are prepared to deny. None of us is, or should feel, commanded to transcend our loss. None of us should feel we ought to 'get over it'. This is a bold and quite counter-cultural Jewish insight. I'm not sure society at large allows for us to suffer unless some vague threshold of awfulness has been reached. I'm not sure the world out there allows us enough time to experience our individual suffering without chivvying us through our darker moments and dragging us from our experience of loss into normalcy.

I often feel this at funerals for those who have passed away at

---

[1]   60a.

the end of a long life, perhaps a great life, a life full of achievement blighted only in its last years by illness or loss of faculties. So often I hear people expressing relief, which is of course understandable, but then, a month or so later they are in tears, they can't work out why they are still in pain. I often feel they've been dragged too quickly out of being allowed to be a mourner. We, those of us who suffer, shouldn't be pulled out of our moments of darkness just because society might think we've cried enough, just because society moves too fast and cares too little for our private grief.

So this is the first Jewish insight into the nature of bad news. Suffering and pain are bad, and should be allowed to be so. We should not rush into deeming everything okay.

The second clear Jewish insight is this – we must reject the notion that our goodness is in any way cosmically significant in terms of increasing our successes or keeping us safe from pain.

As we say in the morning service, *Lo al tzidkateinu anachnu m'palilim lifanecha* – 'We don't pray before you because of our righteousness, dear God.'

Who among us can suggest they are particularly blameless, particularly worthy? Certainly not your rabbi.

This is Rosh Hashanah and Yom Kippur Torah too. We don't ask God to reward us according to our acts of decency and kindness. We ask God to carry away our transgressions, wipe away our sins, cheat the scales in our favour. None of us could stand before the Great Throne of Justice proud of our successes. We all fail too frequently – rabbi, congregant, Jew and non-Jew alike.

There is, of course, a blessing to be said when we survive an encounter with mortality – *birkat hagomel*. It is an interesting response to being saved from disaster. It is a blessing in which we thank God for saving us *despite our failure to deserve being saved*.

So the second clear Jewish insight is that Carmi survived his run-in with the car not because of his goodness, or mine, but because of a grace unknowable and unquantifiable and beyond.

Sure, there are plenty of biblical passages that warn about impending disasters with a stark and simplistic 'you had better do

this or else' kind of logic, but – and here I agree with my frien
teacher, Rabbi Jonathan Wittenberg – these texts should be understood only as warnings before disasters occur. We are forbidden from using these texts, and the logic they might suggest, after
a disaster to try and explain why one child or another did or did not
survive, faculties intact. This is to claim a knowledge of God that is
beyond human grasp.

A third reflection – a reflection on our relationship with an unknowable and impossibly mysterious divinity.

Dear God, it's just not good enough.

I know all about the doctrine of freedom of choice and the Garden of Eden. And I know I, and the other 4.9-something billion people on this planet, need to take responsibility for our actions. We
need to accept responsibility for holding onto our kids so they don't
run into the road. But dear God, it's just not good enough.

The doctrine of freedom of choice moves me not at all.

Not if I want to pray to a good and kind God.

A couple of years ago, John Humphrys interviewed the Orthodox
Chief Rabbi, Jonathan Sacks, as part of a short series. Humphrys
couldn't get past the problem of the seemingly random nature of suffering, and Sacks couldn't find a way to justify a belief in a good and
kind God amidst the sorts of experience that haunted Humphrys.

"Twenty years ago", said Humphrys, "I went up to Lockerbie on
that terrible night when the Pan Am aircraft was blown up and the
bits fell on the town. Some bits fell on houses and some bits fell on
fields, and those people who were in the houses that were hit were
killed. And the thing that struck you walking around that ghastly
evening was the entirely arbitrary nature of it. The people who lived
in number 17 survived, the people in number 21 did not survive."

How could it be possible for a good and kind God to be behind
such cruel randomness? Humphrys wanted to know, and Sacks had
no good answer, for he was not prepared to give the answer I feel
compelled to give.

I don't believe in an all-powerful, wholly good and kind God.

I believe in a God, if such human emotions can be ascribed to the

God, who *sometimes* is good and kind, and *sometimes* is cruel, and *sometimes* is recklessly negligent in leaving us humans alone to do our worst. And *sometimes* walks away, and *sometimes* over-reacts, and *sometimes* is there for me and *sometimes* is not.

My images of God, drawn from the massive, sprawling, and uneven history of Jewish discourse, can't be subsumed into a single simplistic whole. There is too much variety in God's behaviour, too much variety in the tales we tell of God.

But this theology prompts a problem. If I, if we, don't believe in God as wholly good and wholly kind, what are we doing with our prayers? Why bother with all this fulsome praise if a bit of a plane could fall on our house without warning, without reason, without justice?

I had an insight into the answer to this question while in Africa. I was spending six weeks in Ghana, in a very under-developed community with a lot of cockerels. And the cockerels crowed at 2am, 3am, 4am, 7am, 9am, midday...

It turns out that cockerels don't only crow at dawn.

This came as a surprise to me, since the very first blessing we say as part of our synagogue service is one praising God for giving the cockerel the ability to distinguish between day and night.

Now I might have been surprised, but the rabbis wouldn't have been. They would have known, far better than I, the nature of the cockerel. So why would they institute a blessing thanking God for giving the cockerel the ability to distinguish night from dawn, when the cockerel crows all night and all day?

It must be that the rabbis want us to pray, not for the world as it is, but for the world we want to live in – a world of well-behaved cockerels.

It must be that the rabbis want us to pray, not about the God we experience, but the God we would wish to experience. A God who orders the chaos of the world, waking us only at dawn with the crow of the cock, and rewarding our efforts and forgiving our trespasses.

It must be that the rabbis want us to pray about a God who is good and kind in the hope that every time we open our lips and meditate in praise of the Divine, we fill the earth and heavens with more praise, more kindness and decency, and that this somehow helps.

Well, I believe that.

How could it be, asks the great twentieth-century theologian Franz Rosenzweig, that our pouring of goodness and kindness into the world doesn't result in the world being more full of goodness and kindness?

> Love cannot be other than effective. There is no act of neighbourly love that falls into the void. An act performed blindly must appear somewhere. This is the effectiveness of prayer. Prayer, though it has no magic powers as such, nevertheless, by lighting the way for love, arrives at possibilities of magic effects. It can intervene in the Divine system of the world. It can provide love with direction toward something not yet ready for love, not yet ripe for endowment with soul. Thus, prayer is always in danger of tempting God.[2]

We pray in the direction we want the world to be.

Non-one could pray for the world in which we now live. A world of comas and cancers, breakages and loss. We pray to tempt God, and to tempt the world in which we live into becoming a more decent, kind, and magical place.

Prayer works even if God doesn't deserve every word of our unadulterated prayer.

Prayer works, as it were, even if it doesn't snap us out of comas and cure us of cancers at that moment.

Three insights into a Jewish relationship with bad and scary news.

The first truth is that suffering and pain should be allowed to be bad. They should not be rushed into being deemed OK.

The second is that we are to be prohibited from claiming that success is anything other than grace, and we are to be prohibited from claiming that any suffering is deserved.

And the third is that prayer works, even if God is not all good and all kind, even if we fear our words fall into the void.

So I conclude these words with a prayer – the *birkat hagomel* I spoke of. The prayer to be said when a person has come into contact

---

[2] Franz Rosenzweig, *The Star of Redemption.*

with the threat of great injury. And a prayer that expresses a gratitude for a grace I know I do not deserve.

The sermon concluded with the blessing.

The Presumption
of Blindness

{2008}

Balak was my first Shabbat back after paternity
leave following the birth of our second son, Harry.
This sermon was given in his honour.

I feel a certain sympathy for Bilaam, whacking away at his donkey while we, gentle readers, know far better. It's a bit like watching poker on television. We know how the cards have been dealt. We know there is an angel, standing, sword drawn, in the way. It's only Bilaam who doesn't get it, who can't see.

And I'm drawn the point at which God opens Bilaam's eyes – *vayigol Adonai et einei Bilaam*.

The rabbis [1] feign surprise. 'What, was he previously blind?' they pretend to inquire. 'No,' they respond, 'this is just done to tell you that what the eye sees is a power held by God.'

This year, this week, this rabbinic comment reminded me of what is surely the most powerful articulation of the miracle of childbirth in rabbinic Judaism. It's from Kohelet Rabba. [2]

It was taught, at the time a babe is formed in the womb, there are three partners in its creation: the Holy Blessed One, its father, and its mother.
Its father implants the white in the child – the brain, the nails, the white of the eye, the bones and the sinews.
Its mother implants the red – the blood, the skin, the muscle, the hair and the black of the eye.
And the Holy Blessed One, may God's name be blessed, places ten things within the child. And these are they: the soul or spirit; the lustre of the visage; the ability to see; the sense of hearing; the speech from the lips; the strength of the arms and the legs' ability to walk; wisdom; understanding; counsel and intellect; and might.
And when the time comes to pass, the Holy Blessed One takes back

---

[1]   Tanhuma 10, Bmidbar Rabba 20:15.
[2]   Kohelet Rabba 5:12.

His part and leaves behind the parts of the mother and father before them. And the father and mother weep.

I want to talk about weeping, about seeing, about childbirth, and about God.

We say every morning, Blessed Are You God, *pokeach ivrim* – who gives sight to the blinded. The Hebrew *pokeach* suggests something being peeled away, like a cataract – bringing into focus that which had been a blur; making distinct that which had impenetrably fuzzy. This is a great blessing. It reminds those of us who have never experienced physical blindness of the gift of our sight. But more than that, I believe, it reminds us of something spiritual.

Kol ha'olam culo – an obscure midrashic text suggests – *b'hezkat sumim, ad shehakadosh baruch hu megalei eineyhem*. 'All the world is presumed blind, until the Holy Blessed One opens their eyes.' [3]

None of us sees until our eyes are opened – not even Bilaam. Indeed, Bilaam's encounter with the Divine on the way is almost a motif of the Bible. Here's an example from the passage we read on the first day of the New Year. Hagar sits cradling her son, who is dying of thirst, until – *vayifkach Elokim et eineha vatereh be'er mayim* – God peels back the blindness from Hagar's eyes and she sees a well of water. She's blind until that revelatory moment. Her ability to see the well which had been there all along required the direct engagement of God. To see is to experience the miracle.

Another example is the moment Joseph finally reveals to his brothers that the great Egyptian vizier they have come to see is none other than their own long-lost brother.

Vayomer Yosef el-echav ani Yosef. And Joseph said to his brothers, 'I am Joseph'.

Ha-od avi chai? Is my father alive?

V'lo-yachlu echav la'anot oto ki nivhalu mipanav. And his brothers couldn't answer him because they were... the verb, *nivhalu*, takes some teasing out – they were terrified, confounded, left stuttering in response.

This is what it is to see, finally, a reality hidden until revealed, as

---

[3]   Torah Shleimah footnote to Bmidbar 22-169, citing *'b'leket'*.

if by magic – revealed by means of the miraculous encounter with the Divine. This is what it is to leave *hezkat sumim* – the presumption of blindness.

One last journey into the tales of our ancestors.

Jacob flees from the murderous intent of his brother Esau and falls asleep en route to Haran. There he receives one of the greatest of all biblical visions – a ladder set on the ground, its top reaching the sky, and the angels of God going up and down.

He wakes and again, his language is broken. You can feel in the Hebrew the crashing impact of a moment's true sight in a lifetime's blindness. *Vayomer achen yesh Elokim bamakom hazeh v'ani lo ya-dati.* And he said, Wow, there is God in this place and I, I didn't know.[4]

There is a stutter, a breaking in.

Jacob is *nivhal* – confounded.

He has seen.

There are, perhaps, two great traditions of God-talk in our faith.

One tradition dates back to Maimonides and the great medieval rationalists. This tradition of God-talk is philosophical. It is theology in the true meaning of the term – the 'science' of the Divine. This tradition of God-talk is committed to rigorous, sober intellectual analysis.

But this dry, philosophical discourse has nothing to do with the experience of Bilaam, the sudden insight of Hagar, the confounding of Joseph's brothers, or the experience of waking in the morning and knowing that God was indeed in the very place where I set my head to rest.

These biblical encounters are connected to a totally different kind of God-talk, a shattering, ineffable, impossible reality that one only knows, that I only know, because on those rare moments when my life has been most precious, when I have felt most alive, I too have seen.

I have known, I have felt, in my soul.

---

[4] Using the translation of Everett Fox, who makes the 'redundant' *anochi* central to the experience of awakening.

These are moments when, just like our ancestors, I've been confounded, *nivhal*, lost in the enormity of what I have seen.

It's a little weird, this experience of the numinous.

We, those of us who have been touched by these moments of revelation, can seem a little bizarre, a little unhinged.

There is a fabulous moment in the Book of Samuel when King Solomon seems to be touched by the experience of the Divine – and the good King dances over the hills. 'Then the people said to one another, what has happened to the son of Kish? Is Saul off with the prophets?' (I Sam 10:11).

The people think their otherwise all-wise and serious monarch has lost it.

It's dangerous, playing with prophets, seeing with the spiritual cataracts removed, experiencing the confounding presence of the Divine.

Indeed, I'm worried that you, dear friends, might think me a bit unhinged; a little too 'off with the prophets' for a sober community such as this.

No doubt I will find out at Kiddush.

But I don't really care. Rabbis should talk about the experience of God from the pulpit.

And in any case, I'm a new father.

And my experiences these past weeks, and most especially the experience of being present at the birth of our son, have been experiences of being broken into, experiences of having the blinkers of rationalism peeled away, experiences of leaving *hezkat sumim*, the presumption of blindness that afflicted Bilaam, that afflicts us all.

Harry was born at home.

It was Josephine, me, and a couple of midwives, and when this gorgeous, wrinkled, pink bag of skin and bones emerged alive, and healthy, a baby boy –

As he arrived in his mother's arms, in my wife's arms –

As I held the two of them for the first time, I saw. I was confounded. I was unable to put a sentence together.

I tried to thank the midwives, and all I could do was sob at the miracle I saw, the miracle folded into the tiny body before me.

And all the joy and happiness collided with all the fears and fragility.

And I saw.

And I was confounded.

There are three partners in the creation of a child. And the Holy Blessed One, may God's name be blessed, places ten things within him. And these are they: the soul, the spirit, the lustre of the visage, the ability to see and the sense of hearing, the speech from the lips, the strength of the arms and the legs' ability to walk, wisdom, understanding, counsel and intellect and might.[5] And when it comes to the time to pass, the Holy Blessed One, takes back His part and leaves behind the parts of the mother and father before them. And the father and mother weep.

We weep at the beginning and we weep at the end.

Maybe this is the real meaning of that special morning blessing, the one that that praises God, *pokeach ivrim* – 'who opens up the eyes of the blind'.

Maybe it's a prayer about the way true sight leads us to tears.

Maybe it's a prayer about the ability to cry tears of joy when we are lifted higher than any rational discourse can lift.

Maybe it's a prayer about the ability to experience the bitterness of loss, deeper than any philosophical discourse can explain.

Maybe it is a prayer about the ability to be confounded, broken in on, lost.

This ability to cry is what lifts our lives beyond the humdrum and into the miraculous.

These experiences don't come often in a life. But they are the deepest experience of faith.

We should never be afraid of the moment of bursting through. We should never be afraid of the experience of true sight in all its confounding, blinding, dumbing enormity. For it is in these fleeting moments of the experience of the world, as it truly is, that we come to know God.

May they come to us all.

---

[5] The more numerically astute will notice that the Rabbis fail to abide by their own prescription of 'ten things.' This is a perfectly common rabbinic failure.

Smurfette and the Un-named Jewish Women

{2011}

Shabbat Korach was my first Shabbat back after the birth
of our daughter, Eliana. Gender issues will always
challenge a community held in a tension between a love
of tradition, where women's roles were so limited, and
modernity, where a parity of opportunities and roles is
expected (if not always realised). This is one of the most
political and broadly grounded sermons I've given – but
being a new father can loosen the soul.

A n unnamed woman plays a significant role in this week's
parashah.

At the opening of the story we are told of three cronies
who support Korach's assault on Moses' authority – Datan, Abiram,
and On, son of Pelet. We hear more of Datan and Abiram – they join
Korah in the test of the fire censers and lose. Datan and Abiram are
swallowed up by the earth. But On, son of Pelet, disappears from the
story. He's not included in the company of Korah swallowed up by
the earth. That leads the rabbis to this midrashic observation.

On, the son of Pelet, teaches Bmidbar Rabbah,[1] was saved by his
wife. Don't get involved with Korach, she told him. You are a minion
under the leadership of Moses, and you will be a minion even if the
rebellion of Korach succeeds – just under a different master. You
are holy already, all the congregation is holy,[2] and you stand to gain
nothing from this revolution. And she gave him wine to drink until he became drunk and fell asleep. Then she sat in the doorway of
her tent with her hair dishevelled, and when Korach's other cronies
came by to pick up their mate they didn't dare cross his wife. And so
On, son of Pelet, slept through the revolution – and survived.

This story reflects the 'behind every great man there has to be a

---

[1]   18:20.
[2]   Citing Num 3:3.

great woman' school of understanding the role of women in life. But here the man isn't great. On, son of Pelet, is – and here Yiddish will serve better than English ever could – a *putz*.

I'm interested in the anonymity of this woman. She's not mentioned by the Bible, only the midrash, and her name isn't recorded. It's as if history left her out. That's not uncommon. Noah's wife is unnamed and, in the list of those who went down to Israel to escape the famine at the end of the Book of Genesis, 69 men's names are recorded and one woman's.

Here is the most remarkable rabbinic example of the un-naming of a woman. The woman is Bruria, usually referred to in the Talmud as 'Bruria, wife of Rabbi Meir' (as if she has lost her independent existence through marriage). Bruria is known as a learned woman from a couple of other stories in rabbinic literature, but there is a legal debate in Mishnah Kelayim that is technical, but fascinating. If someone dies in a room all the metal in the room becomes *tamei* – ritually impure, spoiled. The rabbis are having a discussion about an iron door bolt in a room where someone is dying, and Bruriah suggests taking the bolt out and hanging it on the door of a neighbour. The Tosefta reports that when 'these words were spoken before Rabbi Yehuda, he said, "beautifully put, Bruria"'[3]. But in the Mishnah, the same idea is reported in the name of another rabbi. Bruria's contribution remains, but she is de-named, effaced.

There are women who feature in rabbinic literature, but they tend not to be actors in their own right. They tend to be the objects of other people acting. In rabbinic literature, it's the men who are out doing things, women become passive agents to whom things are done. The problem is perfectly illustrated by the opening of the rabbis' discussion of marriage, in Masechet Kiddushin[4] – *Ishah nikneit*. A woman, teaches the Mishnah, is acquired by the process of marriage. He betroths, she is betrothed. He is the actor, she the object.

And how easy is it to slip from being an object, to being objectivised, to being objectionable.

This is not, of course, a uniquely Jewish problem. The American

---

[3] Kelayim 1:6.
[4] 1:1.

poet Katha Pollitt wrote some twenty years ago about how difficult it was to find female role models amongst the cartoons and TV
shows her daughter wanted to watch. She entitled her article 'The
Smurfette Principle'. 'Contemporary shows', mused Pollitt,

> are either essentially all-male, like 'Garfield', or organized on what
> I call the Smurfette principle: a group of male buddies will be ac-
> cented by a lone female, stereotypically defined. In the worst car-
> toons – the ones that blend seamlessly into the animated cereal
> commercials – the female is usually a little-sister type, a bunny in
> a pink dress and hair ribbons who tags along with the adventurous
> bears and badgers. But the Smurfette principle rules the more care-
> fully made shows, too. Thus, Kanga, the only female in 'Winnie-the-
> Pooh', is a mother. Piggy, of 'Muppet Babies', is a pint-size version
> of Miss Piggy, the camp glamour queen of the Muppet movies...
> The message is clear. Boys are the norm, girls the variation; boys
> are central, girls peripheral; boys are individuals, girls types. Boys
> define the group, its story and its code of values. Girls exist only in
> relation to boys.

This is neither an outdated analysis, nor one that applies only to
pre-schoolers. Just pick a gender for the each of the following cou-
plets. What's the first gender that occurs to you if I say nurse or doctor, chief executive or secretary, headteacher or classroom teacher?
Rabbi, even.

The prognosis, in both traditional Judaism and so much of contemporary society, is, I think, clear. Women are lovely, important,
holy, capable of the enormous miracle of childbirth and so much
else besides, but they are assumed to be behind men, un-named.
They are objects, not subjects.

There is nothing wrong in being a nurse, a secretary, or a classroom teacher, but there is something wrong with the assumption –
explicit or implicit – that these are roles for women, while the more
glamorous positions are to be the sole preserve of men. And part of
the reason why having women disappear into the shadows is wrong
is that it makes life worse for all of us, male and female alike.

Michael Lewis, one of the most astute observers of financial markets for the past three decades, was asked what single thing could
best prevent a repeat of the financial meltdown that struck in 2009.

He responded that he would have women fill 50 percent of risk positions in banks. Tim Adams, writing in the *Observer* last Sunday, cited a study of '2.7 million personal investors' which 'found that during the financial crisis of 2008 and 2009... male investors, as a group, appeared to be overconfident.' The study's author wasn't surprised, as 'there's been a lot of academic research suggesting that men think they know what they're doing, even when they really don't.' I don't know if that comes as surprise to anyone here. It doesn't come as a surprise to me.

The wife of On, son of Pelet, is a hero. She's smart, she spots something her husband doesn't, and she manoeuvres a situation until a life-threatening risk is eased gently into abeyance. But I don't think that's enough. It's not enough for me, and I don't want it to be enough for my daughter, or any of our daughters. She should be named. Her role should be recorded front and centre, not buried in a midrash, and she shouldn't have to resort to underhand supposedly female wiles in getting her man drunk (as Lot's daughters did to Lot, or as Yael did to Sisera). She should be able to face Korach down in public debate, just as Moses did.

When I encounter the question of whether women belong on the margins or in the centre I look at my wonderful, glorious tradition, the rabbinic tradition I love, and I am prepared to part from it. I know of its ancient androcentrism, and I demand that, as Jews living today, with the knowledge we have of the Smurfette principle and financial markets and much else, we need to hear more clearly, more actively, and more in their own name from women – of this generation and the generations to come. As a man I'm not scared, I'm excited to think what such a world might look like. Which is why I offer my daughter the same blessing most famously recorded in the Bible as given from one man (Moses) to another (Joshua) – be strong and of courage [5]. This is, after all, also the blessing given by Moses *el kol Yisrael* – to **all** of Israel [6].

'Be strong and of courage, don't be afraid, for Adonai your God walks with you. God will not forsake you. God will not fail you.'

---

[5] Deut. 31:7; Joshua 1:6, 9, 18.
[6] Deut. 31:6.

CHAPTER 3

Israel

I'm not particularly interested in hearing rabbis, myself included, talk politics unless the subject is rooted in something recognisably religious. There are political theorists and military analysts aplenty. If we, as rabbis, want our voice to be considered we need to speak from a place where we have genuine expertise and command, and that is as guardians and scholars of a multi-millennial history of religious debate. I have tried to do that in the three pieces on Israel in this chapter.

Incidentally, all three of the contributions below end with the same verse from Micah. I considered editing the original content, but this verse is so much at the heart of my dreams for Israel, I've left it in.

Israel – a Case Study in Jewish Discourse

{2009}

This article was originally published in the New London
Synagogue in-house journal, Quest. In it I try to
articulate an appropriate way of talking about a country
I love – a country in which I have spent three years of
my life – but a country that faces significant challenges,
not only from outside, but also from within.

As a Masorti Jew I don't accept any claim as to perfection
as a given – whether it be an observation about the
authorship of the Torah or the practice of the Israeli
Government – but nor do I consider myself absolved of
the need to care, and care deeply, about those parts of a
Jewish identity that belong at the heart of who we are.

The way we talk about Israel serves as a microcosm for
the way talk about any aspect of our Jewish lives.

Jews, famously, agree on very little. That said, at certain times
and in certain places in the history of our people, different
types, or styles, of Jewish discourse have come to the fore.
In this paper I want to survey four such types of discourse, each
typical of a different religious, social, and historical climate. And
then I want to speculate as to how each type, extrapolated into our
current religious and social existence, would respond to the very
contemporary reality of a State of Israel. There is a risk, of course,
of over-generalising, but there is also much to gain in assessing the
masorah – tradition – and relative merits of different types of Jewish discourse.

The discourse of the *navi* – prophet – is the oldest model of Jewish dialogue, beginning with Abraham (say around 1700 bce) and
coming to a close in the last days of the Second Temple (around 100
bce). That of the *talmid chacham* – rabbinic scholar – came to the
fore in the first century of the Common Era and remains a dominant

trope of Jewish engagement to this day. Alongside this scholastic mode another classic style of Jewish discourse emerged – that of the *chasid* or mystic. Finally, there is the discourse of the *maskil*, or enlightened Jew – a product of the onset of modernity. I shall work from most modern to most ancient.

THE MASKIL

The discourse of the Maskil – enlightened one – is characteristic of the last days of the eighteenth century, especially in France and Germany. This was the moment when Jews were given the opportunity to leave the ghetto and become full members of their surrounding culture; able to trade freely and, most significantly, able to learn from and contribute to the debates and academic institutions of the day. The Maskilim adopted with alacrity the garb, the tone, and the intellectual mores and values of the culture surrounding them. In so doing they cast off many of the traditional mores (or 'fetters' as they would have it) of traditional Jewish commitments and values. In part this casting off is seen as the price of acceptance into the surrounding non-Jewish culture, a price deemed worth paying; but more than that, it is seen as a corrective to what are deemed Jewish errors. The Judaism of the Maskil is, quite literally, made smarter by that which comes from outside of Judaism. 'Sacred cows' – literal and figurative – are rejected, at times, almost with glee.

Berr Issac Berr[1], writing in 1791, mere months after the French National Assembly passed legislation to emancipate the Jews, urged his fellow religionists,

> to divest ourselves entirely of that narrow spirit, of Corporation and Congregation, in all civil and political matters, not immediately connected with our spiritual laws; in these things we must absolutely appear simply as individuals, as Frenchmen, guided only by a true patriotism and by the general good of the nation.

The greatest spokesperson for Jewish enlightenment, however,

---

[1] A merchant and banker who, among other achievements, represented the Jews of Alsace and Lorraine in an attempt to win civil equality in 1989 and subsequently sat on the Parisian Sanhedrin. Text from Paul Mendes-Flohr and Jehuda Reinharz (eds.), *The Jew in the Modern World* (Oxford University Press, Oxford, 1995), p. 119.

would not have used the patriotic nationalism of Berr. For Moses Mendelssohn, the opportunity afforded by modernity was not the opportunity to replace Jewish parochialism with French nationalism, but rather the opportunity to show that Judaism embraced universal truths free of any nationalist tint. The core claims of Judaism (as distinct from our rituals and historic narratives) were truths that could be applied and worked out the whole world over:

> I recognize no eternal truths other than those that are not merely comprehensible to human reason but can also be demonstrated and verified by human powers... I consider this a central point of the Jewish religion. [2]

Being a good Jew, taught Mendelssohn, meant refusing to make claims that ran contrary to ideas the whole world held to be true.

THE DISCOURSE OF THE MASKIL
APPLIED TO THE STATE OF ISRAEL

The Maskilim were behind the foundation of Reform Judaism and, in the nineteenth century most especially, Reformers were forthright in their rejection of Zionism. The principles adopted at the American Reform 'Philadelphia Conference' of 1869 included the following:

> The Messianic aim of Israel is not the restoration of the old Jewish state... involving a second separation from the nations of the earth, but the union of all the children of God in the confession of the unity of God, so as to realize the unity of all rational creatures, and their call to moral sanctification.

Rabbi Kaufmann Kohler, one of the foundational thinkers in American Reform Judaism, is held to 'repudiate the idea that Judea is the home of the Jew – an idea which "unhomes" the Jew all over the wide earth', in the entry on 'Zionism' in the 1911 Jewish Encyclopaedia. The 'problem' of Zionism, and by extension modern Israel, is twofold. First, it impinges on the ability of modern Jews to be treated as fully committed citizens of their respective countries. Second, it is all just a bit too particularistic. Rabbi Kohler and the

---

[2] Mendelssohn, *Jerusalem*, trans. Allan Arkush (Brandeis University Press, London, 1983), p. 88.

early Reformers would have doubtless recoiled from the messy ugly realities of governing a particularly Jewish State.

By extension, we are on fairly safe ground in supposing how the Maskilim would have spoken about the contemporary State of Israel.[3] The discourse of the Maskil, extrapolated into the contemporary debate on the State of Israel, would be, if not anti-Zionist, then clearly deeply uncomfortable at the way the particular Jewish claims behind the actions of the Israeli Government reflect on Jews both within and outside the country's borders. In the contest between the particular and the universal, the particular carried little weight with the Maskilim. They would not consider it a duty to defend the honour of the State. We can even imagine the descendants of Mendelssohn leading a campaign for a 'one-state' solution: an end to a particular Jewish state and its replacement with some kind of international universal entity in and around the current Jewish capital. And there are Jews who, even today, find themselves in the position of the Maskil.

THE TALMID CHACHAM – RABBINIC SCHOLAR

The archetypical model for the discourse of the *Talmid Chacham* comes in the well-known story of the Oven of Akhnai – an encounter where the massed ranks of rabbis prove Rabbi Eliezer wrong by citing a biblical verse.[4] In the technical matter under discussion (the ritual status of a certain oven), Rabbi Eliezer, by any objective standard, is correct. He brings proof after proof of his position, followed by various miraculous events that support his case. Even God thinks Rabbi Eliezer is right – a Divine voice comes from on high to say so. But the rabbis nonetheless reject Rabbi Eliezer's view, and what is more, they do so by ripping a biblical verse so far out of its natural context that it comes to prove the complete reverse of its straightforward meaning.

What the rabbis cite is, 'Incline after the majority', but the full

---

3 Nothing here, of course, should be considered a comment on contemporary Reform Zionism. Indeed, if there is a model of discourse discussed here that is most embraced by contemporary Reformers, it is the model of the Prophet, not the Maskil.
4 BM 59b, citing Exodus 23:2.

biblical citation is 'You shall not incline after the majority to do wrong'. The mark of the Talmid Chacham is the moment when the seemingly obvious is turned on its head in a display of hermeneutic pyrotechnics that owes nothing to cool objectivity or Aristotelian logic.

Indeed, in many ways the entire Talmudic endeavour can be understood not as an attempt to understand biblical verses in some objective logical sense, but rather as an attempt to justify the practices the rabbis know, subjectively, to be correct with reference to some kind of proof which often has to be scraped, pulled, and forced into position.

The opening mishnah in Tractate Pesachim, for example, suggests that the search for leaven is to be carried out in the 'or' of the 14th day of Nissan. The problem for the rabbis is that the Hebrew word or means light, suggesting a morning-time search, and the rabbis 'know' that the search for leaven takes place at night. It takes them three folios to 'prove' that or, at least in this context, means darkness. This is not to suggest that the rabbis are making up their arguments, but rather that rabbinic discourse is often built backwards from a known end result. The known result determines the engagement with the proof, not the other way round. [5]

In terms of our case study – how a Talmid Chacham would speak about the State of Israel – it is important to note one other characteristic of the discourse of the Talmid Chacham: it is fiercely sectarian. The claim to be the true inheritors of the biblical covenant is hotly disputed, most particularly in the first centuries of the Common Era. Scores of rabbinic texts both explicitly and implicitly record or imagine the Talmid Chacham battling the non-Jew for the

---

[5] This classic piece of rabbinic humour is only a mild exaggeration of a genuine Talmudic passage (Chullin 113b). The Bible repeats the injunction 'you shall not boil a kid in its mother's milk' three times (Ex 23:19, 34:26 and Deut 14:21). We are encouraged to imagine a thrice-repeated dialogue between God, giving dictation on Sinai, and Moses, hasty scribbling notes on the Divine Will. 'You shall not boil a kid in its mother's milk,' says God. 'What,' says Moses – 'no eating milk and meat together?!' 'You shall not boil a kid in its mother's milk,' says God. 'What,' says Moses – 'we need to wait three hours between eating meat and eating milk?!' 'You shall not boil a kid in its mother's milk,' says God. 'What,' says Moses – 'we need entirely separate sets of crockery and cutlery?!' 'Fine,' says God. 'Have it your own way!'

right to claim that they, and no other sect, people, or faith, have a right to claim inheritance of the covenant of Sinai.

The texts which record meetings between rabbinic Jews and outsiders to rabbinics almost invariably end in the outsider being defeated in a test of hermeneutic bravado. In one rabbinic text a group of heretics, pagans, and Gnostics or possibly even Christians are reported suggesting to Rabbi Simlai that a plurality of gods (or a Trinitarian godhead) were engaged in the creation of the world.[6] The rabbi responds with various proofs and the heretics leave, defeated.

What is remarkable about this particular text is that Rabbi Simlai's students, watching the disputation, are curiously unmoved by their teacher's arguments. 'You have brushed them off with a reed, how would you answer us?' they demand, almost acknowledging Rabbi Simlai's arguments as too 'rabbinic'; in contemporary terms, too full of spin, lacking in a grounded reality. There are, of course, moments in the vast rabbinic corpus of talmidei hachamim celebrating the claims of the non-Jews around them, but they are few and far between.

THE DISCOURSE OF THE TALMID CHACHAM
APPLIED TO THE STATE OF ISRAEL

Surely the sectarian nature of so much of rabbinics would translate into a rejection of the claims of the non-Jew, either absolutely or partially. But the hermeneutical training of the Talmid Chacham would see them engaged in debate and argument. This type of Jewish discourse, translated to the contemporary political arena, would surely involve a defender of Israel showing how, at every turn, the Palestinians have rejected this peace offering or that, or demonstrating how anti-Semitic Ahmenajad or Hamas really are. And they would reject this or that independent report on grounds of flawed methodology or ideology. The details and the facts would have to be worked over and made to fit into the underpinning conviction that Israel's right to exist needs to be justified and defended not only physically, but

---

6   Bereishit Rabba, 8:9.

also in Jewish discourse. The discourse of the Talmid Chacham extrapolated into contemporary politics would surely be recognisable in the discourse of Israeli Government spokespeople and pro-Israel lobbyists associated with the right wing. And indeed, there are many who speak about Israel in the discourse of the Talmid Chacham.

THE CHASID, OR MYSTIC

The Mystic is entranced by matters of the spirit – by the magical quality of life and, often in the history of the Jews, by nature. To the Mystic the world exists to lift one's eyes above and beyond the material and the corporeal. I am not speaking here of the theosophists who by mathematical formulas of great complexity mapped out the precise dimensions of the heaven and the human relationship to it, but rather the more ecstatic pietists.

A story is told of two brothers, students of Dov Baer, the Maggid of Mezeritch (1710-1772). One, Elimelech of Lizensk, went on to create schools of study and publish an important work of Torah. The other, Reb Zusia, published nothing and left only a collection of tales. How is it possible, we are bidden to ask, for two brothers to study in the same manner and still to turn out so differently? The answer is that every time the Maggid began to cite a biblical text, 'And God said...,' Zusia would reel in ecstasy: 'GOD SPOKE! Extraordinary, amazing, incredible!' Eventually they would have to carry him out of the study hall and he would miss the lesson.

Before the onset of modernity it was, surely, the mediaeval Jewish poets of Spain who were most entranced by the natural world around them. This is from the Divan of Abraham Ibn Ezra:

> Wherever I turn my eyes, around on Earth or to the heavens
> I see You in the field of stars
> I see You in the yield of the land
> In every breath and sound, a blade of grass, a simple flower, an
> echo of Your holy Name. [7]

The Zohar, from the early thirteenth century, is the classic Jewish religious work most noted for its attention to the natural world.

---

[7] From Rabbi Daniel Swartz, 'Jews, Jewish Texts and Nature', in Roger S. Gottlieb (ed.), *This Sacred Earth* (Routledge, London, 2004), p. 98.

Rabbi Eleazar and Rabbi Abba were staying together one night. When night had fallen they went out into the garden by Lake Tiberias. As they did so they saw two stars moving in different directions. They collided with one another then disappeared.

Rabbi Abba said, 'How great are the works of the Holy One, blessed be He... Who can possibly understand the significance of these two stars that have come from different directions and collided with one another and then disappeared? [8]

The companions of the Zohar are in their natural habitat, walking through the orchards, sheltering under the trees, [9] and gazing at the sky above the eternal home of the Jewish people. For them the natural world – the land – is at the heart of their relationship with the Divine, a relationship untrammelled by governmental or political machinations.

THE DISCOURSE OF THE MYSTIC
APPLIED TO THE STATE OF ISRAEL

When it comes to politics... the Mystic just doesn't do politics. [10] Mystics don't read the papers, they *daven*. When it comes to the tough political decisions that face the State, they believe in God's providence and the coming of the Messiah.

The Mystic extrapolated into contemporary Israel would be the lover of the land, off hiking through the hills, plunging into the sea, blind to what happens behind the security fence, or wall, or whatever, and just wishing the whole political problem would somehow go away so they could be left to commune with the land they love. And there are many whose relationship with the contemporary State of Israel is the relationship of the Mystic.

THE NAVI, OR PROPHET

The Hebrew prophet is not to be confused with the Greek oracle. The prophet's telling of the future is not a tarot-card trick; it is more

---

8 Zohar II 171a, trans. Yeruham Fishel Lachower and Isaiah Tishby in *The Wisdom of the Zohar* (Littman and Oxford University Press, Oxford, 1989), vol. 2, p. 663.
9 See Zohar II 127a.
10 I am taking a particular and narrow example of mystic discourse. Some Jewish mystics have been deeply engaged politically. Akiva's support of Bar Kochba and Mendel of Rimanov's support of Napolean are but two examples.

a holding up of a particular kind of a mirror where the inevitable consequence of current behaviour is reflected back at the viewer. The prophets must turn the people from their sins by confronting them with their stumbles and failings. They do this by speaking truth to power and exposing our failings, sparing no blushes, accepting no excuses, cowering before no-one. They do not care who might be listening in, nor do they choose their words with tact or delicacy. Their barbs are designed to shock the people out of their stupor.

> Hear this, you who trample on the needy, saying, 'When will the Sabbath be over so we may offer wheat for sale, so we may make the ephah small and the shekel great, dealing deceitfully with false balances, buying the poor for silver and the needy for a pair of sandals, and selling the refuse of the wheat?' Shall not the land tremble on this account and every one mourn who dwells in it, and all of it rise like the Nile, be tossed about and sink again, like the Nile of Egypt? [11]

The retreat into mystical piety is not for the prophet. Nor is the prophet tempted by the universal philosophical truths that so entrance the Maskil. And, most of all, the prophet rejects the legal curlicues that exemplify the rabbinic scholar. Abraham Joshua Heschel's expanded and anglicised dissertation, *The Prophets*, articulates these tendencies better than anyone.

> To the prophet, no subject is as worthy of consideration as the plight of man. Indeed, God Himself is described as reflecting over the plight of man rather than as contemplating eternal ideas. [The prophet's] mind is preoccupied with... the concrete actualities of history, rather than the timeless issues of thought.
>
> The prophet is intent on intensifying responsibility, is impatient of excuses, contemptuous of pretence and self-pity. His tone, rarely sweet or caressing, is frequently slashing, even horrid – designed to shock rather than to edify.
>
> The prophet makes no concession to man's capacity... he seems unable to extenuate the culpability of man. [12]

But this coruscating pounding aspect to the classical biblical prophets is not the only mode of prophetic discourse. The contem-

---

[11] Amos 8:4-8 (extract).

[12] Heschel, The Prophets (Harper & Row, London, 1969), pp. 5, 7, 9.

porary biblical scholar Yochanan Muffs notes:

> The prophet has another function: He is also an independent advocate to the heavenly court who attempts to rescind the evil decree by means of the only instruments at his disposal. He is first the messenger of the divine court to the defendant, but his mission boomerangs back to the sender. Now, he is no longer the messenger of the court; he becomes the agent of the defendant, attempting to mitigate the severity of the decree.[13]

Indeed, Muffs argues, one could claim that the role of prophet as defender is older even than the role of prophet as accuser. After all, Abraham is seen as the first great prophet not because he confronts the people of Sodom and Gomorrah with their failings, but rather because he intervenes with God to save them: 'Should not the just one of the entire world behave justly?!' (Gen 18:25). Moses too is at his most 'Navi-like' defending the children of Israel before God, most especially in the aftermath of the Golden Calf debacle, where the rabbis imagine God as a father about to kill his child before Moses steps in.[14]

The vaguely paradoxical idea is that God wills the prophet to oppose God by championing the people against the decision of God to punish them

> Like foxes in the ruins were your prophets, Israel. You have not gone up into the breaches, nor have you built up a fence for the House of Israel to stand in battle in the Day of the Lord.
> (Ezekiel 13: 4-5)

> And I searched for a man, a fence-mender, someone who would stand in the breach against Me [God!] on behalf of the land, that I not destroy the land.
> (Ezekiel 22:30)[15]

The prophets must be engaged in defending the people's ultimate goodness and value. They must stand up for Israel, even in her failings, even in the face of great opposition.

---

[13] Muffs, *Love and Joy: Law, Language, and Religion in Ancient Israel* (Harvard University Press, New York, 1992), p. 9.

[14] Brachot 32a, expanding on Exodus 32 and Deuteronomy 9. See also Psalms 106:23.

[15] Muffs cites 1 Sam 7:5-9; 1 Sam 15:10-11; Jer 14 and Amos 7:3 as other examples of this fence-building quality of prophetic discourse. Loc cit. p. 29.

THE DISCOURSE OF THE NAVI APPLIED
TO THE STATE OF ISRAEL

It is safer, perhaps, to begin with what would not appear in the discourse of the Navi – or prophet. The Navi would not attempt to 'contextualise' or explain away the more discomforting actions of Israeli governments or officials. The Navi would castigate 'collateral damage' as unacceptable. They would be repelled by attempts to justify what they would see as unjustifiable. Prophets do not win elections with manifesto commitments dripping in bravado. They do not win friends with flattery and small talk. But the Navi would also refuse to give up on Israel. They would preach of its deeper goodness and ultimate worth, even beneath its contemporary failings. Lovers of Israel would find the words of this 'extrapolated Navi' hard to hear. The words would sting, but ultimately it would be impossible to close one's heart to their oratory, power and truth.

This combination of sharp critique allied with great love is perhaps the least-heard voice when it comes to speaking about Israel. There are few who speak about Israel with the discourse of the Navi.

A PERSONAL CHOICE

I reject the approach of the Maskil. Indeed, this is one of the great lessons of the last century – we need to find a place for nationalism, it can't be sublimated or rejected. Emancipation with no Jewish homeland is no protection from the forces that led to Stalinism or Holocaust, nor can Judaism survive free of its connection to the Land.

Nor do I accept the discourse of the Talmid Chacham. It's impressive, but it feels hollow, disingenuous, and even self-serving on occasion. While some of Israel's actions may indeed be justifiable if properly understood, and some accusations levelled against the Jewish State may indeed be misplaced, I feel deeply uneasy when confronted by the indefensible. I might be able to persuade interlocutors real and imagined some of the time, but I fear I am pushing off arguments with a reed.

Equally I reject the discourse of the Mystic. My Judaism, and the Judaism of the synagogue I lead, cannot close itself off from truths, no matter how uncomfortable they may be. I bless God every morning for the gift of my sight, and I cannot close my eyes to what goes on behind fences and walls.

Ultimately I choose the approach of the Navi. In fact it is no choice, I am compelled. I believe the most powerful, the most holy and the most modern response to the State of Israel is the most ancient of Jewish discourses. This is not an easy path to tread: I risk being accused of a lack of love on the one hand and a lack of guts on the other. But I commit myself to speaking more prophetically of Israel, more passionately in love with her, more sure than ever of her ultimate righteousness and worth, but also brooking no failures and speaking out when she falls short. The aim, and it should be the aim of all of us, is to prove ourselves worthy descendants of Abraham, Moses, Ezekiel, and Amos. If we can do that we may even live to see the dreams of another great prophet fulfilled.

> They shall beat their swords into ploughshares, and their spears into pruning hooks; nation shall not lift up sword against nation, nor shall they learn war any more.
>
> But they shall sit every man under his vine and under his fig tree; and none shall make them afraid.
> (Micah 4:3-4)

May it come speedily and in our time.

Israel and Other Broken Relationships
{Rosh Hashanna 2008}

This was as brave as I have dared to be on the first day
of Rosh Hashanah, on what is the hardest day in the year
for a congregational rabbi – for me. The rabbi faces a
vastly increased number of congregants, with a
correspondingly decreased level of familiarity with
synagogue life. The service is long and the sermon is the
last thing holding people back from lunch. There are
expectations aplenty and the temptation is to warm
hearts and do whatever possible to ensure rare attendees
will like the sermon/rabbi/service/synagogue enough to
come back again. In the aftermath of a very painful year
for lovers of Israel, I took the other option and chose to
talk about the pain in a way that offered no easy solutions
and attempted no easy point-scoring. Sadly, this sermon
could be given again today.

I t's been a tough year for lovers of Israel. Again. This year it was
the Gaza Flotilla, last year it was Operation Cast Lead.

Admittedly, for the first time in two years there are direct
peace negotiations between Israelis and Palestinians. But I detect
no change in the mood in Anglo-Jewry when it comes to Israel. The
mood is still pretty dismal.

I rang up a friend who lives in Jerusalem and works as a facilita-
tor taking Jews to meet Palestinians in the West Bank. I asked him
what he was hearing from his contacts about the negotiations.

No-one talking about them, he told me, everyone thinks it's a joke.

A joke! Here's a joke about Israel. Four Jews are sitting in a café
enjoying a cup of coffee. 'Oy', says one. 'Oy vey', says the next. 'Oy
vey zmir', says the third. 'Listen', says the fourth, 'if you keep talking
about Israel, I'll take my coffee elsewhere.'

I have some sympathy with the fourth Jew. But I refuse to despair.

Actually, despair isn't even the most serious problem. It would be bad enough if we were just bored of talking about Israel. It's worse than that. The issue of Israel has become divisive – even amongst Jews. God help us, what has become of us. If I were to honestly talk about how I feel about Israel today, whether my position was hawkish or dovish there would be some of you, some of us, up in arms. How could I possibly... God help us. You used to be able to rely on Israel to unite us.

When Israel gets mentioned, we – lovers of Israel – are finding ourselves stiffening up – like a circus strongman before accepting the punch to the stomach at some fairground sideshow. We worry about what happens when Israel gets raised as a topic of conversation at dinner, at the office, on the college campus. We are worried and are retreating from being able to speak out. Our love of Israel feels like an open wound – painful to touch, easily inflamed.

Our love of Israel is being conditioned into one of two responses. One is a retreat behind a thick wall where everything Israel does has to be justified and every critique, whether it comes from outside or inside Israel, has to be fought off – often with allegations of anti-Semitic this or self-hating that being hurled at whoever has the temerity to criticise. And cultivating that kind of belligerence can't be good for our souls.

The other response is the 'oy' of our coffee drinkers. It's a relationship with Israel that has become so battered that we are finding it harder and harder to say anything nice about anyone associated with Israel and her neighbours. Soldiers, the media, Netanyahu, the Palestinians, Amnesty, the UN – we're struggling to find a good word to share.

There is something broken at the heart of our love of Israel and our Jewish identity, and that's why I feel I have to speak about Israel today.

And for those of you who will disagree with every word I say on the subject, I want to say this as clearly as I am able – we are a community, and I am a rabbi, who value debate more deeply than we value dogma. This is a community which has always looked at the possibility of speaking in bland, easy-going generalisations and preferred instead to speak about that which is difficult and potentially divisive.

I want to share, today, three Rosh Hashanah lessons that I hope will help us mend a relationship with Israel. And, actually, this isn't just a sermon about Israel, it's about all our broken relationships and the possibility of rebuilding them.

The first Rosh Hashanah lesson – the first religious response to broken relationships – is this: Change is possible.

There is an incredible optimism at the heart of Rosh Hashanah.

Like many of us here, I am sure I'm dealing with my own issues that go back years, and seem intractable, and my *yetzer hara*, my evil inclination, encourages me not to bother trying to change. But the message of the season is that that pessimism and the attitude of resignation have to be fought back at every turn. We are called upon to believe that things can get better, we must refuse to accept things must always be as they are today. I believe this is a response we need to feel desperately deeply when it comes to Israel.

Believing in the possibility of change isn't the same as being hopelessly naive. Opening a door in hope to a cousin we have never really got on well with risks the door being slammed back in our face. And when that cousin has a history of violent aggression, the risk is very real.

But if we don't believe change is possible we are doomed to repeat only the same old, same old. And the same old, same old is not only not good enough, it's getting worse.

And to those who think that change – peace – is an entirely unreasonable dream, know that at least Bibi Netanyahu, Labour leader Ehud Barak, and Kadima leader Tzipi Livni are all united in making the claim that things can be better. This is Livni, speaking just this week in Israel: 'I say to [the naysayers] that they have no right to take hope away from the citizens of Israel. An end to the conflict is achievable. There is no such thing as "I can't".'[1]

They are being very frum by trying again, and again.

The first Rosh Hashanah lesson is that despair is forbidden and change is possible.

---

[1]   http://www.jpost.com/Israel/Article.aspx?id=187318

The second Rosh Hashanah lesson is even harder to accept.

It involves letting go a little of what we know is right to admit our own fault.

It's so tempting to think that we become stronger by conceding nothing. But that's not a very Rosh Hashanah attitude.

I don't mean to suggest that the Palestinians and Hamas in particular are blameless. Far, far from it. And on every other day in the year we are absolutely justified in pointing out all the offensive failures of everyone else. But on Rosh Hashanah we are commanded to turn that gaze inward.

On every other day of the year it's possible to construct every occasion when we reached out a hand in friendship as utterly genuine, and every failure of the other to shake our hand as their perfidy. But on Rosh Hashanah we are called to stand before the One who knows our inner thoughts and our hidden actions and makes us doubt ourselves. What else we could have done?

On Rosh Hashanah we are encouraged to focus on what else WE can do, rather than focus, always, on the shortcomings of the other. This is a necessary focus because it's rarely possible to heal, or even normalise, relationships with others by increasing our focus on how right we are. To heal relationships we must increase our focus on what we can do to encourage that healing. And that might require us to reduce our focus on matters of strict legalist accuracy and instead pursue paths that create a rapprochement.

An example, drawn from the Talmud.[2]

Suppose someone stole a beam and uses it in a building. Shammai says we should compel the person to give back the beam, even if they need to tear down the building to do so. A thief has no right to the beam. But Hillel says the thief ought to pay off the owner of the beam. They don't have to give back that specific beam.

And the law follows Hillel's position. It's supposed to make it easier for people to achieve a rapprochement.

Now here is a call, for both Netanyahu and Abbas – what can you do to focus on paths that create rapprochement?

---

[2] Gittin 55a.

And here is a call for any of us living in broken relationships – the sort of relationship which has, for years, floundered over accusations and counter-accusations, where we too readily blame the other and too rarely have been prepared to look inside and double- and triple-check ourselves.

Rosh Hashanah demands we admit that we have made mistakes.

There is another problem with this over-reliance on proving that we are right, and the other is wrong. It is that this kind of approach to life – right versus wrong, black versus white – is more Greek than Jewish. A Greek philosopher would say that if I'm right and you disagree with me, you must therefore be wrong and I must prove you are wrong. We live in a Greek world massively influenced by this Greek approach.

We grow up thinking that our winning means that the other person loses. We are schooled to think that being strong means standing firm. But Judaism is more subtle, more willing to admit the presence of conflicting alternate rights.

It's hard to explain this to someone who has never studied the Talmud, but a Talmudic argument that seems to pitch Rabbi X against Rabbi Y doesn't tend to end with Rabbi X winning and Rabbi Y losing. It ends up, often some pages later, agreeing that Rabbi X can indeed feel one way and Rabbi Y can indeed feel another way.

Judaism would suggest that we need to find ways where both parties to an argument can be right. Judaism is willing to admit that we may disagree, and yet we must both be acknowledged, recognised, given something that can make us feel at peace. This is an important insight, because beating the other in argument might make us feel better, but it doesn't stop making the other feel worse. And that alone makes peace harder to find.

Eizeh hu gibor, asks the Mishnah – who is mighty? Ben Zoma answers, *hakovesh et yitzro* – one who conquers their evil inclination.[3] He doesn't say, one who wins every battle.

---

[3]   Avot 4:1.

I wonder if he means that a real hero realises that other people need to be allowed to win also.

I wonder if he means that a real hero doesn't allow himself to be puffed up by his own rhetorical prowess to the point where he insists on defeating everyone he meets.

I wonder if the really heroic way is to pull back from being convinced of our exclusive right to be right in search of ways to compromise and heal.

This is the opening of the Mishnah in Baba Metzia[4]:

Two people come before the court grabbing hold of the same tallit. One says, it's all mine. The other says, it's all mine.

You see the problem. Intractable. They both claim the whole tallit. They both want to be acknowledged as right, but their claims are mutually exclusive.

So, continues the Mishnah, 'You get both of them to swear an oath that not less than half of the tallit is theirs, and then you split it in half.'

You find a solution, a solution that appeases both claims even as they are both forced to compromise. Both make an oath on which they can agree. Then both get something. Less than they hoped to gain, but more than they feared losing.

Peace, in this dispute over a tallit, comes at the moment when the disputants accept that the other has a claim, or rather when the disputants acknowledge that their own claim is not total. That's a huge spiritual, not to mention political, achievement, but it is a necessary precursor to finding peace.

This is the third Rosh Hashanah lesson I wish to share today: *If we wish for peace we must acknowledge our own claim cannot be total.*

This is the challenge for the Netanyahus and Abbases and all of us.

Can we find the way to acknowledge that our own claim is not total, and what is claimed by both of us will need to be split if we are both to find peace?

---

[4] BM 2a.

Of course I'm not living in Israel, I'm not serving in the army or at a checkpoint. I don't expect to get a vote to the same degree as an Israeli. But I'm a Jew and a Zionist.

Israel is at the heart of my Jewish identity and I pray daily for its peace.

And that, especially now, means that I feel the need to share these Jewish truths, these messages for Abbas and Netanyahu, and the rest of us.

Change is possible.

I have made mistakes.

My own claim cannot be total.

I know the Palestinians have made lousy partners for a lasting peace for decades.

But I believe change is possible.

I know that sick Palestinians have received world-class treatment at Israeli hospitals, but, today, I don't claim that Israel has done everything it should have done to encourage an economically self-sustaining Palestinian state where trade, not violence, would be the central concern of its leaders. We have our share of guilt to carry also.

I believe that Jews have a right to live in a Jewish state in the land we have loved for thousands of years. But I believe in the right of Palestinians to self-determination in the land of their forefathers also. I believe the tallit needs to be divided.

To everyone involved in the negotiations, I pray for your heroic strength.

May this at last be the year when Micah's vision of swords being beaten into ploughshares comes true – a time when every man or woman, be they Jew or Palestinian, will sit under their fig tree with no-one to make them afraid.

To all of us living with long-term broken relationships, I hope these insights help. And that Micah's vision of secure, restful peace be granted to us all in the year to come.

Shanah Tovah.

Jewish Reflections on War and Peace – For Muslims, and Others

{2011}

I was contacted by the editor of the journal Arches Quarterly, asking if I would consider contributing an article on Jewish approaches to 'War and Peace', the theme for an upcoming edition. Arches Quarterly is published by the Cordoba Foundation – an organisation, founded by a British Muslim, 'committed to ensuring that a clash of civilisations is neither inevitable nor necessary.' 'In particular', their statement of aims goes on to say, they look 'to bridge the gap of understanding between the Muslim World and the West and vice-versa.' The only time I have actually seen a copy of the journal, other than on my own shelves, was at an interfaith meeting at the Central London Mosque, where one of the imams there waved it at me, amused to see his dialogue partner appearing in the journal. I accepted the invitation to make a contribution knowing the majority of its readers would be Muslim.

How much explicitly refers to contemporary matters in Israeli politics? Not so much. How much is implicitly about contemporary matters in Israeli politics? Everything.

Judaism believes in peace, loves peace, and prays and works towards peace. The greatest visions of the Bible are of the wolf lying down with the lamb (Isaiah 11) and of swords being beaten into ploughshares (Isaiah 2). Beyond the Bible, the rabbis, in their codification of Jewish life, infused every major prayer experience of the Jew with the yearning for peace. The second-century sage Rav Shimon son of Halafta says 'a blessing is useless unless it comes with peace'. The great medieval commentator Rabbi Yom Tov Isbili, known as the Ritba (Spain, d. 1330), collated a list of codified Jewish prayers that have as their conclusion the plea for peace[1]; it includes the grace after meals; the principal doxology (Kaddish); the central prayer of evening, morning and afternoon services (Amidah); the priestly blessing (Numbers 6)[2]; and others. Judaism believes in peace.

But the Hebrew Bible also knows violence. The commandment lo tirzach (Exodus 20:13) is inaccurately translated in the King James Bible as 'thou shall not kill'. The correct rendition of the original Hebrew is 'thou shall not murder'. The Bible justifies and even demands violence, even unto killing, on too many occasions to list. That said, there is a noteworthy attitude towards violence that suffuses not only the Bible, but also the project of rabbinic Judaism. Time and time again in the Bible and rabbinic texts one can see the impulse to violence and war subjected to controls designed to ameliorate the destructive potential of military brutality.

The Bible mandates (Deut 20 and 21) that an invading army should offer peace to a city before waging war against it. It demands that fruit trees around an ancient city are not destroyed by siege warfare, asking rhetorically 'is a tree a person, to be besieged by you?' It insists that any beautiful woman captured in combat is not to be treated as chattel to be 'used' and/or abandoned at will... and the list goes on.

One can see the same tendency in rabbinic texts. Maimonides (d. 1204), the greatest of medieval Jewish sages, set out precise laws of war in his code the Mishneh Torah. One mandate prescribes that 'when besieging a city in order to capture it, you should not surround it on all four sides, but only on three sides, allowing an escape path for anyone who wishes to save his life'[3]. Aside from the seeming military lunacy of a three-sided siege, there are two other points to note when considering the significance of this kind of religious engagement with war. Firstly, while Maimonides is able to produce a biblical verse to justify his injunction (Numbers 31:7), on the face of it the verse mandates no such behaviour. Maimonides need not

---

[1]   B'midbar Rabbah 11.
[2]   Ritba Megillah 18a d.v. U-Mah C14.
[3]   Hil Melakhim 6:11. See Sifrei Bmidbar Mattot 157 beshem Rabbi Natan.

have included this mandate; he's willing the mandate into existence, driven by a greater sense and understanding of what Judaism
must stand for. Secondly, this militarily self-defeating mandate has
had practical impact for the contemporary Israeli army, as will be
discussed below.

The messy business of Israel's contemporary engagement will
be treated more extensively later in this piece, but it's important to
understand that for close to two thousand years Maimonides'
injunctions were of no practical import whatsoever. The dominant
norm governing Judaism's engagement with violence was not that of
a military power, squaring military necessity and morality, but that
of a wandering, stateless, army-less people subject to the attitudes
to violence of other nations and nationally enshrined faiths. In 70
CE the Romans destroyed the Israelite state based around Jerusalem; in the years before and after this all the other vestiges of Jewish
national and military presence were also erased. Jews became a
people with no physical border to protect, no army and no possibility of waging war.

From Seleucids to Romans to Christians to Muslims, across time
and place Jews have been persecuted, beaten, burnt, and, in a period as dark as humanity has experienced, been subject to a level of
genocidal brutality beyond imagination. Throughout almost two
millennia of Diaspora existence Jews were forbidden from bearing
arms and, by and large, accepted this and other externally imposed
regulations as the cost of survival, of 'doing business', in a world
governed by foreign might. Jews became pacifists by circumstance.
Any drive to conquer territory was sublimated into mercantile endeavour or the exegetical engagement characteristic of rabbinic
Judaism. In place of soldiers Judaism valorised scholars. The rabbis even turned the soldiers of the Bible into intellectuals. The Book
of Samuel refers to David, slayer of Goliath, as 'a brave fighter and
man of war'. The Talmud explains this means he knew how argue
his point in 'the war of Torah'. [4] Offered only the opportunity of military surrender, Jews and Judaism waged war on the entire notion of

---

[4]   Talmud Bavli Sanhedrin 93b.

military bravado and, playing by rules they themselves constructed, declared themselves victorious without recourse to sword or bullet.

But by the beginning of the twentieth century Jews were growing weary of a purely exegetical triumph. The pacifism was being beaten out of them. By the dark years of the '30s and '40s, the suggestion that Jews could respond to anti-Semitic violence with words alone seemed more than vapid, it bordered on the offensive. The great pacifist Mahatma Ghandi wrote, in 1938, that the Jews of Germany should protest against Hitler using only non-violent means. 'I am as certain as I am dictating these words that the stoniest German heart will melt [if only the Jews] adopt active nonviolence... I do not despair of his [Hitler's] responding to human suffering even though caused by him'.[5]

The Jewish philosopher Martin Buber (hardly known as a militarist!) took Ghandi to task. The Jews of Germany, as Buber knew from personal experience, were dealing with a genocidal mania that would not respond to non-violence. Non-violent resistance in the face of utter brutality was capitulation. Of course, said Buber, the violent response was one that could only be employed with 'fear and trembling', but 'if there is no other way of preventing the evil destroying the good, I trust I shall use force and give myself up into God's hands'.[6] Alongside its abnegation of violence and love of peace, Judaism began to place increasing weight on the value of self-defence.

Then the wheels of history turned and Israel found itself with an army, a state and, arrayed around and even inside its borders, armed aggressors. Now what? Certainly ethical and religious factors have always been central to the vision of the defence of the Israeli State. The Israel Defence Forces (IDF) have an ethics code, drafted by religious leaders, professors, lawyers, and generals and drummed into soldiers during training. The code articulates the values of

---

[5] *The Collected Works of Mahatma Gandhi* (Ministry of Information and Broadcasting, Government of India) v. 68, p. 189. Cf loc cit, pp. 191-92, 205.

[6] Published in Martin Buber, Nahum N. Glatzer, and Paul Mendes-Flohr, *The Letters of Martin Buber: A Life of Dialogue* (Syracuse University Press, 1996). The full exchange may be found in P. Mendes-Flohr (ed.), A Land of Two Peoples: Martin Buber on Jews and Arabs (Oxford University Press, Oxford, 1983), pp. 106-126.

'human dignity', 'responsibility', and 'purity of arms': 'IDF servicemen and women will use their weapons and force only for the purpose of their mission, only to the necessary extent, and will maintain their humanity even during combat. IDF soldiers will not use their weapons and force to harm human beings who are not combatants or prisoners of war, and will do all in their power to avoid causing harm to their lives, bodies, dignity and property'.[7]

When soldiers fail to live up to values espoused in the code they can expect investigation and reprimand. But the challenges faced by the Israeli State do not fit easily into categories outlined in a document written in ivory towers. Terrorist aggressors, usually dressed as civilians, tend to launch attacks from and/or into densely populated areas full of civilians; both Arabs and Jews are liable to suffer the consequences of terrorist actions.

In the aftermath of Operation Cast Lead, December 2008, the philosopher Moshe Halbertal, a member of the team who drafted the IDF Code, expressed his empathy for Israeli soldiers confronted by recognisable military violence but no recognisable army. 'By disguising themselves as civilians and by attacking civilians with no uniforms and with no front', he wrote, 'paramilitary terrorist organizations attempt nothing less than to erase the distinction between combatants and noncombatants on both sides of the struggle'.[8] Israel faces what Halbertal calls acts of 'assymetrical warfare'. It's hard to balance out risks of loss and risks of collateral damage even in moments of security, let alone in the heat of incoming mortars and Katyusha rockets.

The aftermath of an incident now fifty years old will serve as a test case from which to consider more contemporary religious responses. In 1953, Palestinian terrorists launched attacks on Israel from Kibiya, a village on the then Jordanian-controlled West Bank. The Israeli military responded ferociously. The village was all but destroyed; many villagers were killed. It was an action with uncanny echoes for our times. Some religious leaders expressed

---

[7] Available at http://dover.idf.il/IDF/English/about/doctrine/ethics.htm.
[8] Writing in the *New Republic*, 6th November 2009. Available at http://www.tnr.com/article/world/the-goldstone-illusion.

no compunction in accepting the validity of violence in the face of terrorist attack on Jewish lives. Rav Shaul Yisraeli, who went on to become one of the heads of Yeshivat Mercaz Harav Kook, justified the use of force as follows: 'There is a place for acts of retribution and revenge against the oppressors of Israel... They are responsible for any damage that comes to them, their sympathizers, or their children. They must bear their sin. There is no obligation to refrain from reprisal for fear that it might harm innocent people, for we did not cause it. They are the cause and we are innocent.'[9]

This is the tough uncompromising perspective of a hawkish politician, but Yisraeli justified the attack on Kibiya with reference to a classic rabbinic concept. The community of nations, he claimed, believed these kinds of military actions were permissible, therefore Israel could avail herself of this international consensus in an application of the classic rabbinic principle *dina d'malkhuta dina* – the law of the land is the law.[10] 'The foundation of *dina d'malkhutah dina* relates not only to what transpires within a state, but also to international matters as is the accepted custom', claimed Yisraeli.

Putting aside the issue of whether the international community would have accepted the legality of actions taken in Kibiya, Yisraeli's claim is that Israel should be judged by the ethical standard of the world at large. If the British bomb Dresden and the Americans lay waste to Hiroshima (both examples cited in support of his position), the Israelis can lay waste to Kibiya not only as a matter of military expediency, but also without religious qualm.

More critical positions also crystallised in the aftermath of the attack on Kibiya. The philosopher and commentator Yeshayahu Leibowitz acknowledged the attack could be defended with reference to rabbinic tradition or the standards of other nations, 'but let us not try to do so. Let us rather recognize its distressing nature'.

[9]   See Arye Edrei, 'Divine Spirit and Physical Power: Rabbi Shlomo Goren and the Military Ethic of the Israel Defense Forces', *Theoretical Inquiries in Law* (2006), Vol. 7, No. 1, Article 11. Available at: http://www.bepress.com/til/default/vol7/iss1/art11 at p. 70. I am indebted to Prof Edrei for his original research.

[10]   Talmud Bavli, Ned. 28a; Git. 10b; BK 113a; BB 54b and 55a. There is an irony, of course, in the notion that *dina d'malkhuta*, by its very essence a diasporic invention, is turned here into a staging post for bullish nationalism.

Leibowitz compared Kibiya's destruction to the biblical tale of Dinah.[11] Dinah, daughter of Jacob, was kidnapped, taken to Shechem and raped, an action that led her brothers to destroy the town and kill its male inhabitants. Leibowitz claimed the brothers

'had a decisive justification [for launching the all-out raid]. Nevertheless, because of this action, their father Jacob cursed the two tribes for generations... Let us not establish [the modern State of Israel] on the foundation of the curse of our father Jacob!'[12]

Both these responses – the hawkish and the cursing – can be observed in contemporary Jewish and Israeli discourse responding to contemporary acts of Israeli military violence, but there is a third way which, I argue, is truer to Jewish discourse and analysis. Rav Shlomo Goren (d. 1994) founded the Israel Defence Forces rabbinate and served as its first chief rabbi for about two decades, subsequently serving as chief rabbi of Israel. Much of his vast scholarly output concerned military matters. His formally collected Responsa on Matters of the Military, War, and Security[13] alone run to four volumes and cover a vast range of issues, theoretical and practical, as applied to generals and to privates.

Goren was no apologist. In a radical and broad application of principles learnt from an obscure law in Deuteronomy[14] he deems Israelis responsible for any death that occurs anywhere in the occupied territories.[15] In 1982 Goren was chief rabbi of Israel and used his position to insist that an escape path be left open during the siege of Beirut (in accordance with Maimonides' mandate as discussed above).[16] Responsa literature is technical, and there are many competing factors to be balanced as religious aspiration and ugly brutality come into conflict. It also requires deep scholarship and an understanding of religious sensitivities and military

---

[11] Genesis, Chapter 34

[12] Y. Leibowitz, 'After Kibiyeh', trans. Eliezer Goldman et al., in Eliezer Goldman (ed.), *Judaism, Human Values and the Jewish State* (Harvard University Press, 1992).

[13] *Meshiv Milhama: She'elot U-teshuvot Be-inyene Tsava Milhamah U-vitahon* (1983-1992).

[14] Deuteronomy 21:1-9: If a dead body is found between two Israelite towns, the priests of the nearer town must accept responsibility for the bloodshed and seek forgiveness.

[15] See A. Edrie, loc. cit. at p. 286.

[16] Rav Goren's letter on the subject appeared in *Hatzofeh*, 6th August 1982.

necessity. Goren's approach is untidy, often unpopular, and even occasionally unsafe. But it is, I argue, the truest reflection of a Jewish tradition torn between dreams of peace and harsh political and historical realities. Those who wish to speak on the validity, or otherwise, of various acts of military violence need to study much, speak carefully, and know that the safety of certainty is not given to human beings. 'Who knows if your blood is redder', asks the Talmud. 'Perhaps their blood is redder.' [17]

Ethics and war make for uncomfortable bedfellows. Military ethicists, particularly those who speak in the name of a religious tradition, should be troubled sleepers, uneasy and unsure, afraid that their pronouncements could condone the spillage of a single drop of blood. No matter whose blood may be shed, every drop is sacred, 'for the soul of all flesh is in its blood'. [18] At the heart of Judaism lies an extraordinary articulation of the value of human life. All people, the book of Genesis tells us, are created from one original template – Adam. This is so, state the rabbis, in order to teach us that 'whoever destroys a single soul, is considered as though they had destroyed an entire world; and whoever saves a single soul is considered as though they had saved an entire world'. [19] This is, of course, an articulation that Muslim scholars will recognise from their own scriptures. [20] The demand of the One God shared by both Jews and Muslims is that this message be taught and taught again and again until the day when swords can indeed be turned into ploughshares, nations and individuals will cease lifting up swords against one another and none shall learn war any more. And then every person, Jew and Palestinian, shall be able to sit under their vine and under their fig tree and none shall make them afraid. [21]

---

[17] Sanhedrin 74a.

[18] Leviticus 17:14.

[19] Mishnah Sanhedrin 4:5, dated to the second century. The text has been cited according to the Kauffman manuscript, acknowledged as bearing the correct original version of this text. See Ephraim Elimelech Urbach, *Kol Hamekayem Nefesh Achat... Gilgulav Shel Nusach* [Whoever Saves One Soul ... The Evolution of a Text], 40 Tarbitz 268 (1971).

[20] Kuran 5:32.

[21] Micah 4:4.

CHAPTER 4

Theology

*The three pieces in this chapter cover
a span of ten years, from 2003 – not long
before my ordination as a rabbi – to 2013.
Despite the passage of a decade, I don't
think my theology has changed all that much.
I leave it to the reader to decide.*

Just So - A Senior Sermon on Parashat Bereishit

{2003}

This is the one 'cheat' in this volume, a sermon I wrote while still a student.

Rabbinical students, at JTS, are invited to give a sermon in their last year in the main synagogue of the Seminary. It's a big deal and a central part of the culture of becoming ordained – a sort of second bar mitzvah. The weeks are drawn by lot and I ended up swapping to get Bereishit (how could anyone turn down Bereishit?).

I'd spent five years hearing senior sermons, and hearing about senior sermons, and I felt the pressure. How could I distil my six years of full-time rabbinic learning into something simple – and brief – enough for a sermon? Looking back on what I shared, I'm still proud of it. It's the first time I felt I had truly cracked that most rabbinic of disciplines – the set-piece sermon. It also touches on something at the very heart of my theology: the notion of brokenness.

Shabbat Shalom.

How do you feel about the world?

Big question, I know, but it's that kind of a week, a week when we are asked to consider the biggest questions. This is Shabbat Bereishit.

How do you feel about the world? More specifically, how do you feel about those parts of the world that are out of your control?

The societies in which we live, I argue, lead us to two responses in the face of a world we cannot control.

Firstly, we are led to feel a failure.

We feel a failure if we can't shoot the hoop, if we can't find a partner with whom to spend the rest of our lives, if we can't control our children, if we can't afford a new car, a picket fence or a foreign vacation. We feel a failure if, after five years of rabbinical school, we can't read *tosefot*, or if after five months of dieting we still can't fit into those jeans we last wore in our twenties. We are conditioned to believe that everything in our life will work out just so, and if it doesn't we are conditioned to feel a failure.

The second response is even more disturbing. Our second response to a world we cannot control is to jump blindly into action – the danger being that our actions are, most likely, ineffective responses to the inevitability of the struggles life places before us.

How do you feel about getting older, the hairline receding and the belly rounding? Does it make you want to reach for the Botox, the Rogaine, the nip & tuck?

Or to draw our map a little more broadly – as rabbis, how do we feel about Jews who marry out or who don't keep Shabbat? What about those who come out as gay? Do we want to close our hearts and communities to these people as if they simply don't exist?

Or more broadly still, how do we feel about the seemingly ever-present threat of terrorism? Does it make us want to run off and invade Iraq, or Syria, or North Korea? Does it make us want to round up '*all 'dem Arabs*' and deport them somewhere far away?

When we feel out of control, we are drawn to react. But too often our best efforts seek only to mitigate the symptoms of our unease. Too often we fail to engage with the root cause of our discomfort.

Ernest Becker, in his book *Denial of Death*, unfolds an understanding of the human condition predicated on our failures to act well in the face of that which is most beyond our control. It is an understanding of the human condition predicated on our inability to cope with mortality.

We are terrified of that which is most inevitable in our lives, and in the face of this fear we deny our failures and we deny our death. We bury these fears deep in our subconscious. And then we begin to transfer. We take our fears and act out towards others, any other.

We will grasp at anything as a possible saviour. Any passing fancy can become the one thing that would let us feel a success, give us a glimpse of immortality, if only we could trap it.

Or more dangerously, we blame our own mortality on any passing scapegoat. We blame anything, pummel anyone in the attempt to preserve ourselves from own stark death fear.

We are prepared to take the most dramatic steps to impose a semblance of order on the world, to render the world how we would wish it to be. But the truth remains – our world is beyond control and all our efforts to tame it are not only useless, they may even be the source of our inability to live well in the world.

So how did we get here, how do we come to live so poorly? Feeling as though we are failures, transferring our fears of mortality onto false messiahs or passing punch bags?

What is driven so deeply into our souls to cause such a malaise?

Let us be clear, we are dealing with a Western problem, so perhaps we should begin with the single pre-eminent myth of Western society.

Bereishit bara Elohim et hashamayim v'et ha'aretz.

And God said, Let there be light: and there was light.
And God saw that it was good.

And God said, let the waters be gathered.
And it was so –
And God saw that it was good.

And God said, let the earth bring forth grass.
And it was so –
And God saw that it was good.

And God said –
And it was so –
And God saw that it was good.

And God said –
And it was so –
And God saw that it was good.

And God said –
And it was so –
And God saw, and behold it was very good.

The first chapter of the Bible sets a standard for all Western civilisation – and what a standard it is. God speaks and it is, and it is good.

Again and again, everything just falls into place for our Super

Deity. Chaos is effortlessly banished. Not a hair out of place, every blade of grass, every ant, every raindrop obeys the Divine fiat, and it is all so effortlessly done. No wonder we are so nagged by a sense of failure. We can't help comparing our futile attempts at creativity with this picture of unadulterated perfection.

God created an entire universe without breaking sweat, and I get tired running for the bus. No wonder I feel inadequate. No wonder I take out my frustrations on those around me.

No wonder the more I read and reread the first chapter of Genesis, the more I feel this is an extraordinarily dangerous text.

It is a text which brooks no dissent, and it calls on us to brook no dissent. It is a text which crushes all trace of chaos, and it calls on us to crush all trace of chaos.

The first chapter of Genesis sets forth a standard of perfection so high that our every action seems rotten in comparison.

But as I began to think more deeply about this passage, what strikes me is not merely how profoundly emotionally dangerous this narrative is, but also how profoundly untrue it feels. The world simply doesn't feel 'just so' and 'good' and 'good' and 'very good', and it doesn't feel as though it ever was.

I'm aware this might sound a little blasphemous to the Karaites among us, but as I read through hundreds of years of rabbinic grappling with this narrative, I began to feel I was in good company in my heresy.

Rabbinically we have glimpsed the creation of the world in a very different manner. Through our rabbinic lenses this tale of 'just so' and 'good' and 'good' and 'very good' melts away.

A rabbinic text, dating back to the second century of the common era:

> And why begin the Torah with the letter bet, the language of *bra-cha*, a blessing, as opposed to *aleph*, the language of *arur* – cursed. Said the Holy Blessed One, 'I can only create my world with the letter bet, for otherwise the entire world would say, 'How could a world created from *arur* survive?' Rather let Me create it with a bet, the language of blessing – and then perhaps it will survive.[1]

---

[1] Yerushalmi Hagigah 2:2.

There is tension in this midrash, an acknowledgement that the world is dangerous and scary. Its order and perfection cannot be taken for granted, and even though the world begins with blessing there is no guarantee of survival. *Hareni bore oto b'bet b'lashon bracha v'ulai ya'amod* – Rather, let me create it with a bet and *perhaps* it will survive.

In this early text God doesn't tower above all creation intimidating and perfect. God reaches down and offers us a hand as we begin, tentatively, to make our way in the world.

Let me bring another text, one that speaks more clearly of the nature of the fragility in the world. For I am not, today, focussing on the fragility of human behaviour, but rather the fragility inbuilt in the very fabric of the world itself.

The first midrash in Midrash Tanuhuma claims that God consulted the Torah before creating the world, and that the continued existence of the world depends on each tiny marking in the black fire. It continues:

> It is taught about the verse *v'lo t'chalelu et shem kadshi* – 'And they shall not profane my holy name' – that if you make the letter het into a hey you destroy the world.

But of course you do. If you make the Hebrew word *t'chalalu* into *t'halelu*, the verse 'They shall not **profane**' becomes 'They shall not **praise**'– and the world is destroyed. Back to the midrash:

> It is taught about the verse *col haneshama t'halel ya* – 'All that breathes should praise God' – that if you make the letter *hey* into a *het* you destroy the world.

And of course you do. The Hebrew word *t'halel* becomes *t'chalel*, and you chant that 'all that breathes should **curse** God'.

And if, the midrash continues, by some slight slip the letter *dalet* becomes a *resh* – the opening verse of the Shema is found to proclaim 'Hear O Israel, Adonai our God, Adonai is... **Other**'. And the world is destroyed.

And if you confuse a *resh* with a *dalet*... Or a *kaf* with a *bet* or a *bet* with a *kaf*... *Atah machriv et ha'olam*: You destroy the world.

Where now that secure vision of perfection we thought we knew?

But we are not done yet.

We will not be done until we have seen that God too is unable to sustain the fib of the 'just so', the 'good', the 'good', and the 'very good'.

We have reached the cosmic mythology of Isaac Luria. This comes from Etz Chaim, the greatest compendium of Lurianic teaching.[2]

> And now we will explain the order of emanation of the lower parts of the Godhead and how they shattered.
>
> Know that of these seven rulers, none was greater than the other. Each had the same size perimeter as the other. And therefore there was not enough power in any one of these lower vessels to withstand any more than that part of the supernal light that was its portion.
>
> There was not enough power in any one vessel to withstand all the light and they shattered and fell down.

The Lurianic cosmogony is an abstruse tale that rambles and repeats itself and is weighed down in its own technicalities. How unlike the Genesis narrative with which we began. It is a narrative that is built, if built is the right word, on a gaping void and the shattered fragments of a creation unable to cope with the perfection we thought to seek. It is not just that the world is broken, it is that God is shattered. God is no more able to make this mortal and finite world 'just so', 'good', 'good', and 'very good' than any of the creations in it.

Thankfully, we rabbinic Jews are not called upon to take the tale of the first chapter of Genesis literally. I argue we shouldn't take it as true at all. Rather, we should view this chapter as a symptom of the very malaise we have been investigating. The first chapter of Genesis is a desperate attempt to avoid the struggles and complexities of existence by holding tightly to a vision of perfection that can never, could never, be. The more broken and perilous we perceive our lives, the more we are drawn to the first chapter of Genesis, but the attraction is flawed.

---

[2]   Etz Chaim II:1:5.

The truth is otherwise. The truth can be found hidden in midrash, folded up in folios where we don't like to look too often, for fear of what we might find.

We live in a broken world, my friends, a world of orphaned children and bereaved widows, a world of savaged natural resources and puffed up consumerism. It is not 'just so' and 'good' and 'good' and 'very good', no matter how much we might wish that it were.

And now what?

Actually it might not be so bad, this re-calibrated vision of the Universe.

Indeed, it might even be that we are only capable of saving this planet, and its human cargo, if we are prepared to let go of the dangerous and false notion of a perfect, ordered, 'just-so' creation.

In a world in which everything is 'just so', what is the role of the individual? What are we supposed to do? Despite its superficial lure, would you really want to live in a perfect world? Who would ever wish to spend an eternity in a garden that had everything you could ever want? The terrifying truth of living in a world of fragility is that now, all of a sudden, our actions count. In a world balancing precariously on the cusp of collapse our every action becomes crucial. We are called to action. And there is more.

Firstly, our perception of *suffering* is transformed. In a world where we do not expect everything to be 'just so', the existential challenge is no longer 'Why do things go so badly wrong?' but 'How could anything ever possibly go right?' If the first question threatens despair, the second inspires radical amazement. It propels us into acknowledging there is still tremendous beauty in the world. It makes it possible to smile, again, at even a butterfly.

Secondly, if we give up on the notion of a creation that is 'just so', we might find a way to live more gently in this world. We would see the interconnectedness of all things and the fragility of existence. The world is surely safer if we let go of the need to force it to be something that it can never be.

If we no longer took the might of Creation for granted, maybe we would no longer need to extract every last penny from the sweat-shop and every last log from the rainforest. Maybe we would con-sign authoritarianism and bigotry to the history books. Maybe, in allowing our fellow human beings to be flawed – in absolving our-selves of the need to force them into our version of a perfection for which they are not suited – we would find it easier to love others. Maybe we would even find it easier to love ourselves.

And finally, in abandoning the notion of a creation that is 'just so', we might gain the reward of being able to see the world as it truly is – and it is beautiful. In the 'just so' world everything is forced into a monochrome of darkness or light, sea or dry land, one thing or its opposite. And never the 'twain shall meet. But in our new vision of the world, with our rabbinic lenses, we see a myriad of gradations between the black and white poles of the foolish search for certainty and perfection. In this new vision of the world we become witnesses to sunsets – melting the edges of darkness and light. In this new vision we become witnesses to rainbows – born out of the dance of raindrop and sunbeam.

It is scary, this fragile, precarious existence – as a human being, as a senior rabbinical student, as an Englishman counting down his last months in New York, as a single man counting down his last months of bachelordom. And there is no solid ground beneath me.

But when I look up and see rainbows and sunsets – when I look up and see the smiles of those I love and those whom I have had the enormous honour of learning from these last 32 years – then I know I would choose no other path, and that is the greatest gift I know.

It is the gift I wish for you all.

Shabbat Shalom.

More 'Theos', Less 'Ology'
{2010}

I first met (then plain old) Elliot Cosgrove – now Rabbi Cosgrove PhD – over email before I arrived in New York. As a student he had a part-time position helping others navigate the Seminary's entry procedures. I took up a lot of his time. Elliot has strong connections to my own rabbinic journey. For a time he flew into St Albans to provide SAMS with rabbinic support, and he wrote his PhD on Rabbi Louis Jacobs. We only met in person seven or so years after our first correspondence, and I was honoured to be invited to contribute to a collection he edited – *Jewish Theology in Our Time: A New Generation Explores the Foundations and Future of Jewish Belief.*

The title for my contribution owes – of course – a debt to Maureen Lipman's peerless creation, 'Beattie', though I'm not sure any of the book's American readers would have caught that. I discuss both brokenness, and also what I think of as my 'substantiated' theology – a theology that is driven not by escape into abstraction and purity, but instead by corporeal encounters in the real world; a theology that turns towards the more substantiated, corporeally infused parts of the rabbinic theology.

As I received proofs I heard of the passing of Yochanan Muffs. Yochanan, in his pomp a colossus of JTS's Bible faculty, was struck low by illness by the time I arrived at the Seminary. But every semester a couple of students would get a chance to sit with him and attempt to navigate the path between his written works and vast mind. I remember him thumping his fist on the desk and demanding of our pallid reading of some prophetic passage, 'Juice, you have to extract the juice!' I dedicated the contribution to his memory.

A s a junior rabbinical student with a passion for philosophy, I decided to tackle a modern Christian academic's 'Systematic Theology'. It seemed a sensible thing to do if I was planning on studying for a Master's in Theology. I lasted fifty pages. It was a mind-numbingly dull book, stuffed with logical proofs, determined to avoid any whiff of contradiction and set on tidying up the whole messy business of God. It was a Christian work, but it wasn't, so much, the Jesus-ness of the work that got to me, as the notion of a systematic relationship with the Divine. It left me cold and I ended up studying for a Master's in Midrash.

I prefer literary raids on the Divine to systematic logical posits; I'm very concerned with my 'Theos' and only peripherally with 'ology'. I like my theology full of colour and contradiction, anthropomorphism and emotion. Attempts to construct watertight philosophical arguments about the nature of God and my Jewish relationship to the Divine feel unsuited to the messy uneven world in which I find myself. My theology is 'new', if it is new at all, in that I don't share the concerns of the philosophically-minded theologians I have read. Unlike the founding rabbi of the synagogue I now serve, Louis Jacobs, I'm not that interested in articulating a theology that the Orthodox Jewish world would consider acceptable.

Unlike Franz Rosenzweig, the early twentieth-century German theologian, I'm not that interested in a theology which passes muster according to the standards of Western universities. Unlike Rambam, I'm not that interested in dogmatic assertions which allow me to test who is and who is not a proper Jewish theologian. None of these theological endeavours seems to help me be better: a better husband, father, rabbi... They don't even seem to help me understand the world with more accuracy or insight.

If my theology has a foundation it is this verse: 'And God created the human in the image of God, male and female God created them' (Gen 1:27). To me this verse is more than the foundation of our conception of human rights, democracy, and the equality of all people (though that would be enough). It is also the key to the map which allows me to find a path towards the heavens. The problem is this: I am finite and limited. There is so much I will never understand. I believe in infinity as a place where contradictions cease and everything makes sense. I call that place (literally *hamakom*) God, but I can't directly engage with that infinity. Direct engagement with infinity is impossible mathematically, philosophically and emotionally, so I need a path. All religious people avail themselves of techniques which illuminate a path towards divinity/infinity. Temple Jews tried sacrifices, Abulafia tried mystical combinations of letters. I use the images and tales passed down in the Jewish tradition I inherited, claim and love. The Bible and older rabbinic texts are full of images of a God expressed in human terms: outstretched arms, flaring nostrils, remembering and forgetting. I don't think the rabbis believed in a literal Zeus-like caricature any more than Michelangelo (painter of the Sistine Chapel ceiling) believed God has a white beard and a pointy finger. It's just that these images allow us to negotiate a path towards that which is beyond comprehension in ways our human hearts and human minds can grasp. The verse suggesting the creation of human beings in the image of God teaches me something about the nature of humanity, but it teaches me more about the nature of God – or more precisely more about the way in which I have to think about God, if I am to find any way of bridging the chasm between the human and heavenly realms.

But I'm not sure my theology arises from a single foundation, no matter how powerful a verse like Genesis 1:27 might be. My theology arises in the space between circumstance and sefer (book) – between experiencing something and the response that more slowly emerges from my encounter with my faith. The process also works in reverse. Study produces the raw material that enters my mythical 'theologiser', life happens somewhere in the middle, and out the other end appears – on a good day – a coherent reflection on the space that exists between God and human (me).

An example: From circumstance to sefer.
I'm the father of a three-and-a-half-year-old boy who recently followed a cat he had been playing with from the pavement into the middle of the road, where he was struck (thankfully only a glancing

non-serious blow) by a passing car. My wife and I had spent a lot of time talking about road safety with our son and we were standing five metres away at the time, but he hadn't learnt well enough and we didn't manage to stop him. And then it struck me, God had the same problem in the Garden of Eden, and in the desert, and once the Israelites crossed into the Promised Land. God wants children who independently make their own decisions, but God also wants them (us) to behave precisely as God would wish. Our failure to prevent our son from breaking his leg was God's failure to prevent Adam and Eve from eating the fruit. It is the failure of wanting our dearest creations to have life and meaning, and we've always failed this way – God, you and I.

Another example: From sefer to circumstance. [1]

The Bible says of Noah that he walked with God, and it says of Abraham that he walked before God. The rabbis suggest God had to support a stumbling and fallible Noah, but that Abraham was called forth from Mesopotamia to illuminate the path before a stumbling God – a deity staggering in the darkness like King Lear's blinded Lord Gloucester on his way to Dover. The Talmudic master Reish Lakish suggests an analogy to a Prince who needs his elders to lead the way before him. God needs us. Abraham Joshua Heschel has the perfect title for his major theological work, *God in Search of Man*. Needed as I am, as I believe we all are, I feel I have a role, I am called to action – I should be doing what I can to light up the way.

When my teachers (Neil Gillman, Paul Tillich, and James Fowler) have written of 'brokenness' in the context of theology they have meant the brokenness of a believer's beliefs about God – childish literalisms broken into myths. But that has never been my experience. I never thought God, literally, had a 'white beard', I never felt the loss of that kind of innocence. The brokenness of my theology haunts God, not my faith journey. The brokenness of my theology is the brokenness articulated by the sixteenth-century kabbalist

---

[1] Bereishit Rabba 30:10

Isaac Luria. In Luria's cosmology, God begins by creating a hollow void in the suffusing light of God's goodness – this is the origin of chaos and disorder. And then God tries to trickle-feed goodness into this empty space. The result is what happens when an electrician fails to use wire of sufficient thickness to cope with a mighty power surge. The 'lower vessels' shatter and in the mess of order, chaos, good and evil that results from the explosion we find ourselves, and our God, all trying to get along as well as we can.

I've had more insight, more comfort and better instruction (literally, *torah*) reflecting on biblical and rabbinic narratives of Divine-human encounters than in the hundreds of pages of discourse on the nature of etiology, determinism and the rest of the classic subjects of academic theology I encountered before I gave up on 'systematic theology'.

There are perhaps two problems with building a theology from texts like these, narratives about a broken and/or human-like deity who needs human support to realise 'His' lofty potential. First, we don't live in a world which appreciates the way narratives serve as carriers of profound truths. We live in a world which prefers its truths wrapped in philosophy, couched in the language of the academy and buttressed by logic. We consider stories to be playthings for children, but these texts are not childish; they are brave, bold, self-aware and profoundly adult, and they communicate more in image than logical positivism ever could.

Second, these kinds of texts feel dangerous, blasphemous almost, especially since Rambam's decrying of anthropomorphism. Whenever I share texts like this in educational settings, I get challenged by those who insist on a Jewish theology in which God is a philosophical entity, too aloof for the corporeal sensibilities of midrash. (It's not that my challengers necessarily sign up to this aloof version of God, but this is, nonetheless, the kind of God they demand I offer for them not to believe in.) But I have sources on my side, verses, *sugyot* – Talmudic passages – and midrashim. There are texts like this throughout our tradition and they must be considered authentic by dint of their canonisation in the classic collections of our faith.

These texts become the bulwark of my faith when I struggle to find a relationship with God. When the sun is shining and the birds are singing I can find Divinity everywhere, but when life seems nasty, brutish and short I turn to these texts and they are there for me. They give me insight and strength. The bad stuff, cancer, Alzheimer's and much worse, break any attempt to construct an image of a wholly powerful and beneficent God. But the bad stuff doesn't force me outside my religious tradition. I don't feel the need to reformulate or reconstruct a new Jewish relationship with the Divine, unknown in history. Instead I excavate and dust down canonised images of God that speak to me in my brokenness. And from this exercise in literary archaeology God emerges as a companion for my suffering (literally, *ach letzarah*; Talmud Sanhedrin 46a), and that helps.

I am sometimes asked, usually by those who disavow a faith in God, if I ever have crises of faith. I find this an impossible question to answer in the terms of my questioners. I don't have crises of faith because my theology is built off existential crisis. It is a theology immune to being shattered by the slings and arrows of outrageous fortune precisely because it comes pre-shattered. I live in peace with my broken theology.

It could be that with all this emotion and wish to find meaning I am kidding myself. It could be that God is really no more than a fig leaf strategically placed over an existential vacuum. Or it could be God really is all perfect and perfectly unknowable. But, despite my disavowing of much of the scientific aspects of theology, I do believe in testing my theological hypotheses. I test my theology in hospices and at Holocaust memorials. I test it in the context of my rabbinic workload of 'hatch, match and despatch'. I test my theology as I open prayer books and study books, when I sit in my home and when I walk on the street. The more I test, the more I feel that this exercise in textual archaeology in search of a broken Deity who is in search of Man – me – is true, and the more I test the more I feel existential nihilism and aloof perfection are equally false.

I claim and treasure the authenticity of articulating my theology in the language of the biblical and rabbinic tradition. It's not that I have a fear of being excommunicated – every decent rabbi should be excommunicated at some point – but rather that I want to be held by my *masorah* – tradition: its people, its history, its wandering and wondering, especially when I am struggling to find a response to pain and suffering. I can't practice my theology in a cave or an ivory tower; my theology belongs in a community, in dialogue with my congregants and my teachers and their teachers and their teachers' teachers going back to Sinai.

In the opening of this reflection I cast doubt on whether my theology is really a 'new voice'. It's not supposed to be. It's supposed to be a theology for today in which the echoes and resonances of the tradition can be heard as fresh and powerful voices able to help us live better when facing the challenges and opportunities of the current age.

Damien Hirst - Open and Closed Systems
{Yizkor, Yom Kippur 2013}

I enjoy the sermonic challenge of Yizkor on Yom Kippur. As rabbi and High Holy Day crowd we have, by now, got used to one another. For me, there is only one subject for the Yizkor sermon, something about death and the things that survive it. I keep a document open during the year with thoughts that could make their way into a High Holy Day sermon, and it's usually the Yizkor sermon that coalesces first in my mind. I've often turned to contemporary art in search of a parallel language in which to express religious ideas, and I knew, the moment I saw the installation that provided the springboard for this piece, that I had a sermon waiting to be written.

This summer I finally got to see Damien Hirst's *A Thousand Years*. It's a big glass box – a vitrine – in which lies a severed cow's head: big mournful eyes, blood gently seeping into a pool. And around the head are flies – it revolts: vast numbers of densely packed tiny winged insects, breeding away as the cow lies rotting. Then, above the head, suspended inside the vitrine is a fly killing machine, blue light radiating, every couple of seconds a flash as another fly wanders too close and dies. Actually not all the flies die in the insectocutor. Some seem dead of natural causes, lying on the floor on the far side of the glass box, away from the bright blue light.

The piece feels as if it is about me. Here I am, inside this big ol' vitrine, buzzing around and facing only a singular certainty. Like a withering leaf and a passing dream.

But the thing that struck me most, looking in at this stark eco-system, was its sealed quality. I expected the work to smell, but the smell is sealed in. You expect the zapping insectocutor to make a noise, but you can't hear anything. Nothing emerges from within. Nothing goes anywhere. It's a closed system. And that was the thing that struck me as false, emotionally and spiritually. That's the element that felt inaccurate. We buzz around and we die – for sure. But my question is this. Is there a possibility of transcending, is there something beyond or is everything forever to be locked inside a sealed box? My question doesn't seem to interest Hirst much, either in this work or any of the others at the exhibition. But it nags at me. Are our lives lived in a closed-in ecosystem, sealed inside a glass box, or is there a permeability to existence? Can we touch something beyond, can that which is beyond touch us?

I admit I desire a permeable universe. If our lives are truly lived inside a hermetically sealed box, what's the point? If there really is nothing that can emerge from all this strife, then frankly, none of it matters. Even humanity's greatest achievements, from Ghandi to Einstein to Mozart, amount to no more than a brief buzz inside a vitrine. This is the game Hirst plays with his choice of title, 'A Thousand Years' – as if the flies exist for more than a measure of days; as if any length of time could make any 'real' difference if everything we are, everything we were and everything we will become exist only inside a glass box. On the other hand, if there is permeability, some point of connection from this mortal world to somewhere beyond, then even my most paltry of actions might count, might emerge in some unpredictable way in a parallel universe, an unknowable future, an *Olam Haba* – a world to come. If we live in a world where the realities of life and death are, somehow, permeable, then there is the possibility of a link or bridge connecting me with those I have loved and lost. It might still be possible to talk about a living relationship with the loved ones we remember on this day.

I'm no physicist, but I'm fascinated by astral physics and quantum mechanics – tales of parallel universes and a strange subatomic existence which scramble my sense of what we know about our Universe. Black holes seem to suck in matter, which goes where, exactly? Electrons disdain normal laws of motion, travelling from place A to place C not via B, but by every point in the known and unknown Universe. Off they go, escaping from their vitrines left, right, and centre and in directions and dimensions that evade human understanding.

And what of memories, emotions, our sense of self? Will it, could it, be possible to download everything we are onto a circuit board, will it be possible to create a human being purely inside a test tube? Or will there always be something about being human that needs to be created in a world beyond measure? Today is a day for speaking about memories of those who have passed away, leaving imprints upon us. Is that all happening in a sealed ecosystem, or is there a place from which and into which memories and emotions emerge in ways that cannot be contained, replicated, measured or understood?

Certainly religion, my religion anyway, has an answer to these questions. My faith is predicated on just such a notion of permeability. Judaism teaches that our actions permeate beyond the realms of classical physics or any other force known to humanity. The Talmud teaches, *Gedolah teshuvah shemiga'at ad kiseh hacavod* [1] – how great is *teshuvah*, for it reaches the Throne of Glory. Judaism is theurgic: we believe our actions can change God, change everything. That relationship between a person and God is called *bein adam laMakom* – literally, between a person and The Place. God is That Place which lies beyond the vitrine, beyond our ability to reach, understand and order – but a Place no less real for its lack of a quantifiable location. Religion can be rational, and there are all kinds of vital things rationality can teach us about our lives inside the vitrine. But religion is ultimately about that which is mysterious. It is about what lies beyond the observable and the measureable.

Julian Barnes, in his wonderful book *Nothing to be Afraid Of,* [2] cites a passage from *Madame Bovary* in which Homais, who he calls 'the bigoted materialist', declares the Christian notion of Resurrection to be not only 'absurd' but 'contrary to the laws of physics'. This is a nonsensical argument, suggests Barnes, predicated on things we can't understand being ridiculous because we can't understand them. It's the spiritual equivalent of the drunkard who looks for his fallen keys only in the small pool of light emanating from a streetlamp. The drunkard rejects the notion that the keys could have fallen outside what he can see, and so is doomed to never find them.

---

[1]   Yoma 86a.
[2]   P. 77.

It's easy to misunderstand religion by imagining God is somehow part of the world we are supposed to understand. This is an error made by both atheists and fundamentalists. There is a certain kind of atheist who believes that if they can just manipulate a beam of electrons sufficiently quickly they will understand everything there is to know about the Universe and its creation. There is a certain kind of fundamentalist who is wont to believe that God can be manipulated by obeying certain prescriptions; if you keep kosher and light Shabbat candles you will be rewarded with good exam results and a new tricycle for Chanukah. But that is to misunderstand God as part of the measurable and manipulable Universe – existing inside a vitrine along with us flies. That's not how religion works. God is the space beyond measurement, permeating inside as our actions and inactions permeate beyond in ways we cannot understand.

Religion is often accused of tending towards authoritarianism,[3] but the kind of religion I'm trying to describe doesn't incline towards absolutism. The only thing I absolutely believe about that which is beyond is that there is such a Place. I can't understand it, but my actions permeate to it as it permeates through me. More than that is mysterious.

Perhaps the two most honest and holy lines in the entire Yom Kippur liturgy are to be found in the Book of Jonah. The first is the speech of the captain of the ship, being tossed around in the sea, while Jonah sleeps, having fled to Tarshish. *Ma l'cha nirdam kum kra el elohecha **ulai** yitashet ha'elohim lanu v'lo noved* – 'What are you doing asleep? Get up, call to your God, and **perhaps** that God will save us and we won't perish.' *Ulai* – perhaps.[4] And then later – the King of Ninevah, having been told his whole city is to be destroyed, seeks to repent. He calls on the city to turn away from their violent, evil ways. ***Mi-yodea** yashuv v'niham ha'Elohim v'shav meharon apo v'lo noved* – '**Who knows**, maybe God will return and take pity and turn from God's anger and we won't be destroyed.' *Mi-yodea* – who knows.[5]

---

[3] Even by the more 'gentle' atheists; e.g. Julian Barnes, *Nothing to be Afraid Of*, p. 82.

[4] 1:6.

[5] 3:9.

Ulai – perhaps; and *mi-yodea* – who knows.

The point, I think, is this. Far from turning us into bigots or fundamentalists, living with belief should make us throw in our lot with those who are trying to create a more decent and kind world for us all. It should make us better. Living with belief is not a crutch to prop up a childish fantasy or a tool to ensure we are all given tricycles for Chanukah. Belief isn't about certainty. Indeed, there is less certainty in this kind of religion than in many brands of atheism. Belief is the attempt to engage with the permeable walls of the vitrine in which we buzz around. It is about the courage to engage with that which we cannot know, with the sea captain's sense of *ulai* – maybe this will work.

I had a strange experience at a funeral this year. One of the mourners, not a member of the family, accosted me as I was washing my hands on leaving the cemetery. 'Will I see my father in heaven,' they wanted to know. 'I asked– [here they mentioned the name of a well-known rabbi] – and they told me I definitely would. What do you think?' I told him I didn't know. I wanted to offer the answer of the captain of Jonah's ship – *ulai*. He was having none of it. What use was I, he insisted, if I couldn't even promise him this?

But there is use in this gentle form of faith, a belief in something beyond comprehension, but there nonetheless and permeable. Not only does acting with such a belief improve us, it also trains us to listen out for the whispers of that which is beyond. It's a kind of mindfulness in which we can experience that which we cannot understand. It's a state of life which allows for moments of transcendence, permeability. On this day, when we stand and knock at the permeable walls of our mortal selves, it is the blessing I have for us all – that we should feel that sense of the transcendent, that sense of something beyond knowledge but nonetheless present. And for those of us here to touch the memory of a departed loved one, my blessing is that we can find a way to keep the impossible connections alive so the memories of those we have loved and lost can continue to be a blessing.

Yehey zichronam l'varuch.

May their memories be always for a blessing.

CHAPTER 5

Religion and Science

Some perceive the encounter between religion and science as a zero sum game, one which either religion or science must 'win' and the other lose, absolutely and unconditionally. These souls, whichever faction they adhere to, regard those in the opposite camp as ignorant at best, and stupid at worst.
Yet there have also always been people of faith and people of science who see the two as inhabiting complementary conceptual worlds. As I said in the Yizkor sermon reproduced in the previous chapter, 'religion is ultimately about that which is mysterious. It is about what lies beyond the observable and the measureable.' For this group – and I count myself among them – the line separating religion from science is a place of meeting rather than confrontation.

Playing Dice with Einstein, God, and Suffering

{2008}

I have a lay person's love of science (nothing is as
dangerous as a little knowledge). Walter Isaacson's
masterful biography of Albert Einstein made a great
impression on me and this article, published in
Conservative Judaism but based on material originally
shared in the *Jewish Quarterly*, is my attempt to find
a meaningful debate between two worlds so often seen
as diametrically opposed to one another.

I am grateful to Professor Louis Lyons, University
of Oxford, for looking over the physics discussed in
this piece.

I've never been interested in hearing whether one person or
another claims to believe in God, or is or is not religious. As
Thomas Merton noted, 'our idea of God tells us more about
us than Him'.[1] Neither question seems to offer insight into how a
person might face a world in which bouquets and brickbats fall
equally on those who claim faith and those who deny it. Rather, in
search of a central religious–philosophical way of understanding
the world I have always been more interested in this question: how
do you understand its relationship with order and chaos? Do you
look at the world and see a universe basically in order, with the occasional challenge or mystery, like an unfilled answer in a crossword
puzzle that will eventually all make perfect sense? Or do you look
at the world and see an unpredictable, unknowable chaotic pit with
any semblance of order we might encounter no more than a veneer
stretched over a nihilist chasm, a fig leaf over an existential vacuum?

This is hardly a new way of posing a foundational theological
cum philosophical question, but, perhaps surprisingly, its most

---

[1]   T. Merton, *New Seeds of Contemplation* (New Directions, 1972), p. 15.

passionate and articulate respondents are neither professional theologians nor philosophers, but particle physicists. In this paper I want to look at one of the most significant debates in twentieth-century science and suggest some implications for those of us who are struggling to articulate a relationship between order and chaos in our own lives.

PHYSICS, CAUSE AND EFFECT

Until the 1900s, physicists believed it would be possible to reach a precise understanding of the relationship between cause and effect. If you dropped a weight from a certain height it would take a certain amount of time to reach the ground – that sort of thing. As long as a physicist had enough information about a system, they expected to be able to work out precisely how any part of that system would respond at any given time.

The doyen of all modern physicists, Albert Einstein, was an archetypal classical physicist in that he believed in this type of approach. He was a self-defined 'determinist': a passionate believer in strict rules of cause and effect. He didn't have the arrogance to believe he understood all these rules; indeed, his humility when confronted by the majesty of the world was the prime source of his special kind of religiosity – but he believed such rules did exist and that they applied to every element of the Universe, 'for the insect as well as for the star. Human beings, vegetables, or cosmic dust, we all dance to a mysterious tune, intoned in the distance by an invisible player.'[2]

Then came quantum mechanics. The discovery of quantum mechanics in the 1920s was built on the foundations of Einstein's own discoveries, but Einstein never fully accepted the single most provocative truth of the field of studies his own work begat.

It is possible to 'charge up' a cloud of atoms by pumping electricity into it. This results in some of the atoms in the gas absorbing energy and emitting photons. As long as one doesn't wish to look too closely it is possible to use these emitted photons very precisely

---

[2]   W. Isaacson, *Einstein* (Simon & Schuster, London, 2007), pp. 391-2. Subsequent references to Einstein's quotes, followed by a page number, refer to this work.

– this, after all, is how lasers work. But while an applied physicist might be content working out how to focus a laser beam to perform any particular task, a theoretical physicist, as Einstein was, has to grapple with how this stream of photons is produced. And this is where the science becomes murky.

The problem is that atoms in a gas do not emit photons according to precise laws of cause and effect. There is no way to determine which atoms in a gas will emit a photon at any given time, and there is no way to determine which direction any particular emitted photon will travel. In general terms the majority of atoms will behave in a particular way, and that is fine for practical applications, but on an individual basis no amount of information about the system of gas and charge can allow a physicist to predict which atom will behave in which way under any given set of circumstances. Three identical atoms could undergo identical experiences and two might emit photons in completely different directions while the third atom might emit nothing.

While classical theoretical physics speaks in terms of causality and predicts certainty, quantum theoretical physics speaks in terms of indeterminacy and predicts only probability. Quantum mechanics is not nihilism. It doesn't reject order, but rather the attempt to pin down the precise nature of this order. As long as one is content to generalize, a certain order can be predicted. It is only when individual explanations are sought that clear-cut answers become impossible.

Einstein doggedly refused to accept what experiment after experiment seemed to prove – that on an individual level, sub-atomic matter failed to behave according to laws of cause and effect. 'I find the idea quite intolerable that an electron exposed to radiation should choose of its own free will not only its moment to jump off but also its direction', he wrote to his colleague Max Born. 'In that case, I would rather be a cobbler, or even an employee of a gaming house, than a physicist' (p. 324). Indeed, it is another letter to Born that contains the first appearance of the now-famous aphorism. 'Quantum mechanics is certainly imposing,' wrote Einstein, 'but an inner voice tells me that it is not yet the real thing. The theory says a lot, but it does not really bring us any closer to the secrets of the Old One. I, at any rate, am convinced that He does not play dice' (p. 335).

Does the world operate according to strict rules of causality, or is there another ordering power? This is the essence of the argument between Einstein and the school of quantum mechanics led by Niels Bohr. It is no minor detail; it threatens not only the determinist position of classical physics, but also the central claim of anyone who, like Einstein, believes that the Universe is, at its essence, a place of order and regulation. The philosopher C.P. Snow suggested that 'no more profound intellectual debate has ever been conducted'.[3]

Turning the clock forward some seventy years, Bohr seems to have won. Despite the best efforts of Einstein, and classical and quantum physicists since, physics – at a quantum level – has abandoned the absolute ordered determinism that was the marker of Einstein's world view. The jury has returned. The Universe, at its core, is uncertain; not without structure, not chaotic, but aloof and unwilling to be bound down. The Universe is unknowable not merely as a fact of our current state of knowledge, but essentially, irredeemably and ultimately so.

RABBINICS, CAUSE AND EFFECT

This scientific reality impacts on what is surely the greatest challenge to faith, a challenge articulated perfectly in words the Talmud reports as coming from Moses in the aftermath of the Golden Calf debacle.

> Moses said before God: Master of the Universe, why is it that there are righteous people who do well, righteous people who do poorly, wicked people who do well and wicked people who do badly?[4]

The problem is, of cause, an enquiry into the nature of cause and effect. If a person does good they should get good back, and vice versa. While this approach to life is often equated with a somewhat simplistic notion of God sitting like some Divine accountant keeping track of our various existential credits and debits, the belief in a

---

3 In A.P. French (ed.), *Einstein: A Twentieth Century Volume* (Harvard University Press, Cambridge, MA, 1979), p. 3.
4 TB Brachot 7a.

connection between the good we do and the effect we expect to see in our lives need not involve any deistic intervention at all – this after all is what non-deistic Eastern faiths call karma, or what determinist scientists might be tempted to consider an application of doctrines of cause and effect.[5] The challenge comes when the available evidence appears to contradict such claims as to the ordered nature of life.

There are two possible approaches to this challenge. We can reject the apparent evidence, so preserving the nexus connecting cause and effect. Or we can reject the nexus, and accept the evidence. It's worth unpacking a little more gently these two possible approaches.

REJECTING THE EVIDENCE, PRESERVING THE NEXUS

Rejecting the evidence means either rejecting that the suffering good person before us is genuinely good, or alternatively rejecting that the suffering they experience is genuinely bad. Both approaches have rabbinic precedent. Rabbi Yossi suggests that when confronted with Moses' question, God responds by suggesting that the suffering righteous person is really suffering a cosmic hangover brought on by their wicked and unpunished parents: 'The righteous one who does badly is the righteous child of a wicked one', and vice versa (loc. cit.). In other words, the evidence presented at first instance is set in a broader context whereby the causation merits suffering rather than reward, contrary to what an observer might have originally thought.

The other nexus-preserving approach, the approach which denies that the suffering is indeed bad, finds its *locus classicus* in the Talmuda few folios earlier than Moses' question to God (5a-b). Here the rabbis suggest that unexplainable suffering in this world will result in greater reward in the world to come. These are the *isurin shel ahavah* – sufferings of love – which, it is suggested, should be accepted with grace and even delight.

---

5   Though it is odd to see literalist theologians and determinist scientists lining up on the same side of an argument.

REJECTING THE NEXUS

Rejecting the nexus – rejecting the relationship between cause and effect – seems, if anything, even more terrifying than rejecting the evidence that not all good causes result in good effects. Rejecting that there is a necessary connection between reward and punishment begs the question, 'Why be good?' Of course, there are by-ways in our tradition that suggest just such a rejection (the conclusion of the *isurin shel ahavah* passage suggests that a suffering person should reject not only their suffering, but also any possible reward). Nonetheless, rejecting the operation of a nexus of cause and effect feels, if not immoral, then amoral. It threatens personal morality and even the fabric of society.

THE LESSONS OF PHYSICS

Initially these two paths seem mutually exclusive; one might think we are forced either to preserve the nexus of cause and effect, or reject such an ordered system of earthly and/or heavenly operation. But this isn't the message of quantum mechanics. Neither Einstein nor Bohr rejected the generalised operation of doctrines of cause and effect. Neither denied that cause and effect is, in general terms at least, the operating default of the Universe (the example of the laser). It is only when one is forced to look specifically at individual cases that the holes in the generality are exposed. This, perhaps, is the approach of Rabbi Meir, again responding to Moses' great question to God (loc. cit.). Rabbi Meir held that God refuses to answer the question:

> As it is said: 'And I will be gracious to whom I will be gracious', although he may not deserve it, 'and I will show mercy on whom I will show mercy' (Ex 33:19), even if they do not deserve it.

It's not that Rabbi Meir should be considered a nexus-anarchist, but rather that he seeks to preserve God's 'wiggle-room' in specific cases. The twin doctrines of reward and punishment and cause and effect both apply and remain aloof, unknowable and beyond our lepidopterist's desire to pin every specimen down for microscopic examination.

The question of whether the Universe operates, on an individual basis, with or without cause and effect is of pastoral, as well as theological, significance. If we suffer but feel the Universe is ordered along determinist principles (per Einstein), we will, consciously or otherwise, attempt to fit our pain into a mechanistic system. This, in turn, often leads to a search for causation: why did this happen to me? While for some this kind of questioning can provide instruction or comfort, it's not a path I tend to offer those who turn to me for guidance in their suffering. Searching for answers where none exists is thankless at best and can lead only to more pain, guilt and/or recrimination. On the other hand, if we are prepared to accept that cause and effect are ultimately indeterminate – if we accept that, ultimately, there may be no reason why one small baby dies and another lives – it might be easier to return to the real world, leaving some of the existential pain behind.

A RIGHT AND A WRONG JEWISH APPROACH

Many Jews (especially those who are distant from religious study) assume that, on the question of causation of suffering, Judaism sides wholeheartedly with the determinist Einstein, but that is incorrect. A more nuanced and accurate representation of the tradition should acknowledge precisely what Bohr suggests – at a certain level we can predict order, but when it comes to individuals we need to acknowledge an absence of causation. Nowhere is this common fallacy and accurate reality better expressed than in the first verses of the Hebrew Bible. The opening of the Bible as translated in the Christian King James Version reads, 'In the beginning God created the heaven and the earth. And the earth was without form, and void; and darkness was upon the face of the deep. And the Spirit of God moved upon the face of the waters. And God said, Let there be light.' This is a beautifully balanced, ordered reading of Genesis 1:1-3. It's a translation that might make a person think the Hebrew Bible believes that everything in the world is in order, determined. But as a translation it is wrong. It fails to communicate a clear element of the original Hebrew. The Hebrew suggests a far less ordered creation, and the Jewish JPS translation is more accurate when it translates, 'When God began to create heaven and earth – the earth being unformed and void, with darkness over the surface of the deep and a wind from God sweeping over the water – God said, "Let there be light."' In other words, at the first moment of creation there is a void – *tohu vavohu.*

Mystics from Isaac Luria to Nahman of Braslav have understood this emptiness – also referred to as a place of *tzimtzum* or the *hallal hapanui* – as the primordial location of indeterminism. In the beginning chaos and order stood side by side, each competing for the upper hand, just as we find in the argument between Bohr and Einstein.

There are, in these encounters between Judaism and physics, different ways of framing very similar perspectives on the Universe and everything in it. The science acts as a testing ground for the religious claims (if it fails the test of science it cannot be claimed as 'true'), while the religion provides a broader framework for the claims of science – a way of setting scientific claims against broader theological, pastoral and psychological canvases. At the very least, engaging seriously with Einstein's dice playing (or otherwise) deity has to be an improvement on arguments about whether God does or doesn't exist and, if he does, whether he gave dictation on Sinai all those years ago.

Religion and Contemporary Medical Ethics

{2008}

This is the first major presentation I gave at New London off the bimah. I arranged an evening with responses from a geneticist and a chaplain from Great Ormond Street Hospital and attempted to articulate a role for Judaism in one of the most important conversations of our age. Using religion to engage in these kinds of issues is something I would love to spend more time doing – but the day job is hectic.

The presentation was given shortly after the passing of Sidney Mann, a beloved senior warden at New London who passed away in my first month as its rabbi. I dedicated it to his memory.

THE UNDERPINNING OF MEDICAL ETHICS

I want to start with an observation about what seems to be the driving force behind medical ethics in the societies in which we live. The first basis of most attempts to articulate an approach to medical ethics, from a secular perspective, is autonomy.[1] In other words, the general approach of secular medical ethics is to assume that 'I have the right to decide what treatment I want and what medical science should do or not do for me.' For instance, in the General Medical Council's guide to Good Medical Practice we find the following: 'The Doctor registered with the General Medical Council must respect patients' right to reach decisions with you about their treatment and care.'[2]

Professor Raanan Gillon, Professor of Medical Ethics at Imperial College, puts it more circumspectly:

---

[1] T. L. Beauchamp and J. F. Childress, *Principles of Biomedical Ethics*, 3rd ed. (Oxford University Press, New York and Oxford, 1989). A full bibliography of all the writing which has been of use developing this lecture is would be a vast undertaking. Citations are only provided where primary texts have been referred to.

[2] http://www.gmc-uk.org/guidance/good_medical_practice/duties_of_a_doctor.asp

Respect for autonomy is the moral obligation to respect the autonomy of others in so far as such respect is compatible with equal respect for the autonomy of all potentially affected. Respect for autonomy is also sometimes described, in Kantian terms, as treating others as ends in themselves and never merely as means – one of Kant's formulations of his 'categorical imperative'. [3]

Autonomy isn't absolute, a patient's will is not inviolate, but it is the basic starting point of future conversations.

This is something that, as a Jew, I would want to recognise also. Human individuals are of exceptional importance in Judaism. We are all created in the image of God, and, therefore, to trespass against an expression of human will is to trespass against an expression of the will of the image of the Divine. But I can't build a Jewish ethics from this foundation. In Judaism, notions of responsibility are far, far more important than the rights-based notion of autonomy. Investing absolute importance in an individual's autonomy – a supposed right to exercise their own desires – is problematic for a number of reasons. I want to detail two.

First, the human will is fickle. In religious terms we are governed by the interplay of *yetser hatov* and *yetser harah* – the good and the evil inclinations. We wish for strange things – sometimes. We live our lives by strange values – sometimes.

We don't really know how to measure the value of life in terms other than material productivity. We live in a society that offers us a scale of values by which to judge our decisions, and the scale is marked up in pounds and pence. That's a problem.

We live in a society that values its best footballers as 250 times more valuable than our best nurses. That's a problem.

Our ethical compass is erratic, and we are drawn magnetically to a direction that is not good and holy.

And that is the case when we are healthy.

When we are ill, particularly if we are afflicted psychologically or mentally, the notion that we – fragile humans – should be trusted with the ultimate say over how we are to be treated seems particu-

---

[3]   R. Gillon, 'Medical Ethics, Four Principles Plus Attention to Scope'. *BMJ* (1994), vol. 309, p. 184. Available at http://www.bmj.com/cgi/content/full/309/6948/184.

larly dangerous.

In the world of Jewish approaches to medical ethics, nowhere is this clearer than in the way Jewish law approaches suicide.

Suicide is forbidden in Jewish law. I will have more to say about this later. At present I want to pick up on how the codes of Jewish law treat someone who seemed to take a decision to take their own life. Simply put, the codes mistrust such decisions. They don't assume the autonomous action of a suicide is a genuine reflection of that in them which is divine.

Before a person is classified under Jewish law as a suicide, before taking one's own life is recognised as an autonomous decision, a vast range of requirements – checks and counter-checks – need to be met.

This quote comes from the *Aruch HaShulchan*:

> The general rule in this matter is that we look for any mitigating circumstance such as fear or anguish or insanity on the part of the victim [4] or if they thought that suicide was [somehow] meritorious. [If either is the case they] are not judged as a wilful suicide because it is so rare that a person would commit such an act with a clear mind.[5]

Feeling suicidal is not an autonomous feeling to be respected, but an illness that needs to be treated, to be responded to. In other words, an action which might by the standards of the world be considered autonomous is disregarded, and should be disregarded.

This is the first problem with basing an ethical approach on autonomy. We are not, even in health, the best judges of what is best for us, and when we are suffering it becomes even more dangerous to claim that an individual's decision is worthy of ultimate respect.

But the greater issue is this. In Jewish terms, this is not my life to use as I would wish.

This comes from the very opening moments of the daily liturgy: *Elohai neshama shenatata bi* – 'God, the soul you have placed in me is

---

[4] Note how the suicide is considered here a victim, not a perpetrator.
[5] Aruch haShulchan YD 345:5.

pure. You created it, you formed it, you breathed it into me, you tend it within me and in the future you will take it from me.' *Kol zman shehaneshama bkirbi modeh ani l'fanecha* – 'As long as the soul is within me I recognise my debt of gratitude to you, my God.'

To live is to pick up the responsibility to repay a debt of gratitude to our Creator. Central to Jewish thought – the foundation of Jewish ethics – is not human rights, but rather human responsibilities. We are not free to choose any path. Not all choices are ethically acceptable. Moses puts it bluntly:

> I call heaven and earth to record this day against you, that I have set before you life and death, blessing and curse; therefore choose life.[6]

Religion – the term – has at least a folk etymological root in the Latin word for being bound – obliged. Autonomy is the wrong starting point in the attempt to respond to the debt we incur through the gift of our souls.

Kant's recasting of his categorical imperative – the notion of treating every human being as an end in themselves – ultimately is not an attractive starting point in this ethical discussion. That said, Kant's first articulation of a categorical imperative is much more promising for our current purposes. The first articulation states that one should 'act only according to that maxim whereby you can at the same time will that it should become a universal law'.[7] We should act in such a way that we can hope that our actions should become universally appropriate.

A Jewish response to the theoretical primacy of autonomy in contemporary medical ethical thought is to say this – one should do what is good, not whatever one desires. And, moreover, it is incumbent on all of us to recognise that we might not always know what is good.

THE PRACTICAL PROBLEM

So much for the general underpinning theory of medical ethics. I want to move on to address a serious practical ethical concern.

When I was working as a hospital chaplain in America I came up

---

[6] Deuteronomy 30:19.

[7] Immanuel Kant, *Grounding for the Metaphysics of Morals*, 3rd ed. (trans. James W. Ellington), [1785] (1993). Hackett, p. 30.

against one problem again and again.

Doctors trained to remove ailments from their patients often struggle with this most basic truth – life is an ailment from which, ultimately, there is no cure. And indeed, many of the more complex challenges that present themselves to doctors, particularly in hospital settings, cannot be cured, and the role of the doctor in these places is to provide comfort and to limit pain and not to fight desperately to solve a physical problem when there is little to be gained from drastic medical intervention.

Dr Judith Nelson, an intensive care physician, noted that of the patients in her unit, 25 percent would die in the ICU and a further 5 to 10 percent would die before hospital discharge. She wrote:

> I became aware that despite 4 years of medical school and 6 years of residency and fellowship, I was almost completely unprepared for the tasks that occupied most of my time as an ICU attending physician – counseling patients and families in crisis, giving bad news, defining end of life care and ensuring comfort and dignity for those who were obviously dying. [8]

It's getting better. More and more medical schools are increasing the emphasis put on teaching palliative care. More and more doctors speak of cure care and comfort care. Chaplains, working with medical staff, can help patients be healed into death when being healed into life isn't a possibility. But too many doctors (surgeons perhaps most especially) consider cases where a medical cure is not possible as failures, and they find it hard to support patients and families in these places.

The world of science offers the promise that everything is possible – every disease can be conquered, every injury healed. But the world of faith teaches us that we are mortal and that, at the end of our days, the greatest thing we can wish for is to meet death well. We cannot run forever.

> The Angel of Death could never get close to Rav Hiyya. One day he dressed up as a pauper and came and knocked at his [Rav Hiyya's] gate. He said, 'Bring me some bread.' Others brought it out. He said

---

[8] J. Nelson, 'On Being a Doctor, Saving Lives and Saving Deaths', *Annals of Internal Medicine* (1999), vol. 130, no. 9, pp. 776-7.

to Rav Hiyya: 'Don't you, Sir, have compassion for the poor? Why don't you have compassion for me?' Rav Hiyya opened the door to him. The Angel of Death revealed himself, showing him a fiery rod, and Rav Hiyya yielded his soul to him. [9]

Many of us, doctors and lay people, see medicine as a discipline that treats only the physical needs of the patient. Therefore, a successful treatment is one that meets the patient's physical needs and an unsuccessful treatment is one that fails these physical needs. But a more Jewish perspective would insist on a more holistic approach to life. Our bodies are important, but so too are our souls.

Religion ought to help us find a more holistic way to engage in matters of medical ethics, one which insists that we treat not just the physical symptoms, but the entire person before us – acknowledging that we are a product of both physical and mental health, both corporeal and spiritual beings.

Despite the well-known passion, in Jewish teachings, for life – physical life – the importance of the soul is never denied. And sometimes it is the needs of the soul that should shape our approach to medical care.

Perhaps the clearest example of this in the rabbinic tradition is the story of the death of Rabbi Yehudah Ha-Nasi in the third century. The rabbi is mortally ill, but the rabbis have decreed a public fast and are praying for his recovery. They've also announced that anyone spreading rumours that he is dead will be stabbed with a sword. They are desperate to assure their leader's physical recovery.

The rabbi's nurse climbs to the roof and prays, 'The inhabitants of heaven want Rabbi and the inhabitants of earth want Rabbi. May it be the will of God that the inhabitants of earth overpower the inhabitants of heaven.' But when she sees how often the rabbi is forced to the toilet, when she witnesses his intense physical distress and lack of dignity, she prays again, 'May it be the will of God that the inhabitants of heaven overpower the inhabitants of earth.'

The nurse's first prayer is for the rabbi's physical recovery; her second is for his death. The story ends this way:

---

[9]   Moed Katan 28a (all Talmudic references are taken from the Babylonian Talmud).

But the students didn't cease in their prayers, so she took a jar and threw it from the roof to the ground. [The students'] prayer was interrupted just for a moment, and the soul of Rabbi departed to its eternal rest. [10]

This Talmudic story is clearly reported in praise of the actions of the nurse. The students are cast in the role of those unable to see that, from a holistic standpoint, they shouldn't be seeking a physical cure. It's an important story, particularly in the context of a faith that loves life above almost all else.

This same approach to the importance of spiritual issues, and anguish in particular, also characterises Judaism's attitude towards abortion. The Hebrew Bible is clear that the foetus is not to be considered a full human being, [11] but it doesn't consider abortion on demand to be acceptable either. So when may abortion be permitted? The answer is that where the foetus threatens the life of the mother it must be aborted, on the grounds that it is a *rodef*, or pursuer – i.e., one who pursues another in order to kill them. Jewish law mandates killing a *rodef* if they cannot be stopped in some other way. [12]

But then the question becomes, what counts as a threat to the mother's life? There is almost unanimous consent that abortion is permitted in cases of pre-eclampsia (toxemia of pregnancy). But what is noteworthy is the attention paid to the case of a foetus who pursues the mental or spiritual health of the mother – for instance, if the pregnancy arose as a result of abuse, or if a mother fears for her mental health having realised that the foetus has a severe illness.

In these cases there is rabbinic opinion, admittedly not unanimous, but noteworthy nonetheless, that permits abortion on the grounds that the foetus should not be allowed to pursue the mental and spiritual well-being of the mother.[13]

The Pandora's Box of that most combustible medical-ethical issue, abortion, is open. But I don't want to go further here. The point is that a holistic, mind and body, spiritual and physical approach to

---

[10] Ketubot 104a.
[11] Exodus 21:22-23.
[12] M. Ohalot 7:6, Sanhedrin 72b.
[13] Pri Ha-Aretz 3 YD 2.

the needs of the individual is a religious and ethical demand, and a demand that, at least until recently, many medical professionals have struggled to meet.

GENETICS

Genes are, of course, a modern discovery, but the notion of inherited characteristics is old and rabbinically understood. Isaac, for example, is held by the rabbis to have had the same facial characteristics as his father Abraham.[14] The Mishnah, a text some 1,800 years old, prohibits a person from marrying into a family who suffer from particular hereditary disease.[15] And the Talmud counsels against a very tall man marrying a very tall woman lest their children be tall like a mast.[16] There is even a contemporary authority in Jewish medical ethics who attempts to explain the story of Jacob mating the sheep of Laban as a demonstration of a biblical understanding of Mendelian inheritance,[17] though that seems anachronistic.

It is clear that the obligation to protect life and bolster health makes many contemporary and even future developments in gene therapy and similar fields exciting and acceptable. As Jews we made our peace with the role of human beings as partners, with God, in creation some time ago. We are not placed on this earth to step back from engaging in creation. As the good book says, 'Be fruitful and multiply and fill the earth.'

Most Jewish medical ethics, in what is still an underdeveloped field largely sees genetic therapy of all sorts as merely an extension of a general approach to the role of doctors. We have faith in God who controls who shall live and who shall die, but we are also commanded to take preventative measures to ward off illness, and to seek to cure illness when it occurs.

In one ancient text two rabbis are trying to heal a patient, only to have the patient accuse them of interfering in God's will in making

---

[14] BM 87a.
[15] Yevamot 64b.
[16] Bechorot 45b.
[17] Avraham Steinberg, *Encyclopedia of Jewish Medical Ethics* (Feldheim, 2003), vol. 2, p. 441.

him ill. The rabbis ask the man why he interferes with the God-given state of his vineyard by fertilizing and weeding. When he responds that without human care the crops wouldn't grow so well, the rabbis respond,

> Just as plants, if not weeded, fertilised and ploughed, will not grow and bring forth fruit, so too the human body. The fertiliser is the medicine and the means of healing and the tiller of the earth is the physician. [18]

Maimonides, with customary clarity, puts it like this. A person who sees a contradiction between the use of science to heal and pure faith in God,

> is like a person who is hungry and seeks bread to eat – which heals him from great pain. Should we say that they have failed to trust God? 'What fools!' is the proper retort to [those who say so]. For just as I, at the time of eating, thank God for having provided me with something to relieve my hunger, to sustain my life and strength – so should I thank God for having provided a cure which heals my illness when I use it.[19]

As Jews we are skilled at seeing God's guiding hand in human achievement. As Rabbi Louis Jacobs has noted, when we eat bread we praise God as *hamotzi lechem min ha'aretz*, the one who brings forth bread from the earth, even though we know a farmer planted the seed and harvested the crop and a miller ground the flour and a baker kneaded the dough... Human engagement need not be seen as contrary to the natural order, especially when there is the possibility of saving life. That is the Jewish way, even among the most ultra-orthodox of Jews.

Perhaps the most interesting example is that of Dor Yesharim, also called the Committee for Prevention of Jewish Genetic Diseases, which was founded by Rabbi Joseph Eckstein, a Tay-Sachs carrier who fathered Tay-Sachs children. Eckstein's organisation tests teenage Charedi boys and girls before they start dating and attempts to ensure that carriers of this horrid disease, and others, are

---

[18] Midrash Temurah, cited in David Feldman, *Health and Medicine in the Jewish Tradition* (Crossroad, 1986), p. 16.
[19] Commentary on Mishnah Pesachim 4:6.

not introduced one to the other. His work has had the backing of the unimpeachably orthodox authority Rav Moshe Feinstein.[20]

Genetic therapy is to be welcomed. That said, there is an important caveat that should be addressed.

The Talmud teaches:

> There are three partners in the human: The Holy Blessed One, its mother and its father. The father is responsible for the white, and from it come the bones, the sinews, the nails, the brain and the white of the eye. The mother is responsible for the red, and from it come the skin, the flesh, the hair and the black of the eye. And the Holy Blessed One sets within it spirit and soul and the brightness of the face and the eye's sight and the ear's hearing and the mouth's speech and the leg's ability to walk, and wisdom and sense.[21]

Pursuing genetic therapies in order to eliminate any role for the Divine is dangerous. It leaves us, as human beings, thinking we control too much. We are tempted to begin to see ourselves as gods, and this – aside from breaking the second of the Ten Commandments – creates the ethical problem of this work. We are in danger of glorifying too much in the work of our own hands.

Again, this is not a Luddite, anti-science approach, but rather a call that scientists hold themselves in check and don't allow their undoubted skill to cross over from the attempt to save life and increase health – entirely good – to the attempt to demonstrate their own brilliance and line their own pockets.

There is a beautiful prayer of Maimonides, himself a physician whose stature and skill allowed him access to the halls of power in Cairo, that I think should be on the laboratory benches of anyone working on the edges of medical possibility:

> Inspire me with love for my art and for Your creatures. Do not allow thirst for profit, ambition for renown and admiration to interfere with my profession, for these are the enemies of truth and of love for mankind and they can lead astray in the great task of attending to the welfare of Your creatures. In the sufferer let me see only the

---

[20] http://www.jewishgeneticscenter.org/rabbis/overview/, citing Moshe Feinstein, *Iggrot Moshe, Even Ha-Ezer*, Part 4, no. 10.

[21] Niddah 31a.

[22] Cited in D. M. Feldman and F. Rosner (eds.), *Compendium on Medical Ethics*, 6th ed. (Federation of Jewish Philanthropies, New York, 1984), pp. 144-5.

human being. [22]

Of course researchers have egos, of course they want to win awards, publish papers and even earn a decent living, but to pray to suppress these all-too-human desires, to pray to work always for the healing of suffering, is an ethical demand I make today.

END OF LIFE

The room of a person who is terminally ill is the most holy space I know. I suspect that sounds a little strange. It probably only makes sense in the context of a faith that seeks, not fairy stories and pious blandishments, but a clearer understanding of life in all its beauty and all its pain. The room of a person who is terminally ill is a place of truth.

As he approached his own death, Francois Mitterrand, the late President of France, wrote of his mortality in this way:

> At the moment of solitude, when the body breaks down on the edge of infinity, a separate time begins to run that cannot be measured in any normal way. In the course of several days, sometimes with the help of another presence that allows despair and pain to declare themselves, the dying take hold of their lives, take possession of them, unlock their truth... It is as if at the very culmination, everything managed to come free of the jumble of inner pains and illusions that prevent us from belonging to ourselves. [23]

For Maimonides, the physician, the moment of death was a moment of prophecy, true insight.

But preceding and surrounding this momentary glimpse of ultimate human knowledge is terrible pain. And indeed, for many the moment of death comes not with the insight afforded to President Mitterrand, or Tolstoy's Ivan Ilyich, but drugged up with morphine and lost to any possibility of conscious interaction with loved ones.

And here is the ethical problem. Medical science is capable of sustaining physical life far, far beyond what used to be possible. We can keep a person alive in vegetative states for decades. We can hold on to every last breath long past the point where medical cure is possible. But when science allows us to keep a shell of a life alive, how

---

[23] Cited in Marie De Hennezel, *Intimate Death: How the Dying Teach Us To Live* (Knopff, 1997), p. ix.

does one make a decision to let go, to pull back, to desist from medical intervention, or even to take active steps to foreshorten a life?

I began to address this terrible problem in the context of the nurse of Rabbi Yehudah Ha-Nasi. Let me take a step back and address the issue more systematically. Judaism loves life. The Bible states: 'You shall keep the laws and ordinances and by doing them, live by them.'[24] The early rabbinic commentary known as Sifra provides an echo for the last part of the verse: 'Live by them and not die by them.'[25] This is the textual proof at the heart of the well-known Jewish commitment to saving a life.

The classic discussion of how far our desire to save a life extends is the case of person discovered beneath a collapsed building on Shabbat. According to our earliest rabbinic text, the Mishnah, 'If a person is found alive under a fallen house [on Shabbat] the debris may be removed.'[26] The problem the later Gemarah has with this Mishnah is that it is blindingly obvious to the Jew that the laws of Shabbat should be over-ridden in this case. 'Isn't this obvious?', asks the Talmud. 'No', it answers its own challenge. 'It needs to be stated to specifically include the case of the life of a moment' (Heb. *chayei sha'ah*, idiomatically 'a moment of life').

The life of a moment overrides Shabbat. Even one moment is precious. This is the starting point of a Jewish approach to end-of-life issues.

But the sacred nature of life – even of a moment – is not absolute in every circumstance. There are, hidden in the margins of our faith, traditions and stories that demonstrate an understanding of what we might call the 'quality of life' issue. There are tales that condone intervention, of one type or another, in order to bring forward the physical death of a person whose real grasp on life has passed some time before.

Perhaps the best known is the tale of the death of Rabbi Hananiah (or Haninah) ben Teradion, a tale referred to in the liturgy for Yom Kippur. The Romans find Rabbi Hananiah breaking several of

---

[24] Lev 18.5.
[25] Ad loc.
[26] Yoma 85b.

their prohibitions, prohibitions punishable by death.

They found Rabbi Haninah ben Teradion sitting and studying Torah, gathering students, and keeping a Torah scroll in his bosom.
They took hold of him, wrapt him in the Scroll, placed bundles of
branches round him and set them on fire. Then they brought tufts
of wool, soaked in water, and placed them on his heart, so that he
should not die quickly... [His students said to him] 'Open your
mouth and let the flame come in.'
He said to them, 'Let the One who gave, take. Let a person not harm
themselves.'
The Executioner said to him, 'Rabbi, if I increase the flame and
take away the tufts of wool from your heart, will you bring me to
the world to come?' He said, 'Yes.' 'Promise me.' He promised him.
He increased the flame and removed the tufts of wool from his
heart, and his soul departed speedily. The Executioner then
jumped and threw himself into the fire. And a heavenly voice called
out, 'Rabbi Haninah ben Teradion and the Executioner have been
invited to the world to come.' [27]

The executioner is deemed not to have committed murder. Rabbi Hananiah is deemed not to have committed suicide. They both
enter the world to come immediately. Of course to expect the rabbi
to withstand this brutal torture is to expect something beyond the
realm of human possibility, but the case of the executioner is more
complex. He removes the tufts of wool – withdrawing a treatment
that is unnecessarily prolonging life. He also fans the flames – an active step, designed to hasten the onset of death.

Is this what would be called in contemporary ethical discourse
'active euthanasia'? Where, on the fiendishly slippery slope, does
one find gradations which allow us to recognise the desire to prevent anguish and preserve dignity in the face of death while still
holding true to our overriding concern regarding the preservation
of life?

One key source regarding the active removal of something that
is keeping a terminally ill person alive is from Sefer Hasidim: 'If
there are factors that are preventing a speedy demise – such as a
man chopping wood in the vicinity of a dying man's home, and the

---

[27] Avodah Zara 18a.

noise of the chopping prevents the soul from escaping – we remove the chopping.'[28] How far does a text like this apply? Can it apply to removing a life-support system? In my mind I have the terrible case of Chicago father Rudy Linares, whose two-year-old son was in a technologically assisted persistent vegetative state. In April 1989, Linares disconnected the child's life support system and cradled him until he died, holding the hospital guards at bay with a gun.[29]

Perhaps this too is the sort of case where we should incline towards an understanding of the desire not to needlessly perpetuate suffering. Or perhaps disconnecting life-sustaining equipment is just too dramatic an intervention to be considered covered by Sefer Hasidim's permittance to remove the sound of the wood-choppers.

In contemporary secular ethics, much is made of the difference between withdrawal of treatment that is keeping someone alive and actively treating towards death. And within the category of withdrawing treatment, whether one may withdraw nutrition, and if nutrition, whether one may withdraw hydration... but from an ethical standpoint these gradations seem most fine and a little overly legalistic for a problem of such emotional and spiritual magnitude. Perhaps an example will help us clarify our position.

One of the most heartbreaking legal responsa on Jewish medical ethics concerns a patient who is dying from ALS, amyotrophic lateral sclerosis, a muscle-wasting disease. The disease eventually strikes at the muscles which allow the lungs to operate, and without intubation the patient will die of suffocation. Of course with intubation one only succeeds in extending life until the point where the heart muscles also waste to nothing – but that is the case of *chayei sha'ah*, the life of a moment.

A man suffering from ALS in Tel Aviv expressed his desire NOT to be intubated when the time came. One has to have huge empathy for the victim, but also the medical staff who are placed in a position of having to watch their patient pass away when there is an inter-

---

[28] Sefer Hasidim 234.

[29] A grand jury later refused to return a murder indictment against Linares. See http://articles.chicagotribune.com/1989-05-21/news/8902020978_1_grand-jury-grand-jurors-stein

vention they could make to sustain life.

But is the decision not to be intubated active or passive? Is it euthanasia, or is it the decision not to continue with an ethically optional treatment? The case went to Rav Shlomo Zalman Auerbach, one of the leading ethicists of his day. In the exctract cited below you can hear him wrestling with the issue, consulting with doctors and other great rabbinic leaders:

> And they also banished sleep from their eyes to seek out the proper path to balance between the holiness of life and awfulness of continued suffering of this ill person. And eventually, I came the conclusion I am going to set out here. But before doing so I must emphasise that this is not a general position and it is forbidden to rely on it to cease treatment unless another situation is as similar to this one as two drops of water are similar, one to the other.[30]

Ultimately, the rabbi allows the will of the patient to stand. He is not to be intubated against his will.

The issue is a desperately complex one, and it is noteworthy that one is drawn to individual cases in search of a way forward. The notion that there can be an overarching generalised approach seems dangerous, in the face of such suffering and pain. But there are approaches that can provide assistance, both ethical and practical. One idea, found in the writings of Elliot Dorff, is that we should be guided, when considering these impossible cases, by asking this question: Is the removal of life-sustaining treatment consistent with the individual's creation in the image of God?

This is an awesome question to ponder. The very source of the sanctity of human life is our creation in the image of the divine, but if it comes to a point where that divine image would be better served by being released from what has become a mortal prison, then perhaps one should feel emboldened to be more active in allowing the life to come to an end.

CONCLUSION

Though this lecture leaves many threads hanging, this seems ap-

---

[30] Shut Yachel Yisrael 62.

propriate. An approach to medical ethics which rejects the raw complexity of each and every situation by definition must lack the sensitivity needed to engage with life at the edge of existence.

But to distil this lecture down to four brief points I would say this.

● A religious approach to medical ethics would downgrade the importance of autonomy, and upgrade the importance of Kant's first categorical imperative: Decisions taken should be such that one can desire that the decision should become a universal law.

● A religious approach to medical care would pay more attention to the holistic mind/soul/body balance when treating patients, particularly patients at the edge of life.

● A religious approach to issues around genetic engineering and genetic therapy welcomes and encourages even dramatic interventions in our God-given genetic make-up, but insists that these interventions are made from a place of humility, as a partner with God, seeking the healing of the sick, and not from a place of greed or personal ambition.

● A religious approach to issues around the end of life struggles mightily to tread a path between our love of life and our hatred of suffering. It recognises that at some point removal of treatment is not only allowed, but to be applauded as long as the divine image encoded even within the most sick of humans is cherished and valued.

CHAPTER SIX

History

I didn't go to JTS to study history, and I didn't always appreciate why I had to do so much of it as part of my preparation for ordination. Distance has helped. There is something about having a sense of how the Jewish narrative has unfolded over thousands of years that grounds my rabbinic practice. I know where and when the bits fit together and, to avail myself of a phrase much used by the, then, Chancellor of JTS, Esmar Schorsch, I know the relationship between text and context On a good day I even feel I can extract from a passing historical moment an idea that has very direct contemporary implications.

On the Invention
of the Jewish People
(2009)

In this sermon I'm responding to a book which
drew an enormous amount of attention, especially
beyond the Jewish community. It's also a sermon
about a particular kind of contemporary anti-Semitism.
It was Shabbat Vayakhayl.

O ur portion opens *Vayakhayl Moshe*.
Moses brings us together as a *kahal* – a community. It's
an important moment.

The 2,000-year-old translation-cum-biblical commentary On-
kelos translates the word *vayakhayl* as *uchnas* – brought together.
That root – *canas* – we probably recognise from the term *bet c'nesset*,[1]
the Hebrew term for synagogue. The original synagogue was brought
together as a community on the slopes of Mount Sinai, says Rashi,
the day after Moses threw down the tablets bearing the original Ten
Commandments.

Vayakhayl Moshe et col **edat** *bnei Yisrael* – Moses brought together the **nation** or **citizens** of Israel: the citizenry of Israel.

Of course the religious element is central to being Jewish, but this
term *edah* suggests something more than a mere commitment to
communal worship. It suggests something political, national, ethnic.

We've been doing this for a while – coming together as a people,
as an *edah*, a nation.

If we were to calculate a date for this moment, and classic rabbinic commentary does just that, we would be looking at a moment
some 3,400 years ago.

Or maybe not.

I first came across Shlomo Sand's book *The Invention of the Jew-*

---

[1] The term is usually transliterated as *bet* (or *beit*) *k'nesset*, with a 'k'. It is transliterated
here to show the etymological connection between *canas*, *c'nesset* and *uchnas*.

ish People when it was featured on Andrew Marr's Start the Week. It's had a lot of press attention. Not bad for an academic historian. But it's not a book I recommend. Sand is certainly keen to be seen as a brave and fearless writer, but there is a line between boldness and, intellectually speaking, jumping out of a plane without checking your parachute works properly.

Sand's claim is that the Jews were only ever a religion, not a people, not a culture, until the nineteenth century, when Jewish peoplehood was invented by the great Jewish historian Henreich Graetz. Now Graetz was indeed a great historian. His eight-volume masterwork *History of the Jews from Oldest Times to the Present* was the first great modern history of the Jewish people. But Sand suggests that Graetz, by bringing the entire tradition of Judaism into a single work, suppressed all the variety, the ethnic diversity, and the multi-cultural reality of Judaism. Prior to Graetz, says Sand, Judaism was a religious culture, not a nation. And after Graetz, Sand claims, Jews constructed for themselves a 'long unbroken geneology'. And this, suggests Sand, prepared the way for Zionism, which claimed the Land of Israel as the home for a people thrown out of their ancestral land.

If Sand is right, if the Jews were never a people, then the central claim of Zionism can be debunked. And if the central claim of Zionism can be debunked, then the Jewish nature of the State of Israel should be rejected. And if the Jewish nature of the State of Israel should be rejected, then...

You can see how this might confront some as problematic.

At least Sand is perfectly clear about his intent. He doesn't like the Jewish nature of the State of Israel, he wants that dismantled.

While Sand's work has been picked up by the BBC, and while it attracted support in France, in particular, it's been received with a loud raspberry by Jewish historians. Martin Goodman, Professor of Jewish History at Oxford University, pulls the book's central claims apart in a review in the *Times Literary Supplement*. He asks, 'What has possessed Shlomo Sand, a Tel Aviv historian of contemporary European history, to write about a subject of which he patently knows so little?' Goodman goes on to suggest dubious motives on the part of a number of his colleagues. I quote: 'Worryingly, the book has... received praise from historians and others who ought to have known better. These enthusiasts do not presumably know the material about which Sand writes, but they like his conclusions.' Conclusions, of course, that tear at the heart of the Jewish state.

The reasons why professional Jewish historians find Sand's work so shoddy are partly technical and partly blindingly obvious. I'll share some technical ideas first.

The big problem with Sand's analysis of what happened in the 1850s, with the publication of Graetz's *History of the Jews*, is that he has the story upside down. Sand is right that Graetz was interested in showing the Jews were a nation, but that is only because in the surrounding society, at that time, the idea that Jews were **not** a nation was beginning to circulate for the first time. The doors of modernity were opened to the Jew, and Jews were asked to demonstrate fidelity to the states where they lived. Napolean convened a Sanhedrin – a Jewish court composed of the most notable scholars of his day – to ask Jews a series of questions that boiled down to this: Are you French Jews part of a Jewish nation or a French one? Who, we were asked, would we side with in a battle between France and a Jew from another nation?

One can hear the wish to strip Jews of our national character in the declaration of the eighteenth French Count Stanislas de Clermont-Tennerre that Jews should be 'granted everything as individuals and denied everything as a nation'. Graetz's claim for Jewish nationhood was a response to a suggestion that we should not be afforded status as a nation.

Sand claims that before Graetz, no-one considered Jews were a nation. Graetz, on the other hand, is claiming that before modernity, everyone knew Jews were a nation. Graetz, it has to be said, has the facts on his side.

We have records of a certain Binyamin MiTudela who traveled the ancient world in 1150, some 100 years before Marco Polo. He made his way from Tudela to France, Greece, Constinople, Syria, and Persia, before heading back to Spain via North Africa. In all he visited over 300 cities. And time after time he reports on the Jews he meets, the numbers in any given city, their communal leaders, their buildings, their lives. I'm quite sure Binyamin would have been most surprised to be told that his wasn't an exercise in meeting 'his people' around the world, such a people not existing.

But we can go earlier still.

Goodman, the Professor of Jewish History at Oxford, notes that Romans of the first four centuries of the Common Era would categorise the various people they conquered and would ascribe various terms – secta, superstitio, or religio – to those who shared a religious outlook. But the Jews are also referred to in poems, legal tomes and even the great Theodosian Code as 'natio' – a nation. The Romans thought we were a nation over 1,500 years ago – and perhaps even as they expelled us from the Land of Israel.

Actually, the very earliest reference to Israel in any archaeological record we possess speaks of Israel as a people. The Merneptah Stele was found in the Egyptian city of Thebes, and has been dated to 1200 BCE. That would be something like 200 years after a supposed Sinaitic moment. The famous irony of the oldest surviving reference to the Jewish people, outside of our own texts, is that it celebrates our alleged destruction. The Stele reads: 'Canaan is captive with all woe. The City of Ashkelon is conquered, the City of Gezer seized, the City of Yanoam made nonexistent; Israel is wasted, bare of seed.' Of course, we are still here... But note how Israel is referred to. There are cities mentioned, but Israel isn't referred to geographically. Rather, it is preceded by an Egyptian sign that seems to mean... a people.

In other words, the great constant of the 3,000-plus-year history of the Jewish people is that in each and every generation someone comes along to destroy our peoplehood. Sand, unlike the Pharaoh of the Bible, is quite OK with Jews being alive; he just doesn't want to allow us to live as a people. But that doesn't render his theory palatable – especially since it's rubbish.

So much for the technical problems with Sand's thesis – the stuff you need to know about Jewish history in order to know it's rubbish. The bleedingly obvious problem with Sand's thesis is that it is bleedingly obviously nonsense.

Sand admits that Jews across time and history were united by a religion, but attaches great significance to the claim that Jews can't be a people because we lived in different lands, because Sephardi Jewish culture and language and dress is so different from Ashkenazi Jewish culture and language and dress, and so forth. But it would never have occurred to a Jew in fourteenth-century Morocco that he wasn't part of the same people as a Jew of fourteenth-century Italy, or fourteenth-century France. They would have felt the same kinship to Jews across the world as we still feel today.

Two years ago my wife and I visited Tangiers for a day, popping over from the South of Spain. What did we do? We looked out for the shul, the Jewish trinkets in the market, we went looking for the signifiers of kinship. I wasn't trying to touch people who had the same 'Jewish gene' as I do, because I don't believe that Judaism exists in the genes. I wasn't even trying to find a *minyan* or a kosher butcher I could use to fulfil various religious requirements of faith, as important as religion is in my Jewish identity. I was trying to connect to people who connect to Jewish peoplehood the same way that I do. I was looking for the same *edah* Moses brought together. I was declaring myself to be part of the same *kahal*. I was doing the same thing Binyamin MiTudela did a thousand years previously.

And I know this sort of tourism, this sort of seeking out connections to our past, our present, our future, is at the heart of the identity of so many of us here. And has been part of the identity of Jews for, not hundreds, but thousands of years.

So what is the point?

Sand is wrong, factually misleading, and blinded by his desire to strip from Israel its Jewish nature. But he's not the first person to try and write off the Jewish people. He's not even the first Jew to do so. So what?

The point is this. We ARE part of a people, a great and mighty people, with an extraordinary, mighty and LONG history. We are brought together by religion, but also by peoplehood, by kinship, by our commitment to our fellow Jews through time and space.

And that should fill us with a tremendous sense of pride.

It should drive us to ensure the bonds that bind us are so strong they create a Jewish future in which we, as a Jewish people, are even more clearly *agudat echad* – one entity.

But I'm not sure it does.

It certainly doesn't enough.

Sand, at one point, suggests that Jews across the world can't seriously claim to be a nation since so few Jews bother to learn Hebrew. He's wrong in suggesting that this means we aren't a nation. Yet we are weaker than we would be if we all shared *safah achat*, a common language.

Sand, at several points, suggests that Jews across the world can't seriously claim to be a nation since so many Jews over time have married others who can't trace their genetic heritage back to Sinai. He's wrong in suggesting this means we aren't a nation. Yet we are weakened as a nation by levels of intermarriage that threaten the future of the Jewish people.

This 3,000-plus-year-old story of Jewish peoplehood doesn't write itself.

It's not an accident, and while it may be a miracle, it's foolish at best and blasphemous at worst to suggest that God will take care of our future.

Jewish peoplehood is in our hands now.

Our commitment to deepening our engagement with the Jewish culture and traditions we share, our commitment to sharing a language and so on, these are the tests of our strength as a people.

And we are not strong enough.

We should commit ourselves to prove Sand wrong, not only because he has dramatically misread our Jewish past, but also because he has misread our Jewish present and even, dare we pray it, our Jewish future.

The Jews of England
{2006}

Major Anglo-Jewish communal organisations got excited in 2006. The year was deemed the 350th anniversary of the return of Jews to England after our expulsion in 1290. As is often the case, the reality is both more subtle and more interesting than the misleading headline.

This article was originally published in
The Jewish Chronicle.

We are reliably informed that 2006 marks the 350th anniversary of the re-admittance of Jews into Britain. But the trail is murky. There is no Act of Parliament welcoming the Jews and no statement from 'Lord Protector' Oliver Cromwell. There doesn't seem to be anything. In search of answers I headed for the Rare Books Room of the British Library. There, in leather-bound volumes that rise out of the Library's subterranean vaults, we can find an extraordinary range of pamphlets from the period, mini-essays, often published under pseudonyms.

'Britannia' offers a history of Jews in Britain in the 1260s. While Jews were widely disliked, it seems we were popular with the monarchs: a cheap source of finance through fines or loans (often un-repaid),

> but all these Fines and many other Losses both in Estate, Limbs and Life, were not sufficient to deter these stubborn People from their iniquitous Proceedings in their Manner of getting Money and of their oppressing the native-born *Englishmen* and of ridiculing and blaspheming *Christ*.

Eventually having a friendly monarch proved insufficient. The 'Commons of England' offered Edward I a massive bribe to get rid of the Jews and, in 1290, we were 'banish'd hence, never to return again under pain of being *hanged*.' But, by 1753, Britannia is fighting a rearguard action. His pamphlet, *An Appeal to the Throne against the Naturalization of the Jewish Nation,* is written at a time when others are advocating readmitting Jews. In fact, Jews had never entirely left, and in the aftermath of expulsions from Spain and Portugal several hundred *conversos*, New Christians, came to trade in London. Most had links to flourishing Jewish trading communities in Holland. As another pamphleteer, James Howell, wrote in 1653 to a friend in Amsterdam, 'Touching Judaism, some corners of our city [London] smell as rank of it as yours doth there.'

The leader of the readmission campaign was Menasseh Ben Israel, whose pamphlets describe him as 'A Divine and Doctor of PHYSICK'. He arrived from Amsterdam to plead his case before Cromwell in September 1653, while England was in the grip of messianic excitement. Cromwell had opened Parliament that July with the announcement that 'this may be the door to usher in the things that God has promised... You are at the edge of the promises and prophecies.' Menasseh lost no time stoking the messianic fervour for his own purposes. In 'A Humble Addresse to the Lord Protector' he notes:

> The opinion of many Christians and mine doe concurre herein, that we both believe the restoring time of our Nation into their Native Country is very near at hand; I believing that this restauration cannot be before the words of Daniel be first accomplished, *And when the dispersion of the Holy people shall be completed in all places, then shall all these things be completed,* signifying therewith, that before all be fulfilled, the People of God must be first dispersed into all places of the World. Now we know how our Nation is spread all about, and hath its seat and dwellings in the most flourishing parts of all the Kingdomes of the World except only this considerable and mighty Island [Britain]. And therefore this remains onely in my judgement, before the MESSIA come [slightly abbreviated from the original].

It's fascinating to see Menasseh's theological partnering with the Puritans. He is seducing Christians to let Jews into Britain in order to bring the second coming of Jesus! The 'Addresse' is a masterful work of flattery, requesting a 'free and publick Synagogue' in order that Jews may 'sue also for a blessing upon this [British] Nation and People of England for receiving us into their bosoms and comforting Sion in her distresse.' But it also reminds Cromwell that no ruler 'hath ever afflicted [the Jews] who hath not been, by some ominous Exit, most heavily punished of God Almighty; as is manifest from the Histories of those Kings, Pharaoh, Nebuchadnezer ... and others.' Menasseh also marshals less spiritual and more pecuniary arguments, devoting several pages to a survey of the profitability of 'The Nation of Jewes' in a range of states that have seen fit to let Jews in. This might have been particularly interesting to Cromwell, seeking to find ways to keep Britain ahead of the Dutch economy.

Suitably inspired, Cromwell assembled a conference of merchants and clergymen but didn't get the support he was looking for. Admitting the Jews would be a blasphemy, some claimed. Others spread rumours of child-murder – the recurring blood libel accusation. There were also fears that if re-admittance was formalised, 'every *Vagabond Jew* may purchase the Liberties and Immunities of free-born Englishmen'. Not everyone, and least of all the Guilds, were anxious to see the Jews' economic nous and power in competition with the existing British mercantile classes. Cromwell wound up proceedings before the conference could conclude its report.

So what did happen in 1656, 350 years ago? It seems that this somewhat forced anniversary owes its origin to the imprisonment of a converso merchant, Antonio Rodrigues Robles, on the charge of being a Papist. Robles was threatened with sequestration of his considerable assets and only escaped punishment when he claimed that, rather than being a Papist, he was actually Jewish. Cromwell intervened, Robles escaped punishment and, as the historian Heinrich Graetz remarked, Jews 'made no mistake over the significance of this ruling, [and threw] off the mask of Christianity'. It was, in Cromwell's England, far safer to be an avowed Jew than a closeted pseudo-Puritan who might harbour Papist tendencies.

Devoid of constitutional upheaval, legislation and fanfare, the Jews got on with the day-to-day business of establishing a community on this 'considerable and mighty Island'. How terribly English.

CHAPTER 7

Love – Theory and Practice

This chapter contains two sermons which, despite drawing on very different source material (the Book of Ruth and the Book of Leviticus), attempt to articulate an understanding of love as the foundation of a Jewish approach towards life.

The third essay engages in one of the hottest issues in Masorti discourse – homosexuality. It was written some time before recent decisions by the UK Masorti Movement, and its rabbis, permitting its member communities to celebrate same-sex marriages under a shutafut *(partnership) framework – a decision prompted by passage of the Same Sex (Marriages) Act in 2014. I hope the path I lay out in that essay can help mend divisions in our communities over what remains an emotive and contentious issue.*

Love Theory and Game Theory
{2009}

*Ruth is a wonderful book containing one of the most
stunning verses in all the Hebrew Bible. Though the
language is simple, the idea that underpins the
relationship between Ruth and her mother-in-law craves
sermonic attention. But Shavuot is the least-attended of
the major Jewish festivals and, unlike Kohelet and Song
of Songs, the book of Ruth doesn't get its own
'intermediate Shabbat'. So it's only somewhat to my
surprise that this is the only sermon I've preached on the
book in ten years. It also touches on the economic crash
that dominated news coverage at the time.*

As I was thinking through this sermon, I pulled Matt (Viscount) Ridley's *The Origins of Virtue* – a book I read nine years ago – from the shelf. It contains the story of an experiment in game theory – the study of the decisions we make.

Imagine, says the academic Douglas Hofstadter, a dilemma in which 20 people sit in separate cubicles, each with a finger on a button. If none of the 20 push their buttons for ten minutes, each person will get £1,000. But if someone pushes his button before the ten minutes are up, that person gets £100 and the game ends: everyone else gets nothing.

As Ridley notes, even a fool knows that the best result is for all 20 players not to press the button. But if you are just a little bit clever you will realise there is a high chance that someone else will press their button – so you should probably press your button before they do. As a matter of game theory, pressing fast is the way to go. The risk-reward balance demands it.

'Don't get misled by your morality', writes Ridley. 'The fact that you are being noble in cooperating is irrelevant to the question. What we are seeking is the logically best action in a moral vacuum

– it's rational to be selfish.' Ridley wants us to feel the power of the logic of game theory.

I wanted to share something about this book because I am still thinking about the single moment in the entire Hebrew Bible which most stands most fiercely against this kind of game theory. The one moment, in the entire Hebrew Bible, which looks at logic, calculation and the rest of it and hurls it all away because of a strange, defiantly human quality we call *chesed* – kindness.

The story so far:

Naomi has two sons who marry and die. This leaves three women, devoid of economic possibility and, without a child to carry the name of the family onward, devoid of a future.

'Give up on me', Naomi instructs her daughters-in-law. 'Head back to your own families.' And one daughter-in-law leaves. But Ruth doesn't. Naomi attempts, for a second time, to push Ruth away, and Ruth stops her with this extraordinary speech:

> Do not entreat me to leave you, or to keep from following you;
> For where you go, I will go
> Where you stay, I will stay;
> Your people shall be my people,
> Your God my God;
> Where you die, will I die, and there will I be buried.

I'm in, says Ruth, I'm with you. And the reward for this fidelity – I disregard.

This is the key point, for an understanding of Ruth. When we do something for someone in the expectation of reward, or if we do something for someone because they have done something for us, that is called reciprocity. What Ruth does for Naomi has nothing to do with reciprocity.

'What can I offer you?' continues Naomi. 'Even if I were to marry tonight and bear more sons, should you wait for them to grow up for you to marry?'

Where you go, I will go, says Ruth. I have nothing to offer you, says Naomi. *Where you stay, I will stay,* says Ruth. This is the inverse of reciprocity.

Doing something for someone not only not in the expectation of reward, but in wilful disregard of what one might get back from the relationship – this is love.

Love is doing something for someone with no thought as to the return, the reward, the 'what's in it for me'. This is the meaning of the Hebrew term *gemilut hesed* – doing things for others out of a sense of kindness. The phrase is perfectly encapsulated by the translation 'wanton acts of kindness'.

To be *gomel hesed* is to be gratuitously kind. It is to do the kind thing above and beyond any supposed call of duty.

The rabbis understood precisely how the Book of Ruth carries this relationship with kindness at its very heart. There is a touching midrash which plays with this supposed challenge in the book:

> The book of Ruth contains nothing about ritual, nothing about what is forbidden and permitted. Why then was it written? To teach how great is the reward for *gemilut hesed* – wanton acts of kindness.[1]

The rabbis consider *gemilut hesed* not just a nice thing to do, but a religious, a godly, thing to do.

Here is another midrash on *gemilut hesed* from the collection Yalkut Shimoni:

> Anyone who is *gomel hesed*, it is as if they accept all the miracles which the Holy Blessed One has done since bringing Israel out from Egypt. And one who does not *gomel hesed* is like one who denies the existence of the Divine.[2]

That's a stunning idea. It says that if you do something for someone with no thought for what is in it for you, when you do something out of love, out of a sense of *hesed*, you are in some sense accepting the notion of a God who placed this possibility of love in the human soul and justifies all acts of love in ways beyond human fathom. You accept the notion of a God who demands from us these acts of love.

Try this as a definition of God: God is that which begets the possibility of *gemilut hesed*. God is that which elevates our lives beyond the level of reciprocity. That's the God I believe in.

I began by mentioning Matt Ridley's book *The Origins of Virtue*. Virtue, in Ridley's book, has nothing in common with *hesed*. Rather,

---

[1] Ruth Rabbah 2:14.
[2] Shoftim 64.

the book documents how humans and animals alike end up doing things which appear to be non-selfish, and, without exception, the book reveals how that which appears on the surface to be non-selfish ultimately rewards and turns out to be in our best interests. Ridley's virtue involves acting selfishly, but with a slightly longer-term perspective than one might at first expect. Ridley's book is not theological, it's not about love, it's not about *hesed*.

Matt Ridley came to more public prominence than is usual for an animal behaviourist in 2007 when he resigned as chairman of Northern Rock Bank. Northern Rock's shareholders had put an evolutionary biologist who believed pursuing self-interest was the same as pursuing virtue in the bank's top management position. When it turned out that the bank had gone bankrupt and dragged half the City of London down in its wake, some were surprised. Certainly MPs, leader writers and the rest of them were quick to point a finger at Ridley, who resigned in disgrace.

But what else should we have expected? If you confuse self-interest with virtue you can justify all sorts of economic lunacy.

I don't mean to belittle self-interest. Of course self-interest is a necessary part of life, and the book is certainly a terrific read. It's fascinating to learn why fish travel in schools, how meerkats work out how to avoid predators, or how flocks of doves can fight off a hawk. But these biological truths have nothing to do with virtue.

If you want to understand virtue you would do a lot better reading the Book of Ruth.

What can I offer you? says Naomi. Where you go I will go, says Ruth. I have nothing to offer you, says Naomi. Where you stay, I will stay, says Ruth.

The things we do for those we love –

The things we do for our children, for the members of our family, for our friends, even the things we do for mere acquaintances –

But most especially the things we do for the stranger in our midst, the things we do with no thought of reward – these are the markers of virtue.

Will we, do we, do things for others with no thought as to what is in it for us?

This is the test of virtuousness for all of us.
Gemilut hesed is more than being nice.
Gemilut hesed is the test of our humanity.

It's one of the deepest and most central teachings of our faith.
This is the test. May we rise to meet it well.

Leviticus –
About Love, Really
{2012}

Each year I try to give at least one sermon on why
the sacrificial system that dominates the heart of the
Hebrew Bible is worthy of religious attention.
As a traveller on the yearly journey round the Torah cycle
one rides the crest of a wave through the astounding
vibrancy of the Exodus from Egypt and up to the summit
of Mount Sinai. One can almost feel the screech of
narrative brake as the laws of Mishpatim and the
sanctuary focus of Terumah and Tetzave loom into view.
By then Purim and Pesach and the other markers of
Spring are calling – and they are good distractions from
the Torah reading. But there is no getting away from the
massive hold the sacrificial system has over our
lectionary. It's important to talk about Yom HaShoah and
Israel and there are always good reasons to give a sermon
'off-parashah', but a rabbi who wants to wave the flag for
the value of the entire Torah has to be prepared to
address the sacrificial system one way or another.
This sermon owes a significant debt to Moshe Halbertal's
terrific short work, *On Sacrifice*. It was the Shabbat
before Mothers' Day and we had, as a community,
celebrated a bar mitzvah that morning.

You might know the game Fruit Ninja. It's the sort of thing to
play on a tablet or phone. Pixelated fruit descend from the
top of the screen and you swipe through the fruit, making
squelching noises and amassing points.

My kids love it.

And now, and I kid you not, available on the Apple Appstore: Leviticus! – exclamation point – The App.

Sharpen your knife and your priestly reflexes, demand the
developers. Are you ready for the Ultimate Rule Book? Leviticus!
Play the role of a busy priest working to keep God happy by

sacrificing choice offerings of sheep, goats, and bulls
with frantic speed and slicing precision. Combo your
actions and the rewards get BIBLICAL!
Three sacrificial services a day, seven days a week. Can
YOU make it to Shabbat? Download Leviticus! and start
swiping to find out!
Leviticus! features global leaderboards, long-term
achievements, and high score announcements designed
especially for Facebook bragging.
Cool in-app purchases coming soon!

This is, I suppose, one response to the question – what can we do with the Book of Leviticus? Because it's not obvious.

I would probably download the game if I had an Apple thingy. But ultimately I need to find something else in all this apparatus and ritual other than a child-friendly slasher blood bath.

So that's what I want to share with you. It's very much in debt to Moshe Halbertal's new book, *On Sacrifice*.

Halbertal opens by noting the difference between 'sacrificing to' and 'sacrificing for'.

As Jacob[1] discussed in his devar Torah, we all sacrifice for things, and 'sacrificing for' something isn't bad. But it is transactional. When we 'sacrifice for' something, our sacrifice becomes part of a negotiation, a deal.

I'll go without Starbucks coffee for the year to save the money to go on holiday. I'll go without the chocolate cake to lose the extra weight. That's all 'sacrificing for'. And that's all fine. But it makes us a penny counter, a calorie counter – it doesn't make us a human being.

The Book of Leviticus isn't about 'sacrificing for', it's about 'sacrificing to' – to God, a source of life, creation, possibility and love.

When we 'sacrifice to' we are not focused on what we get out of the relationship. When we 'sacrifice to' we are focused on the relationship.

Halbertal suggests that when you do something for someone not because of what you get out of the deal, that's love. Here Halbertal clearly owes a significant debt to Martin Buber, whose most popu-

---

[1]   Jacob was the boy who celebrated his bar mitzvah that Shabbat, and who gave a short
    devar Torah on a related topic earlier in the service.

lar work, *I and Thou,* is based on exactly the same distinction. 'Sacrificing to' isn't like entering into a contract. It's not like making a deal. It's giving a gift.

That's the first point I want to share. 'Sacrificing to' is about love.

Interestingly, 'sacrificing to' is based on a particular relationship with the one offering up the sacrifice. When we 'sacrifice to', we locate ourselves in relationship to another we deem more significant than we consider ourselves. When we train ourselves in sacrificing to, we train ourselves to acknowledge that there is something 'out there' that is more important than we are. There is a humility that is a part of 'sacrificing to'. We recognise our place in the world and we recognise that the gifts in our possession are not there as a matter of justice or right, but rather as an act of grace. They are bestowed on us by a graceful other, more important than ourselves.

There are clues to this love-centred conception of the biblical sacrificial system in the language used in the Torah. *Korban,* usually translated as 'sacrifice', is etymologically connected to the Hebrew root meaning 'to come close'. It refers to our goal in this process. Minchah, usually translated as 'afternoon offering', is etymologically connected to the Hebrew root meaning 'to set before'. It refers to our position in this relationship. We are like a servant before a king, a pauper before a billionaire or a child before a parent.

When a poor person brings a gift to a rich person, they do so carefully. There is a sense that this needs to be done correctly, there are rituals that need to be observed lest the whole relationship is soured by error. The greater the inequality between the giver and the receiver, the more careful the giver needs to be, the more ritual we should expect. As, indeed, is the case in the book of Vayikra.

The greater the inequality between the giver and the receiver, the more humble we need to be about what we bring. We are not going to impress with the size of the gift – God is not going to be impressed with a piece of dead goat, or even a cow, or even a herd of cows. The only chance to impress is with the heart, the intention behind the giving, the way the giving comes from a sincere place. I wonder if there is an analogy in the context of the homemade Mother's Day card. Cards given by young children to mothers don't impress because of the quality of the artwork (no matter what the mother might claim about their budding Picasso). The cards impress and move because of the way the gift makes the love of the child explicit and even shifts the nature of the relationship. If, let's just imagine for a moment, having proffered a beautiful hand-drawn card, the child promptly does something brattish and ill-behaved – not that that kind of behaviour is ever seen in our house, or Jacob, in yours, I'm sure – then the gift is rendered worthless.

And even if we observe all due propriety in our giving, and even if we behave serenely as we give, there is still an element of faith involved in making a gift to one mightier than ourselves. We can never know how the gift may or may not change anything. A poor person can't bribe a millionaire. A serf can't buy the affection of the king. Sacrificing to one mightier than we are puts us in the mindset of knowing that it all depends on grace. That's the other point.

When we 'sacrifice to' we develop our humility. We recognise how much we depend on grace, the benevolence of our Creator, beyond what we dare demand is our right. When we 'sacrifice to' we build relationships, a relationship of love. We become people who love, who care, who are desperate not to get it wrong.

This ritual reading of the sacrificial system works for me. It reminds me of who I want to be as I stand before the cosmos and everything in it. And the real question is, without the rituals, the bulls and the blood, how do I remain the sort of person prepared to offer 'sacrifices to'? I don't want to become calculating, arrogant and unworthy of love. I'm sure that would apply to us all.

What Should a Gay Jew Do?

{2012}

This piece was written for a Masorti publication on 'Relationships.' My own relationship with the question of same-sex intimacy goes back to my time at the Conservative Yeshiva, before I began formal Rabbinic training. I had a study partner who also began the year hoping to get into the Jewish Theological Seminary (JTS), but part-way through the year she came out. JTS, at the time, had a policy not to accept what they called 'avowed homosexuals.' And, en route to her applying to the Reform Hebrew Union College she asked me how I could apply to a homophobic institution. I took her question as an obligation and, spent hours and hours in my last three years in the States organising and leading a hugely successful pressure group from within the Seminary that played its part in a momentous policy change which has seen the American Conservative movement transformed to become a place open to all regardless of sexual orientation. That said there is still much to do, and in this country also. This article was written before civil legislation gave religious organisations the ability to celebrate, in the language of the statute, Same Sex Marriages. It's not clear to me how that option will play out at New London at this time.

The issue of homosexuality is complicated and tests our legal and practical sensibilities in a vast range of ways. It's also hugely emotive both among those who are gay, or who support others who are, and among those who fear that Masorti Judaism is sliding away from acceptance of the binding nature of our tradition. Faced with these complications we, as rabbinic leaders in the movement have largely kept 'shtum'. [This has changed, to an extent, since the passing of the 2014 Act]. We hoped that members and others would deduce a general welcome of anyone regardless of sexuality without making that welcome explicit, partly out of our own discomfort and partly out of a desire to avoid the inevitable scorn that greets anyone perceived as treading too liberal a path on these matters. I'm not convinced that this silence was tenable or appropriate. For a movement founded on the principle of speaking truths even if they bring criticism, this equivocation failed our raison d'etre.

I don't get asked – 'Rabbi, should I be gay?' The question simply doesn't come to me. Rather, I get what the rabbis call *b'dievad* questions, post-facto questions – Since I am gay, am I still welcome in your shul? Since I have a gay partner, will you recognise us as a family? Since our son has same-sex parents, can you accept him in the Cheder? Actually, even these *b'dievad* questions overstate what passes my rabbinic in-tray on issues around homosexuality. Many gay Jews feel traditional Judaism views them and their hearts inclination with such opprobrium that they simply avoid anything to do with us. Do I want to encourage them to be more involved, or should I watch them disappear for our people? Others sit in the very back rows of our synagogues ducking eye contact, not sure who to trust and from whom they should hide – dishonesty fostered in what should be a house of truth.

I am not, in this short paper, going to offer a fully worked through halachic position. Rather I am going to offer a whistle-stop trip through the principles which underlie how I read our *masorah* – tradition – on this issue.

FALSE PATHS – RIGHTS AND PRIVACY

'Rights'-based discourse dominates much secular discussion of these issues, but that kind of language is largely foreign to Jewish thought. I don't, as a matter of halachah, have a right to free speech, or certainly any right to engage sexually with a chosen other. Judaism is built around systems of responsibility. I have the responsibility to speak carefully and kindly. So when I say halachic Judaism does not recognise the right of a person to choose a life-partner or sexual partner of any gender, that's not because I don't care about ways in which the heart moves a person who is gay, but rather because I don't accept that halachic Judaism should use this sort of discourse.

Equally, I am unmoved by claims that 'what goes on in the privacy of the bedroom' is not a religious concern. Judaism believes that whatever we do, we do it before God. 'Know before Whom You Stand' is a phrase often found above synagogue arks, and it applies equally under the covers. To the traditional Jew, everything matters. There is halachic discussion of the order in which a person should put on their socks, halachic discussion of the materials from which socks can be made, halachic discussion of the way in which the cotton can be picked, and so on and so on. Viewed in the context of Judaism's concern with every aspect of life, the insistence that our sexual practices are of religious concern isn't to obsess over sexuality; rather, it fits into a concern for all parts of life.

HALACHIC NUANCE

The halachic system requires that rabbis show a sense of proportion when opining on matters of same-sex attraction. As a general matter Judaism is very slow to castigate internal emotional states, and feeling drawn to a person of the same sex is no sin in itself. But even when it comes to acts, as opposed to 'mere' feelings, there is more nuance than an oversimplified view might suggest. Male-to-male intercourse is deemed an *issur d'oraita*, or Torah-mandated prohibition, but lesbian sexual engagement is considered *pritzut d'alma*, 'generally lewd' – the same level of disdain as is shown towards the wearing of red clothing (Yevamot 76a and Berachot 20a). Acts of male-to-male sexual intimacy short of penetration are prohibited, but less severely. And there are strange byways in the Talmudic corpus where actions that might be connected to homosexual intimacy are glossed over. This is not the place to fight out the precise meaning of these often elliptical texts but, for example, in Kiddushin 82a the rabbis accept that two men can 'share a blanket' in a context which suggests an awareness of same-sex intimacy.

There are positions taken by the American branch of our movement which do overturn many, if not all, of the prohibitions in the classic halachah. I am not going to argue that the forbidden be deemed not forbidden, but rather that a sense of nuance is preserved, especially when we are dealing with the need a person might feel for intimate companionship.

MORALITY, HALACHAH AND DISOBEDIENCE

Morality (i.e., acts of goodness) and halachah (the Jewish legal system) are not one and the same. Judaism is not amoral, but its web of prohibitions, permissions, compulsions and exemptions are not only about morality. This is a particularly important point to make in light of some of the moral opprobrium directed towards those who are gay by some religious leaders. The Bible outlaws male-to-male intercourse as a *toevah*, but the King James translators perhaps let some of their own discomfort with homosexual intercourse impact on their choice of 'abomination' as a translation of this strange word.

The Bible considers eating pork or shellfish a *toevah* (Lev 11:10, Deut 14:3), but I don't consider a person who eats ham to be acting immorally, even if they are Jewish. The very first time the Bible mentions the term *toevah* (Gen 43:32) it refers to the way Egyptians perceived what it would mean to eat with a Jew. Most frequently the term refers to Jews committing acts of cultic idolatry (Deut 7:25, 12:31, 13:15). In short, a *toevah* is a national and particular wrong; it's not universal, it's not moral. A committed intimate relationship between two people of the same sex is not immoral, even if it involves a breach of the *halachah*, and I oppose the use of verses such as Lev 18:22 to suggest that it is.

It's worth noting that the halachic system imposes significant limits on physical intimacy between a married couple, and certainly has much to say on intimate relationships between unmarried Jews, let alone relationships between Jews and non-Jews. There are many, let it be said, in our communities who, in their intimate relationships with life partners (and more casual partners) breach aspects of *halachah*. We need to ensure that our response on issues of homosexual intimacy bears a sense of proportion to our responses on issues of heterosexual intimacy.

WHAT SHOULD A GAY JEW DO?

This question goes to heart of the responsibility I feel in my engagement with this issue.

The vast majority of my Orthodox colleagues expect a Jew who is clear about their gay sexual identity to live alone, without a central sanctified relationship with another they can love spiritually, emotionally and erotically. Frankly, this has to be better counsel than the advice to marry a woman in pretence, or the suggestion that a firm gay sexual orientation can be 'reversed' through therapy. But there is a verse which speaks about such a life-sentence of loneliness – 'it is not good for a person to be alone' (Gen 2:18). The Hebrew term used here, *tov*, can only be translated to mean 'good'. Goodness is not cultic or particular. Goodness is the language of universal morality. This verse weighs particularly heavily on me, especially in the context of the huge blessing I find in my own finding of a partner with whom I hope to share the rest of my life in every way. It makes it impossible for me to feel called or able to insist gay Jews live a life devoid of the intimacy which I, as a married heterosexual, enjoy so profoundly. I am deeply moved by this claim, but I accept there is also a theological issue at work. Maybe if my theology was more classically orthodox I would absolutely accept the inerrant truth of halachic prohibitions on gay sexual intimacy and vocally oppose all forms of it. But I am a Masorti Jew. I accept the obligation to observe the mitzvot, but I am niggled by the belief that human discomfort with gay sex may be influencing our halachic sources, and that compounds my refusal to demand gay Jews live lives of loneliness. Seeing committed gay and lesbian Jews creating passionate and committed Jewish lives together also strengthens me to push towards the edge of what traditional Judaism has maintained in previous years.

What do I want? I want Jews to find other Jews with whom to make lives together. I want them to commit to one another and treat that committed relationship as sacred. As a rabbi I want to support such couples as they build *batim ne'emanim b'Yisrael*, faithful houses in Israel, and if such couples are blessed with children, through natural means or assisted by science or adoption, I will do everything I can to support the children growing as committed Jews who feel rooted and inspired by their Jewish families and tradition. I want Jews who can only find such a partner among members of the opposite sex to do that, and I want Jews who can only find such a partner among members of the same sex to do that also.

When it comes to matters of sexual intimacy I would hope that couples both straight and gay allow the restrictions the halachah imposes on all of us to influence the decisions we make, sexually, and I hope and believe it is possible for couples both gay and straight to find opportunities for meaningful and profound intimacy within the corpus of permissions and regulations the halachic framework allows. But I am not going to use such power as I have as a rabbi to point fingers at those who might fall short of obligations to observe the rules on sexual propriety that both gay and straight Jews face.

When it comes to the question of ceremonies which recognise these committed gay unions, I struggle. For me the ability to perform both religious and civil wedding ceremonies for heterosexual couples is a tremendous honour, and I understand the way in which many gay Jews will want their relationships to be sanctified by a representative of their own faith. Ceremonies are important; public blessings strengthen a commitment between couples and allow friends and family members opportunities to share their own 'Amen'. But many of the elements of a traditional chuppah are not suitable for the consecration of a partnership between man and man, and I don't advocate plucking them from their heterosexual realm and dropping them into a homosexual one.

That said, I know that offering gay Jews what might be perceived as merely a quasi or ersatz marriage is seen as demeaning, even if that is not the intention. It may be that one way forward would be to explore using *shutafut* – partnership – language and ritual for both straight and gay celebrations, moving away from the traditional marriage rituals associated with *kinyan* – acquisition of a woman by a man in ways very close to the patterns of acquisition of chattel. Personally, as the rabbi of New London Synagogue and as a Masorti Jew, I feel there is much more to do in terms of exploring appropriate religious rituals (including, should it be necessary, in the case of separation of a gay couple) around this issue. I welcome and support the governmental sanction and recognition of intimate committed relationships between gay couples not only as a marker of commitment, but also for the important civil legal protections that these arrangements offer.

There is danger in putting these thoughts in writing. The issue can be one which divides and fractures religious communities. My hope and prayer is that we, Masorti Jews, are sufficiently used to the range of opinions which mark our engagement in complex issues such as this and sufficiently convinced of the importance of articulating the nature of our welcome to gay and lesbian Jews to make this contribution nonetheless welcome.

CHAPTER 8

Jewish Law – Halachah

The two pieces reproduced here are responsa
*– formal decisions given in response to
specific questions about religious law.*
Responsa *are technical documents, written
for who already have a grasp of the sprawling
Jewish legal tradition. If you are looking for
an easier read, skip ahead. But I believe it is
vitally important for Masorti Rabbis to write
technically, at least some of the time. We
profess a commitment to Jewish law, and we
surf the edges of what the Jewish system has
ever deemed appropriate. If we can't
articulate precisely how we justify our
actions we forfeit the right to call ourselves
obliged by the world of Jewish law.*

On Cohanim and Converts
{2008}

This is my favourite responsum to share with people who want to know how Masorti 'does halachah'; it encapsulates how we honour the textual tradition while remaining sensitive to historical processes. It also highlights the problems caused by an uncritical assumption that Orthodox halachah is 'better' than Masorti halachah. Writing this responsum was an entirely new field of research for me, since as a student in America – certainly in the circles in which I lived – I never encountered the issue. Returning to Britain I started coming across the situation I describe in the responsum again and again. I suppose I have officiated at around eight wedding ceremonies between converts and cohanim. I've also encountered the deep pain Orthodox approaches have caused converts, cohanim and their families when they have faced rejection on this issue.

THE ISSUE

Restrictions on whom a *cohen* may marry form part of a pyramid of marital possibilities for Jews. Ordinary Jews may marry any Jew. Extra restrictions apply to the cohanim, and further restrictions applied to the High Priest, who according to Leviticus (21:13) is only allowed to marry a virgin. The more exalted a person's status, the more marital restrictions are placed upon them. An almost identical pyramid of restrictions applies to the issue of coming into contact with the dead,[1] and a similar pyramid of restrictions determines who is allowed to enter where in the Temple. In general this form of increasing restrictions serves as a classically biblical way of using ritual to carry a religious message. Moreover, at least in theory, I don't make any claim that there is something unethical or immoral about the prohibition on a cohen marrying a con-

---

[1] Ordinary Jews have no restrictions, cohanim can only 'profane themselves' in the case of immediate kinsmen (Lev 21:3), and the High Priest cannot perform ritual mourning for even his own parents (Lev 21:11).

vert. The American constitutional provision that only a person born an American can become President of the United States is based on a similar sense that, as a matter of theory, our status at birth remains important, even if we change our status in life.

So much for the theory. The problem comes when, in the contemporary world, a male cohen[2] falls in love with a convert or, as is more often the case, a non-Jew who subsequently decides she wants to convert. At the point we, as Masorti rabbis, meet these couples they have taken a decision to spend the rest of their lives together. They have also, often, been refused a marriage license by Orthodox *batei din* and have been placed in a position where they are close to rejecting all, or at least many, forms of traditional Jewish observance and community. There are several possible responses open to a Masorti rabbi.

1) Do everything possible to disrupt the relationship in the hope that the newly single cohen will go on to find a more halachically appropriate spouse.

2) Walk away from the couple – what they do is their own business, we will not look to support them.

   – In the case of a woman who wishes to convert, this leaves the cohen living with a non-Jewish partner and would result in any children being considered non-Jews.

   – In the case of a woman who has already converted, this leaves the cohen living with a woman without being married to her.

3) In the case of a woman wishing to convert we could accept her application to conversion, but decline to officiate at any chuppah.

4) We could accept a candidature for conversion and officiate at the chuppah with or without some limit on the amount of joy brought to bear on the celebration.

We also need to specify the position that would apply to any children of the marriage.

This is an issue that has attracted some contemporary attention. The Committee on Jewish Law and Standards has passed two responsa on the issue,[3] and while both permit members of the

---

[2] There is no barrier on daughters of cohanim marrying male converts. See Mishnah Sotah 3:7.

[3] The first, passed in 1967, is published in I. Klein, *Responsa and Halakhic Studies* (Ktav, New York, 1975). The second can be found at http://rabbinicalassembly.org/teshuvot/docs/19912000/goodman_marriageconvert.pdf.

Rabbinical Assembly to perform these marriages, they are brief documents and predate the sort of systematic analysis that characterises more recent work. I am, however, indebted to Rabbi Isaac Klein, author of the first responsum, who also identified two key responsa from the Orthodox world. I am also grateful to Rabbi Chaim Weiner, who provided me with an unpublished responsum which examines a number of issues relating to the specific role of a rabbi in this matter.

THE BASIS OF THE PROHIBITION

The key verse on who a cohen may marry is Leviticus 21:7:

> They shall not take [*lo yikchu*] a harlotrous and defiled woman [*isha zona v'halahah*], nor shall they marry one divorced from her husband, for they are holy to their God.

On this verse, the early and foundational commentary Torat Cohanim states: 'A harlotrous and defiled woman: The Sages say a convert is the harlot that is mentioned here [*ain zona ele giyoret*].' [4] In the parallel Talmudic discussion, BT Kiddushin 78a, we find the following:

> It was taught, Rabbi Shimon Bar Yochai said, 'A woman who converted aged less than three years and a day is eligible to marry a cohen, as it is said [in the context of a battle against the Midianites, "kill every boy and every woman that has known man by lying with him,] but all the young women, who have not known a man by lying with him, keep alive for yourselves" (Num 31:17-18). And wasn't Pinchas [a cohen] among them!'
> But the Rabbis said, 'Keep them alive for yourselves' means as slaves.

Shimon Bar Yochai understands this verse to permit anyone in Israel (including cohanim) to marry a virgin Midianite who (to put it anachronistically) subsequently converts. He argues that this must be so since the biblical verse permits these women to all the people of Israel, seemingly thereby to include Pinchas and other cohanim.

According to the rabbis, however, this verse from Numbers has nothing to do with who a priest may take as a wife, but only who

---

[4] See also Mishnah at Yev 61a (references, throughout, to Talmudic tractates are to the Babylonian Talmud).

they may take as a slave. Instead, say the rabbis in the continuation of the Talmudic passage above, the origin of the forbidden nature of this marriage is a verse from Ezekiel:

'And no priest shall drink wine, when they enter into the inner court, and they shall not take widows or divorced women for wives [*lo yikchu lehem Inashim*], but they shall take virgins **of the seed** of the house of Israel [*betulot mi zera Yisrael*]' (Ezekiel 44:22).[5]
Rav Yehudah says both parents must be of Jewish **seed**.
Rabbi Eliezer ben Yaacov says only one parent needs to be of Jewish **seed**.[6]
Rabbi Yose says the woman must be one who was **conceived** [using the root form *zera*] as an Israelite.
Rabbi Shimon bar Yochai says the woman must have entered into **puberty** [also using the root form *zera*] as an Israelite.[7]

The major legal codes (while silent on the relative merits of the claims of Rabbis Yehudah and Eliezer ben Yaacov) reject the position of Rabbi Shimon bar Yochai (that a woman who has converted pre-puberty may marry a cohen) and adopt the position that a convert may not marry a cohen, even if the conversion took place when the girl was a very young child.[8]

TWO ORTHODOX RESPONSA
David Tzvi Hoffman (d. 1921) came from Romania to lead the Hildesheimer Rabbinical Seminary in Berlin. He is known for an openness to the world of Wissenschaft, academic scholarship, and a willingness to engage with the challenges of modernity, especially around the issue of conversion.

---

[5] Boldface emphases throughout are my own. Note that in Tos Yev 61a DHM *v'ein zona* this prooftext from Ezekiel is dismissed as an *asmachata*, presumably so that the *issur* can be considered *d'oraita* (no prooftext beyond the superficially vague, but Penteteuchal Lev 21:7 being considered to provide a more weighty prohibition than a verse from Nevi'im). The issue of whether the prohibition should be seen as *d'oraita* or *d'rabanan* is one we will return to. I will follow Zirelson, who assumes it to be *d'rabanan*; see discussion below.

[6] The biblical verse says *zera* and not *zerai* (the plural form). Note the case of a woman born to a Jewish father and non-Jewish mother. She would clearly need to come to a bet din to convert but, at least according to Rabbi Eliezer Ben Yaacov, would nonetheless be permitted to a cohen.

[7] Reworded to aid clarity.

[8] Rambam MT Issurei Biah 18:3 and Haggahot Maimoniot ad loc., SA EH 6:8.

Rav Hoffman[9] examines the case of a non-Jew who is married, in civil law, to a cohen. They have a son who is circumcised, and the woman decides that she wants to convert, marry the father of her child 'according to the law of Moses and Israel' and bring up her child as Jewish.[10]

Hoffman begins by balancing the relative seriousness of a cohen living with a non-Jew or living with a convert. It is hardly a fair fight. The former relationship, in the eyes of Rav Hoffman (citing his father Maharam Shik), is forbidden *d'oraita* – as a matter of Torah law – and its breach is punished by *caret* – one of the most dramatic punishments in the rabbinic system. The latter, in Hoffman's language and that of his father, 'is not permissible, but only considered as a general prohibition – *issur lav*'. On this basis, Hoffman begins by suggesting that converting the woman in order to save the man from caret would 'certainly be a good thing'.

However, since the Talmud insists that a convert must accept the whole of Torah (understood here as including both written and rabbinic law) without exception (Bechorot 30b), it might be thought that converting a woman who wanted to marry a cohen would present a problem, since the woman would be in the paradoxical position of agreeing to accept all of Torah while palpably not doing so.

There is a further problem which would apply to a *bet din* which supervises such a conversion. They would be acting to allow a sin (the *issur lav* of allowing the man and woman to live together), and even though this would save the man a greater sin (the *caret*-invoking sin of living with a non-Jewish partner), there exists a principle that one person should not sin in order to prevent sin in another. (Shabbat 4a)

From a strict technical perspective, or simply to protect himself from any suggestion of laxity, Rav Hoffman should clearly turn away from the couple. But he cannot. Hoffman is not a halachic technocrat, and he is prepared to expend spiritual capital by engag-

---

[9] Melamed L'ho'il 3:8.
[10] Hoffman makes sure the woman knows that the child cannot be considered Jewish, and that even though he has been circumcised, he will need the other essentials of conversion (bet din and mikvah).

ing with the situation. He finds a technical way of getting round the problems he has identified, but from any kind of objective perspective, it is hardly persuasive. Hoffman's solution is to say that as long as the woman never explicitly states that she is going to reject the law prohibiting a convert from marrying a cohen she is to be accepted, even in her breach of the law.

> Even if we [members of the bet din] know that she is going to sin on the matter of this forbidden act, nonetheless for the sake of a repair for the cohen and a repair for his child – *taknat hacohen v'taknat zar'o* – we receive her.

The woman, says Hoffman, should be warned that becoming Jewish results in her instantly being held responsible for a range of different obligations that, as a non-Jew, she was not previously obliged to meet. But Hoffman comes close to suggesting that to benefit the people of Israel, the woman should be encouraged to convert.

Hoffman also raises the issue of the profanation of God – *hillul hashem* – if the woman is not accepted. If the woman is turned away from her serious wish to convert – even if her intention is to live with or marry a cohen – she could be led to feel that 'Israel do not care – *merachamim* – for non-Jews'. This seems so shocking a possibility as to urge Rav Hoffman to action.

But what about a wedding ceremony? Rav Hoffman doesn't go this far.

> Even if we accept her as a convert, we don't officiate at the wedding with the cohen... This being the case, it is better that she should live with her husband [*ba'alah*] in a civil marriage than that there should be a religious ceremony.

In Rav Hoffman's balancing act, the desire to save a Jewish man from *caret*, coupled with the desire to bring the child into the Jewish people, outweighs the complexities of accepting for conversion a woman who wants to marry a cohen. But, for him, the desire to bring the Jewish couple under a *chuppah*, thereby saving them from the general *issur* of living with a partner without *kiddushin*, does not overweigh his commitment to the obligation that a cohen should not marry a convert. *Ad can leshono* – this is his perspective on the issue facing us.

Rav Judah Leib Zirelson (d. 1941) was chairman of the first international conference of Agudas Yisroel, an early religious Zionist
and chief rabbi of Kishinev – a position that even saw him serve in
the Romanian Parliament. He died in a Nazi air attack on the city
he served.

The question posed to Zirelson[11] is perhaps even sharper than
that facing Rav Hoffman.[12] There is a couple who wish to spend
their life together and, with preparations for the wedding well un-
derway, it emerges that the bride is a convert and the groom a cohen
(or more likely someone points out the halachic problem with the
planned union, this not previously having been realised). The wedding is promptly cancelled and uproar ensues. In the words of the
author of the question: 'What a racket... everyone from the greatest
to the smallest [is appalled].' The groom threatens, 'I will accept
baptism in front of everyone and will get married that way for there
is no way I will leave my beloved.'

Zirelson is most anxious to ensure that his response is not to be
relied on as a general change in halachah. 'This is a one-off decree –
hora'at sha'ah – in legislating a case as extreme as this... Do not learn
from this any leniency on any other issue relating to converts and
cohanim.' But he is prepared to permit the ceremony.

Zirelson begins by considering a Talmudic passage.

> There was a female [non-Jewish] slave in Pumbedita who was be-
> ing kept for immoral purposes. Abbaye said, 'If it weren't for the
> fact that Rav Yehudah has said in the name of Shmuel that one who
> frees a slave sins, I would force her master to make a declaration of
> freedom for her.'
> Rabina said, 'Rav Yehudah would agree [with forcing the master to
> free her], because of the forbidden nature of what is happening cur-
> rently [*mishum milta d'isura*].
> (*Gittin 38a*)

Sinning (by freeing the slave) in order to prevent another from
sinning (by having a sexual relationship with the woman) of course
raises the problem that confronted Rav Hoffman, namely that a

---

[11] Mechkarei Lev 72.
[12] Although the scholars were contemporaries, it does not appear that either was aware of
the other's responsum.

person should not sin in order to give merit to his fellow.[13] Zirelson responds to this by making explicit something that has to be deduced implicitly from Rav Hoffman's work: namely that this prohibition is not absolute, but rather depends on the relative seriousness of the prevented sin, or, equally, the relative importance of any mitzvah that becomes possible if such a sin is committed. 'In essence,' states Zirelson, 'the thing depends on the greatness of the mitzvah – *ha'ikar talui hadavar b'inyan mitzvah rabah'*. Indeed, as Zirelson notes, this is clear from the continuation of the Talmudic passage.

> Rav Yehudah has said in the name of Shmuel that one who frees a slave sins... An objection was made since on one occasion Rabbi Eliezer came into the synagogue and didn't find ten there, so he immediately freed his slave to make up the ten. [The rabbis hold] where there is a mitzvah to be performed[14] this is different.
> *(Gittin 38b)*

In a parallel recounting of the story of Rabbi Eliezer and his slave, the Talmud asks, 'But isn't this a case of a mitzvah on the back of a sin – *mitzvah habah b'aveirah!*[15] Nonetheless this prohibition does not apply in the case of a mitzvah of the many – *mitzvah derabim shani'* (Brachot 47b). In attempting to apply this exception to the case of the cohen and his beloved one might, quite legitimately, feel that the case of a *single* cohen is not one of 'a mitzvah of the many'. That said, Zirelson is prepared to take a very bold approach to this phrase, considering it to encompass the case of a single individual who has a lifetime's possibility of fulfilling the mitzvot associated with marriage.[16]

Zirelson is as aware as Rav Hoffman of the problem of a good deed being done on the back of a sin, but his weighing up of the relevant issues takes him to a very different place. If, says Zirelson, it

---

[13] See above (Shabbat 4a).

[14] In this case the mitzvah of allowing a fully constituted quorum for prayer.

[15] This is a well-attested rabbinic prohibition against, for example, using a stolen *lulav* to fulfil the obligation to take a *lulav* on Sukkot.

[16] Perhaps he wilfully re-interprets the phrase *mitzvah derabim* not as 'a mitzvah for many people', but rather as 'many mitzvot'. But this is neither the *pshat* (simple) sense of the Talmudic passage, nor even a comfortable application of grammar.

is appropriate to override the law against freeing a heathen slave in order to allow nine people to be able to pray as a minyan on a one-off basis, then how much the more is it correct for a wedding to go ahead that would allow the cohen and his fiancée to come together in married life.[17]

This is a very bold piece of halachah, using the issue of freeing a slave to overturn a well-established halachic principle and one that may be considered a matter of Torah law – *d'oraita* (though Zirelson, citing various sources,[18] considers it a rabbinic proclamation – *d'rabanan*). I wonder if the rabbi is moved by the way the codes treat the issue of freeing a slave, even though he does not cite these texts directly.

> It is permissible to free a slave in order to do a mitzvah, even a rabbinic mitzvah such as when there are not ten in the synagogue... and similar cases. Equally a female slave that the people are treating as a free-for-all – *shenehagim bah ha'am minhag hefker* – behold she is a stumbling block that leads to sinning, so you force the master to free her so she can get married and the stumbling block be removed, and similar cases.
> *(Rambam MT Hil Avadim 9:6)* [19]

The emphasis in the Rambam, particularly in the context of freeing the woman, is on removing a stumbling block that results in immoral behaviour, and instead allowing a marriage that brings the possibility of holiness. This seems precisely to be the motivation driving Rav Zirelson.

I am reminded of the Talmudic passage about the yeshivah student who is about to bed a prostitute when he is slapped about the face by his own tzitzit. As the student attempts to run off, the prostitute, astounded by his resolve, gets him to write for her the name

---

[17] Zirelson in his treatment seems to focus less on the sin of an unmarried couple living together, and less on any sin that might apply to a celebrant of marriage, and more on the possible mitzvot that marriage allows both the man and woman to celebrate, particularly being fruitful and multiplying – an obligation he acknowledges as a *mitzvah rabbah*, great mitzvah.

[18] Including Tos Yevamot 61a DHM *zona*, Hidushei HaRashba ad loc. Note also that the prooftext is not the verse from Leviticus, but that from Ezekiel.

[19] See also SA YD 267:79, which uses identical terminology.

of his Bet Midrash and heads off to find him again. She arrives and asks Rabbi Hiyya:

'Rabbi, command me so they will make me a convert.'
'My child', he replied, 'perhaps you have set your eyes on one of the students?' She took out the note and gave it to him.
He responds, 'Go, enjoy your acquisition.'
And those very bed-clothes which she had spread for him [in the whorehouse] she now spread out for him lawfully.
(Menachot 44a)

By the standards of any traditional approach to conversion Rabbi Hiyya seems more than a little over-eager, and we should not understand this tale as reflecting normative halachah on conversion. But it does show the rabbinic desire to do anything possible to bring an end to harlotrous behaviour, including bending conversion rules and, in the case of Rav Zirelson at least, permitting this wedding. It would be a serious mistake to say Rav Zirelson abdicates a concern with halachah, as he rides roughshod over the specific prohibition of a cohen marrying a convert. It is rather that he is anxious to support the institution of marriage and the obligation to 'be fruitful and multiply'. Moreover, he seems to wish to avoid losing the cohen as a Jew. He defends halachah even as he seems to disregard it. That said, Zirelson is quite categorical that his leniency in this one-off specific instance should not be relied upon in general. He is motivated by the fact that the wedding had already been planned and the groom is threatening apostasy, and by a fear that prohibiting the wedding would promote anti-Semitism in the community that sought his help. We therefore need to look further for a more general approach.

CONVERTS, COHANIM, ASSUMPTIONS, DOUBT AND PROBABILITY

The key explanation of the problematic verse Leviticus 18:21 – 'the convert is the harlot that is mentioned here' – is, as stated above, found in the Mishnah. In a commentary of the tosafot on that mishnah[20] the prohibition against marrying a convert is explained as follows: 'The reason is that anyone coming from a place of idolatry [*shebah min ha'ovdei kokhavim*] is steeped in depravity [*shutafim b'zimah*].' This commentary goes on to make the surprising statement: 'A female convert is forbidden [to a cohen] because of the prohibition of marrying a *zonah* even if she herself has not acted in a harlotrous manner [*af al gav d'lo zintah*].'

There are two ways to understand this important statement. One is to consider that, in forbidding a cohen to marry a convert, the rabbis have abandoned any connection to any notion of actual harlotry, rather equating the terms 'convert' and 'harlot' without any pejorative comment whatsoever. This seems a forced reading and I do not accept it.

A better 'pshat' reading is to consider that the rabbis sought to forbid all marriages between converts and cohanim without wishing to defame specifically any particular convert. Instead, surely, they relied on their belief that such is the level of depravity in the general non-Jewish world that one ought to assume a pervasive level of harlotry which would make it unsafe to allow any convert to marry a cohen.[21] I wish to engage with this issue in two ways, substantively and technically.

ARE CONVERTS 'STEEPED IN DEPRAVITY'?

From a substantive perspective it seems wholly impossible to treat the contemporary non-Jewish world with the kind of deep-rooted revulsion that would lead a person to consider all non-Jews as 'steeped in depravity'. Yes, there are issues with contemporary sexual mores and norms, but that kind of blanket approach to all converts (even if it was merited in classical times) now rings untrue. In the sort of situation that confronts a Masorti rabbi – that of being

---

[20] Yevamot 61a DHM *v'ein zonah.*

[21] The notion of the rabbis making presumptions based on the pervading majority of a surrounding society has clear precedent. The classic example is of 'nine stores' (Pesachim 9b). In a neighbourhood with nine kosher butchers and one butcher who sells *treif,* any meat found in the street is deemed kosher. The child of a woman who has been raped is considered to have a status dependent on the majority of the men in the town where the abominable action took place (Mishnah Ketubot 1:10).

A person arriving at a city on *erev Shabbat* who sees lights from far off may say the Sabbath blessing over the lights if 'the majority of inhabitants of the city are Jewish' (Brachot 53a).

asked to official at a wedding where the couple have a pre-existing relationship – rejecting the convert as 'steeped in depravity' seems particularly bizarre, not least since the bride and groom are, almost by definition, in the same stage of a relationship – one with the other.

Moreover, from a technical perspective, the blanket accusation that all converts are to be considered 'steeped in depravity' seems to contradict the command to love the *ger* – the stranger or convert. Maimonides' letter to Ovadiah the Convert contains our tradition's most forceful articulation of the point:

> You must know the greatness of the obligation that the Torah imposed on us regarding the foreigner: we are commanded to honour and fear one's father and mother; regarding the prophets – to heed them... But, concerning the *ger* (convert), we are mandated to bear them great love, with the full force of our heart's affection: 'You must also show love to the foreigner' (Deut. 10:19), just as we are bidden to love His name, as it is said: 'You shall love the Lord your God' (Deut. 6:5).

This demand to love comes with a 'thou shall not' obligation attached. 'One cannot say to a convert, "Remember the actions of your ancestors". As it is written, you shall not wrong or oppress a *ger* (Ex 22)' (Mishnah BM 58b). One wonders what could be a more significant reminder of a person's foreignness and a supposed past of 'harlotry' than refusing them marriage.[22]

We are therefore looking at two opposing trends in halachic thought – one which insists we love and do nothing to hurt the *ger*, and the other which associates all converts with idolatry and harlotry. To apply Rav Zirelson's approach we have to weigh up these mutually exclusive positions. Since the first is enforced specifically by the language of the Torah itself (some 36 times) and the second is a rabbinic derivation, based on a verse in the prophetic works and a series of assumptions that cannot be applied in good faith to converts today, one might argue that we have enough even at this point to permit the marriage.

Personally I would consider that this balancing act, rather than overturning the tradition in its own right, instead sets the bar for

---

[22] Indeed, being forbidden marriage is the marker of the clearest instance of Judaism denying a person entry into the community of Israel – *mamzerut*.

any change in approach. We are to bend over backwards to find a way to welcome the convert, but we still need a technical loophole that can be exploited to address the prohibition as it is recorded in our texts.

One possibility emerges from an engagement with the language of the tosafot quoted above: 'The reason [for prohibiting a cohen from marrying a convert] is that anyone coming from a **place of idolatry** [*shebah min ha'ovdei kokhavim*] is steeped in depravity.' Most rabbis do not consider most converts to come from places of idolatry at all. The major source for the relationship between contemporary non-Jewish religious practice and idolatry or *avodah zara* is another tosafot, right at the very beginning of the Talmud's major treatment of this issue. Here the concern is with avoiding engaging with idol worshippers in the three days before and after their *'eid'* or religious festival.

The problem is particularly severe if one considers Sunday a Christian *eid*. That would make any business between Jew and non-Jew impossible seven days a week (as the authors of this tosafot make explicit). The rabbis[23] find a way to consider monotheistic religious practice other than Judaism, while admittedly 'a rejection of holiness', nonetheless not really *avodah zara*. This is a deeply pragmatic worldview, which also articulates an important theological message about Christianity. I would argue that if one is prepared to consider a practicing Christian as not really engaged in *avodah zara*, the same would surely be true of converts who grew up devoid of any religious practice.[24]

A further loophole emerges from an engagement with the notion that the root of the prohibition lies in the requirement that a priest marry only one of the seed of the House of Israel (Ezekiel 4:22, discussed above). Since the eleventh century it has been clear that the convert is considered a member of the House of Israel. Indeed, the convert is considered to have the patriarchs Abraham, Isaac and Jacob (Israel) as their own forefathers or progenitors. Again, the most

---

[23] Tos AZ 2a DHM *assur*.
[24] For a similar approach to Islam see Maimonides' letter to Ovadiah, who converted from that religion.

forceful articulation of this idea is Maimonides' letter to Ovadiah:

All who embrace Judaism until the end of all generations, and all who profess the unity of the Lord's name as is directed in the Torah, are like pupils of Abraham of blessed memory and are members in his household, all of them... The result is that Abraham our forefather was the father of his legitimate progeny who follow the path forged by him, and he, too, *is father to every 'ger' who converts...* [25] For after having entered the Jewish fraternity and accepted Judaism, there is no difference between you and us, and all the miracles that were wrought were wrought for us and for you... There is no distinction or incongruity between you and us in any respect.

In other words, if we take Maimonides seriously the convert is considered 'of the seed of the House of Israel', even if they were born and raised as non-Jews. This is a radical rejection of the approach of the classical rabbinic period, but Maimonides' statement that 'there is no distinction or incongruity between you and us in any respect' could not be clearer, and it is impossible to suggest that the great master somehow forgot about the issue of marriage to a cohen.[26]

Admittedly these are not crushing proofs, and, all other things being equal, they would not allow for the overturning of an ancient and well-attested traditional observance. But all other things are not equal. We are, today, particularly mindful of the injustice of applying an assumption of harlotry and pre-existing idol worship to all converts. We are anxious to strengthen the institution of marriage for those who are living together without the blessings of *chuppah*, and we are particularly anxious to allow Jewish males to find a way to live their lives with their beloved free of any suggestion of 'marrying out'. The balance of proof, for a technical solution to our problem, has been set so as to welcome any way out of this problematic issue. I hold, therefore, that this provides us with the loophole that allows us to yield to the tremendous tug to 'love' and 'not oppress' the convert, and thereby officiate at the wedding.

---

[25] Note also the classic nomenclature for a convert: *Ploni ben Avraham Avinu* – So and So, the *son of Abraham* our patriarch.

[26] I suppose it is just about conceivable that since there is no prohibition on a male *ger* marrying a *cohenet* (the daughter or wife of a cohen), Maimonides didn't feel the need to mention this exception to his male correspondent.

TO CELEBRATE WITH JOY?

The question of whether this wedding should be celebrated with full joy or with some diminution need not delay us. The houses of Hillel and Shammai debate how to celebrate the wedding of an ugly bride. Shammai wants us to 'tell it like it is'; Hillel demands we sing forth of the 'beauty and grace' of the bride – the implication being that we should celebrate a bride's beauty even if she is ugly.[27] Halachah follows Hillel, as does the popular wedding song, 'How does one dance before the bride – with a voice of delight and a voice of happiness'. As well as being impractical and unsustainable, it is halachically inappropriate and even cruel to allow any concerns about the thin ice on which we tread on an issue like this to impair what must be a day of untarnished joy.

OFFICIATING AT THE CHUPPAH WHEN
ONE BELIEVES THE MARRIAGE IS PROHIBITED

Rabbi Chaim Weiner, in an unpublished paper on a related issue, notes that the celebrant is in an unusual position. They are not being asked if they approve, as a matter of halachah, of the union of cohanim and those whom cohanim are forbidden to marry. They are being asked to officiate at a ceremony celebrating the relationship between two people who, at the time of the conversation, are already committed to spending the rest of their lives together.

> The question facing the rabbi in this case is not 'Is a Cohen allowed to marry [this person]?' but rather 'Should a rabbi perform this marriage even if it is forbidden?' It is not a question of what is permitted, but rather – what should be done.... The marriage will take place anyway. The children will be born anyway. Our refusal to perform the marriage will not prevent a Cohen from marrying a [this person]. Our only achievement will be driving another couple away from us, more alienation, less understanding.
>
> This alone is sufficient reason, in my eyes, to perform the marriage. When the only result of enforcing Jewish law is to lose another Jew, when nothing else is achieved, it is preferable to ignore that law in hope that many more will be observed in the future. I do not say that a Cohen is allowed to marry [this person]. When approached,

---

[27] Ketubot 16b-17a.

I advise the candidate of this fact. However, I do not use my position of power to coerce a non-observant Jews to abide by the law. I accept his decision and accept him as a member of my community with love and respect. I do not compromise my own principles. It is not forbidden to perform these marriages – it is forbidden to enter into them.[28] I choose to be lenient in this case because it is a situation in which I cannot win.

If we accept Rabbi Weiner's argument (and I do), we should officiate at these celebrations even if we are not prepared to consider the marriage of a cohen and a convert sinless.

THE STATUS OF THE MARRIAGE AND ANY CHILDREN

If such a wedding does take place, *kiddushin tosfin* – the marriage holds. This is best illustrated by the clear insistence that if, God forbid, there was a falling out in years to come, a *get* – ritual divorce – would be required.[29]

The child of a cohen and a convert is considered a full Jew, but is also a *halal* (i.e., one who loses the prerogatives of the cohanim),[30] and, as such, should not receive the first *aliyah* or engage in the other rights and responsibilities of a cohen. While there is enough of an opening to allow the marriage, I do not feel the same imperative applies to the issue of the status of any children who are, according to all authorities, recognised as full Jews, with exactly the same rights and responsibilities of all Israelites.

SHOULD A COHEN WHO MARRIES A CONVERT STILL BE CONSIDERED A COHEN?

The key text on this is:

A cohen who came to accept the things of priesthood, apart from one thing, we don't receive him, as it says, 'He, among the sons of

---

28 This distinction is based on the opinion of Rava, that the transgression is committed on consummation of the marriage, and not by the act of marriage itself. Kiddushin 78a (footnote in the original).

29 The position of British Orthodox *batei din* on this issue is a little more complex. It might be that if such a wedding was performed by a Masorti rabbi they would not insist on a *get*, deeming the wedding null by dint of the rabbis who officiated. I suspect they would probably insist on a *get* even while rejecting the validity of the marriage, but I claim no particular expertise on this specific issue.

30 Mishnah Kiddushin 3:12.

Aaron, who offers the blood of the peace offerings, and the fat, shall have the right shoulder for his part'. This means all the rituals are passed on to the sons of Aaron and any cohen who does not accept this has no part in the priesthood.

(Bechorot 30b)

Again I would say that while there is room to permit the wedding, it relies on technicalities and is justified only because other issues demand it. I would therefore apply this passage from Bechorot and insist that any cohen married to a convert should step back from the rights and responsibilities of the priesthood, in particular the right to *duchen* and receive the first *aliyah*.[31] I acknowledge that this may prove a major emotional wrench for many cohanim, but it is an appropriate way of recognising the traditional approach to this issue while still allowing the wedding to be celebrated with joy. In addition, while this may be painful, it should be noted that any children of the marriage would grow up not to expect, inaccurately, that their father's role in ritual service would devolve to them. They would grow up seeing their father and mother taking the same role in ritual service that they would grow into themselves.

A PATH NOT TAKEN

Some discussions of this issue focus on the question of 'the doubtful cohen' – that is, the notion that since we are unsure as to whether any presenting cohen really is the direct patrilineal descendant of Aaron, it is possible to deem a presenting cohen who wants to marry a convert a non-cohen and perform the wedding. I feel uneasy with this approach, which comes close to destroying the entire fabric of the *cehunah*. Deeming an individual a non-cohen for the sake of his marriage would mean that one ought to deem his father and any brothers equally non-cohanim. Rather than destroy the institution of the *cehuna*, it seems more honest and far more preferable to engage with the outmoded, unsustainable and unjust issue of deeming all converts harlots.

---

[31] The cohen can take other aliyot and should be considered a full member of the community in all respects, like any other Jew.

SUMMARY AND PRACTICAL CONSIDERATIONS

● A candidate for conversion should not be turned away if she wishes to marry a cohen.

● We should officiate at the weddings of cohanim and converts.

● These weddings should be celebrated with delight and happiness.

● We take these positions since:

– When weighing the relative merits and problems involved in a couple living together as Jew and non-Jew (or even as a Jewish couple outside of marriage) and comparing them to the merits and problems of marriage between a cohen and a convert, or officiating at the marriage, the latter is preferred (following Rav Hoffman and Rav Zirelsohn).

– Performing the wedding removes a great stumbling block that leads to sinning and supports the institution of marriage (see discussion of MT Hil Avadim 9:6 in the context of Zirelson).

– We consider that walking away from these couples creates a problem in the context of the Torah's repeated commands to love and not oppress the ger, convert (see discussion of Deut 10 and Ex 22).

– We reject that contemporary converts should automatically be considered, in their previous life, *ovdei avodah zara* – idol worshippers (see discussion of Tos AZ 2a DHM *assur*).

– We reject a contemporary application of the tradition's blanket assumption of harlotry to all converts (see discussion of Tos Yev 61a DHM *v'ein zona* in the context of Maimonides' Letter to Ovadiah).

● The children of these marriages are considered fully Jewish but *mehalalin* – i.e., the ritual responsibilities and privileges of the priesthood do not apply to them.

● The husband, once married, should no longer serve as a priest, stepping back from taking the first aliyah, etc. He is, of course, to be welcomed as a full member of the community in all other respects.

On Women as Leaders of Prayer Services
{2006}

During my time at SAMS I was asked to lead a process to answer the question, can and should women lead prayers services at SAMS. This was a long process which involved extensive consultations with lay leaders and the membership more generally. But I was absolutely clear that halachah – Jewish law – should be at the centre of the discussions, not only providing a justification, if a justification could be found, but also determining the way in which the question should be approached. An argument that fails to get beyond 'I want X'–'But I want Y' can weaken a community, but an argument about halachah should strengthen a community not only in its relationship to Jewish life, but also in its internal ability to get along. A huge amount has already been written on this subject, but I never felt comfortable with the position of my teacher Rabbi Joel Roth, for reasons detailed below. And nowhere else could I find the sort of systematic approach I wanted to be able to share with the community at SAMS (though my reliance on the work of Rabbi David Golinkin is considerable).

In the last section of this otherwise technical article, I offer some more general thoughts about the complete androcentrism of classical rabbinic Judaism. I don't regard words like 'sexist' or 'misogynist' as appropriate when describing the entirety of the nuanced and complex rabbinic system, but equally I accept that this system (which I love) failed to understand truths available in more modern times and needs radical intervention right at the very edges of normative halachah – on the issue of the role of women in public Jewish life perhaps more than any other.

CAN AND SHOULD WOMEN LEAD
PRAYER SERVICES AT SAMS? [1]

It is an oversimplification, but we can say that there are three tasks of a communal leader of prayer.

1) They must bring the community together, much like a conductor works with an orchestra. This is in part technical – we must be brought in at the right time with the right tune – but it is also a spiritual, emotional and artistic task. A great leader of prayer functions as a vessel, drawing a spiritual response from the community and transforming the printed words of the Siddur into songful prayer.

2) They must fulfil certain key obligations on behalf of members of the prayer community. This is entirely a practical issue.

3) They must also serve as our representatives before God. We, the community, stand to be judged not only in our own right, but also in terms of who we appoint as our leaders.

Each role raises a different halachic question.

1) The role of keeping the community focussed and united in their prayer raises the question: Is there something about women that distracts worshippers or otherwise makes it impossible for them to 'conduct' prayers for a mixed, male and female, community?

2) The role of fulfilling ritual obligation raises the question: Are women technically able, in the same way as men, to fulfil obligations on behalf of both male and female members of the prayer community?

3) The role of representing a fully constituted prayer community before God raises the twin questions: Who *can* and *should* lead a prayer community consisting of both men and women?

---

[1] There is a vast amount of modern material – articles and responsa – on this subject. I have not referred to every useful source at every moment. That said, as will be clear, I owe a deep debt to Rabbi David Golinkin, whose work in this field is considerable. See, in particular, the responsa *B'Inyan HaMehitzah B'Beit HaKnesset*, http://responsafortoday.com/vol2/1.pdf, and *B'Inyan Nashim B'Minyan Ucshlichot Tzibur*, http://www.responsafortoday.com/vol6/1_4.pdf. Both provide detailed bibliographies, including key material produced by Orthodox legal authorities. These materials are in Hebrew, and those only able to access English are directed to http://www.schechter.edu/women/learnteach.htm, where much of the material is translated, reworked and made available to a non-specialist. Rabbi David Fine has also discussed, extensively, the history of Masorti jurisprudence on this issue in his responsum Women and the Minyan, https://www.rabbinicalassembly.org/sites/default/files/public/halakhah/teshuvot/19912000/oh_55_1_2002.pdf

QUESTION 1.

Is there something about women that makes it impossible for them to 'conduct' prayers for a mixed, male and female, community?

In this section I consider two issues: firstly the notion that the woman is a sexual provocation and is therefore a distraction in prayer, and secondly the question of whether the woman's place is in the domestic realm, away from the public sphere of communal prayer.

WOMEN AS SEXUAL PROVOCATEURS

Is there something sexually provocative and distracting about women, and most especially about their voices, which needs to be kept under-cover and away from public worship?

> Rav Isaac said, 'A handbreadth of exposed skin in a woman is a sexual incitement [*erva*]...'
> Rav Hisda said, 'A woman's leg is a sexual incitement...'
> Samuel said, 'A woman's voice is a sexual incitement, as it says, "For your voice is sweet [*arev*]"' (Song of Songs 2:14).
> Rav Sheshet said, 'A woman's hair is a sexual incitement.'
> *(Talmud Brachot 24a)*

We will have more to say about the male-centred nature of this, and indeed all classic rabbinic language, and also the sexualisation of women in classic rabbinics at a later point. At this juncture I want to consider this issue from within the tradition. I will also focus on the most halachically problematic issue – the woman's voice.

The early rabbinic authority Hai Gaon understood the prohibition on hearing a woman's voice [*kol b'isha*] as follows:

> One may not recite [the Shema] while a woman is singing... However, if one can focus on one's prayers while she is singing in a manner that one does not hear her and does not pay attention to her, it is permissible [to recite the Shema].
> *(Otzar HaGeonim, Berachot, Peirushim 102)*[2]

Hai Gaon specifically prohibits singing, and the prohibition applies to any woman, but only as a barrier to the recitation of the Shema. He also introduces the possibility of *kol b'isha* losing its prohibiting power. These are all issues which need to be clarified.

---

[2] See also Ravad, cited in Chidushei haRashba Brachot 25a, and Yosef Caro, Bet Yosef OH 75, which take similar positions.

DOES THE PROHIBITION APPLY TO ALL WOMEN?

The broader context of the passage in Brachot is a discussion of the possibility of reciting the Shema when in bed with one's wife. It therefore might be thought that the prohibition of *kol b'isha* applies only to one's wife, perhaps on the basis that since a husband is permitted, sexually, to his wife, she can therefore distract him in ways no other woman could. However, in a related Talmudic source, we find the following comment on *kol b'isha*:

> Shmuel said, 'A person should have nothing to do with women at all, whether adults or children.' [Rav Nahman asked Rav Yehuda,] would you like to send a greeting to [my wife] Yalta. [Rav Yehuda] responded, 'Shmuel said, "The voice of a woman is a sexual incitement... Don't even ask after her wellbeing."'
> *(Kiddushin 70 a-b)*

In this passage, the problem is someone else's wife. This suggests that the problem is women who are precluded from the male. And indeed, the codifier Rav Falk states that the problem is ONLY with precluded women, and that a permitted woman – i.e. a person's wife –does not count.

> The voice of women who it is permissible to hear [can be excluded from the classification of *kol b'isha*] for they do not awaken the appetite. *(Prisha Tur EH 21:2)*

Several medieval authorities incline in favour of a test from a person's own feelings: Is the enticing only on who the man feels is sexually enticing? This is the position of the Ritva:

> All is in accordance with one's fear of heaven, and so, in the halachah all depends on the way a man recognises himself. Therefore if he requires prohibitive fences to curb his intentions, he should construct them and even viewing the coloured clothing of a woman is prohibited. But if he is aware of himself and knows that his desires are subjugated, then it is permissible for him to look at and speak with a woman who is an *erva* and to exchange warm greetings with a married woman.
> *(Hidushei Ha Ritba Kiddushin 82a.)*

The Ritba believes that 'only one who is thoroughly righteous and recognises his desires may conduct himself in such a manner... fortunate is one who conquers his passions and toils in Torah.' But

I am not sure it is sensible to assume that expert Torah scholars are particularly and uniquely able to withstand a woman's 'siren call'. Indeed, this is acknowledged in the Talmud itself.[3]

According to Cherney,[4] the relevance of how a person, subjectively, feels in earshot of a woman introduces the concept of *regilut*, or habituation – the idea that something which might once have been sexually enticing loses its erotic (and therefore prohibited) character once it becomes customary. This is the position of Moshe Isserles in the leading Ashkenazi articulation of the law: 'But a voice which one is accustomed to hear [*kol haregil bo*] is not sexually enticing' (SA OH 75.3).

We will return to look at the notion of *regilut* later.

SINGING AND OTHER UTTERANCES

The association with song appears to be derived from the prooftext offered in the Talmud, a verse which concerns a singing woman whose 'voice is sweet' [*arev*] (Song of Songs 2:14). It should be noted that while the word *arev*, sweet, sounds similar(ish) to *ervah*, sexual incitement, the two Hebrew words are not etymologically connected.[5] This is a weak proof and should be seen as an *asmachta* – a hook on which to hang an issue that is already prevalent practice. That said, we should note the following specific Talmudic discussion of women in song:

> Rav Yosef said, 'When men sing and women join in, it is licentious; when women sing and men answer, it is like raging fire in flax.'
> *(Sotah 48a)*

The connection of *kol b'isha* to song is explicit in the Shulchan Aruch (Even HaEzer 21:3).[6] However, there are authorities who,

---

[3] See Succah 52a, where Abbaye follows a man and woman as they walk across the meadows together. As they part, having kept far from transgression, Abbaye acknowledges he could not have withstood this temptation. Abbaye is about to throw himself from a bridge in despair when a wise man comforts him: 'The greater the man, the more powerful his evil inclination.'

[4] B. Cherney, 'Kol Isha', *Journal of Halacha and Contemporary Society* (1985), vol. 10, pp. 57-75, at page 63.

[5] The former, *arev*, is spelled ayin-resh-bet. The latter, *ervah*, is spelled ayin-resh-vav-heh.

[6] See also Bet Yosef OH 75. Also restricting the prohibition to singing is Rabad, cited in Hidushei HaRashba Berachot 25a.

based on the Kiddushin passage discussed above, preclude all female utterances.[7] Regardless of the specifics of *kol b'isha* we should note that the medieval rabbis considered all forms of social contact with women dangerous, verging on the unacceptable. The opening line of the just-cited chapter of the Shulchan Aruch sets out the importance of keeping 'men [*adam*] very, very far away from women' (Even Haezer 21:1).

WHAT ACTIVITIES ARE
PROHIBITED WITHIN EARSHOT?

The passage in Brachot clearly concerns the recitation of the Shema prayer, but other Talmudic articulations merely suggest the voice of the woman is problematic without specifying which, if any, activities are prohibited or voided if performed within earshot. Matters are made even more complex by a tradition of interpretation that seems to fly directly against the context of the passage in Brachot. Commenting on the passage in Brachot, the Rosh states:

> This was **not** said regarding reciting the Shema. Rather it is forbidden to hear the voice of women.[8]
> *(Tosafot HaRosh, Brachot 24a)*

This is a surprising statement in view of the apparently clear language of the Talmud itself. But since neither the Rif nor Rambam[9] include *kol b'isha* among the list of things which make saying the Shema forbidden, we should take the Rosh's statement as representing halachah (perhaps since saying the Shema is such a holy and purifying experience?), thereby understanding *kol b'isha ervah* as a general instruction applied to general social interaction, not as a specific bar to specific prayers.

DOES THE PROHIBITION STILL APPLY TODAY?

We have already raised the possibility of a voice that does not actually entice a man not being counted as *kol b'isha* (see the comments

---

7   See J. Blau, *Responsa of Moses ben Maimon, Machzikei Nirdamim* (Jerusalem, 1960) 2:224, pp. 398-400.

8   This and other bold emphases in translations of rabbinic texts are my own.

9   Mishneh Torah Hil. Keriat Shema 3.16.

of Hai Gaon and the Ritva above). We discuss this more fully now.

In the thirteenth century, Ravia wrote – in the context of the full range of sexual enticements listed in Brachot (hair, skin, voice) – that the prohibition

> applies only to those things which are not usually revealed [*she'ain regilut lehigalot*], but it doesn't apply to an unmarried woman with exposed hair because there is no licentiousness [*hirhur*], and the same applies regarding her voice.
> *(1:76 p. 52)* [10]

The early-modern Orthodox authority Rav Yehiel Wienberg, known as the Sridei Aish, was asked how high a *mehitzah* should be. This is a question with direct implications for our discussion, since the sight of a woman's hair is considered *ervah* in the same passage as the Talmud deems the voice of a woman *ervah*. He noted:

> Hungarian [ultra-Orthodox] writers were exceptionally strict and expounded from sources that the *mehitza* needed to be taller than the height of a woman. Moreover... they prohibited going to synagogues without such a *mehitzah*, and moreover forbade women from coming to pray and held it better that they stayed in their homes. And for sure, their intentions were good – protecting the modesty which was customary in earlier generations – but in our time the situation has changed, and human nature has changed [*nishtaneh hamatzav v'nishtanu hatevi'im*], and if women were kept in their homes and weren't allowed to come to synagogue, the Torah of Jewish life would be lost for them totally.
> *(Sridei Aish 1:8 col 20)*

And so, he held, there was no need for a *mehitzah* which removed sight of any female hair. This is an extraordinary document, clearly sensitive to the differences between our contemporary world and the world in which the more ancient of our texts were written. This response is also remarkable in the way in which it recognises a religious need to involve women in public prayer; admittedly not as leaders – but there is a clear rejection of the notion that what goes on in shul belongs to a male-only sphere. Weinberg also notes that, according to ancient texts, it would be forbidden for a menstruant

---

[10] See also Levush, Manhigim, at the end of Orach Hayim, 36, citing Sefer Hasidim, which takes a similar position.

to come to synagogue, but he also rides over this ancient prohibition, in the context of the High Holy Days, since

> It would be a great source of pain [*atzbon gadol*] for them, with everyone gathered inside and them standing outside. In our time women are very sensitive to being kept far from the Synagogue. Also going to Synagogue is, in our time, the possibility of survival of Judaism, for [men] [11] and for matriarchs. [12]

We live in a world where the voices of women and the sight of uncovered hair among even married women are commonplace. There may be some who are so sensitive to the sexual potential in women that they are unable to focus on even as mighty and holy task as prayer in the presence and/or earshot of women, but it would be wrong to use the power of a halachic dictum to proscribe the voice or presence of women for the sake of these troubled individuals. A man who is unable to consider a woman's voice or sight as anything other than a sexual enticement suffers an affliction. He should seek medical and or psychological assistance. He should not be protected in his affliction when this would cause *atzbon gadol* – great pain – to women who feel that being de-voiced is the equivalent of being kept outside.

In conclusion, on the issue of woman as sexual provocateur, I decide as follows:

Kol b'isha does not prohibit the recitation of the Shema or other acts of prayer. It only applies to individual men who are, subjectively, distracted by individual women. A man who is so distracted should follow the advice of the Ritva: 'He requires prohibitive fences to curb his intentions and **he** should construct them.' It is not for the woman or the community to construct fences creating divisions between all men and all women since, as the Sridei Aish has noted, 'the situation has changed, and human nature has changed'. The voice of a woman cannot be presumed to be a distraction in a society where we are used to it, especially when preventing women from having their voice heard in prayer would cause great pain to them

---

[11] Emending the Bar-Ilan Responsa 'manuscript', which has *'nashim'*, to *'anashim'*, thereby preventing tautology.

[12] Loc cit. See also Sridei Aish 2:8, in which boys and girls are encouraged to go to Jewish youth groups where boys and girls sing together.

and a threat to the continuity of Jewish life.

I would understand the obligations of a woman distracted by the voice of a specific man in the same way.

THE WOMAN'S PLACE IS IN THE DOMESTIC REALM

'All the honour of a Princess is internal' (Ps 45:14). This verse is often understood, in Orthodox settings, to suggest that the correct realm for women is private and domestic. It should be noted that this is a matter of *hashkafah*, behavioural guidance, not halachah, legal principle, and as such it does not warrant, nor has it ever received, the sort of legal in-depth analysis that some of our other issues warrant. That said, several points seem appropriate.

We could enter into a sociological discussion of the advantages of having a mother at home to cook and clean, but that would be to stray onto territory at the edge of rabbinic competence. I will concentrate instead on an analysis of two Bible narratives which suggest that women have a vital roles to play in the realm of public prayer and in the 'House of God'.

> Then Moses and the people of Israel sang this song to the Lord, 'I will sing to the Lord, for he has triumphed gloriously; the horse and his rider has he thrown into the sea...'
> And Miriam the prophetess, the sister of Aaron, took a tambourine in her hand; and all the women went out after her with tambourines, dancing.
> And Miriam answered them, 'Sing to the Lord, for he has triumphed gloriously; the horse and his rider has he thrown into the sea.'
> (*Exodus 15*)

Moses's song, the song of the men, is longer, or at least is recorded in far greater depth than the song of Miriam and the women. Moreover, this text does not suggest that Miriam led the men in song. That said, it is evidence of a woman active in the most public way at the single greatest moment of prayerful celebration in the Bible.

An even more important account of female prayer out of the home can be found in the first chapter of the Book of Samuel. Hannah, yearning for a child, travels to the central venue for Israelite worship in that time, Shiloh:

> Hannah rose up after they had eaten in Shiloh, and after they had

drunk. And Eli the priest sat upon a seat by the gate post of the temple of the Lord...

And it came to pass, as she continued praying before the Lord, that Eli observed her mouth. Hannah spoke in her heart; only her lips moved, but her voice was not heard; therefore Eli thought that she was drunk. And Eli said to her, 'How long will you be drunk? Put away your wine from you.' And Hannah answered and said, 'No, my lord, I am a woman of a sorrowful spirit; I have drunk neither wine nor strong drink, but have poured out my soul before the Lord.'

(1 Samuel 1)

This is an important text in terms of showing the acceptability, for women, of prayer in the public ritual realm, in this case in the House of God. Its importance is magnified by the use the rabbis made of this moving narrative.

Rav Hamnuna said, 'How many important laws can be learnt from these verses about Hannah. 'And Hannah spoke in her heart': from here we learn one who prays must direct it from the heart. 'Only her lips moved': from here we learn one who prays must enunciate. 'But her voice could not be heard': from here, it is forbidden to raise one's voice in *tefilah*.

(Talmud Brachot 31a)

Hannah, a woman, is the model for the correct way to pray! One might suggest that this is almost an example of the rabbinic doctrine *ma'asei avot siman l'banim* – 'the deeds of the ancestors serve as guides for generations to come'. This doctrine is usually applied only to Abraham, Isaac and Jacob, but here a female ancestor (appearing in a prophetic work) inspires both men and women in the correct way to pray.

Nor should we consider that women wishing to attend synagogue is a modern invention. It is clear that women would attend the synagogue in Talmudic times; see, for one example, Avodah Zara 38 a-b, where we are told that a Jewish woman may leave an idol worshiper to stir a pot on the stove while she goes to the 'bathhouse or synagogue' without worrying that the food would be rendered tainted by idolatry.[13]

A full collection of sources, from Talmudic and medieval times,

---

[13] See also Sotah 22a for the story of a woman who went daily to the synagogue of Rabbi Yochanan.

detailing women's regular presence in synagogal prayer can be found in Golinkin's responsum.[14] He cites sources detailing practice in Rome, Pisa, Ashkenaz and Jerusalem. Among them is a tale of a woman who prayed Shacharit every day in the synagogue, but 'the woman would leave the synagogue before the community had concluded prayers... Behold [the (male) rabbis found], she has sinned because she left the synagogue.'[15]

In conclusion, on the issue of a woman's place being exclusively the domestic realm, I recognise several important texts which suggest that women have always played a role in public liturgy. Moreover, I am particularly motivated by the way in Hannah serves as a model for all prayer. I hold the verse 'the honour of a Princess is internal' to be irrelevant in the context of considering who may lead congregational prayer.

QUESTION 2.

Are women technically able, in the same way as men, to fulfil obligations of both male and female members of the prayer community?[16]
Most discussions of the ability of women to lead synagogue prayers begin with the following legal principle: If two people share an equal obligation to perform a particular religious act, one may, in many circumstances, meet the other's obligation by their own action. The reverse is equally true: 'One who is not obligated in a thing cannot exempt others from their obligation' (Mishnah Rosh Hashanah 3:8). For example, if a roomful of Jews wish to eat, only one person needs to make the appropriate blessing for everyone to eat. However, a non-Jew has no obligation to say a blessing before eating food, so their blessing would not allow a Jew to partake of food until the (Jewish) individual made the blessing themselves.

This notion of fulfilling the obligation to say the Amidah on behalf of another person is a key function of a leader of prayer. The leader concentrates on saying the prayers accurately, and if there are people in the congregation who don't have the same facility and

---

[14] Golinkin, *Nashim B'minyan*, pp. 6-7.
[15] Sefer Hasidim Section 465.
[16] This section, in particular, follows Golinkin's *Nashim BMinyan* closely.

familiarity with the prayers, they can respond 'amen' and be considered as if they had prayed accurately. We therefore have to ask this question – do men and women have the same obligation to pray, or is the obligation of men somehow different from or greater than that of women?

There is a notion that women are not obligated to perform what are known as 'positive time-bound obligations' (Mishnah Kiddushin 1:7). But, as we shall see, this does not apply to the obligation to say the Amidah, which is specifically and explicitly deemed an obligation NOT dependent on a specific time:

> Women **are obligated in** *tefilah*, mezuzah and Bircat Hamazon.
>
> You might have thought [that *tefilah*] is a time-bound obligation since the verse states 'I pray evening, morning and afternoon' (Psalm 55), therefore the contrary is specified.
> *(Mishnah Brachot 3:3 and Talmud Bavli Brachot 20b)*

It might be thought that the *'tefilah'* referred to here is a general obligation to articulate the praise of God, but it is clear – not least from the following section of Rambam's Mishneh Torah – that *'tefilah'* in this context refers to the Amidah:

> The obligation [of *tefilah*] used to operate like this; a person would beseech and pray every day and speak of the praiseworthiness of the Holy Blessed One, and then ask for their needs to be met... And so it was from the time of Moses until Ezra.
> However when Israel was exiled in the days of the Wicked Nebucanezer, they were mixed in with the Persians and Greeks and other peoples... and when one of them went to pray [they erred or omitted things]. When Ezra and his Bet Din saw this they got up and fixed [*taknu*] the eighteen blessings in order... so they could be fluent for **all**... and in this way they fixed all the blessings and prayers in order in the mouth of **all** Israel.
> *(Rambam, Mishneh Torah, Laws of Tefilah 1:2-6)*

Golinkin suggests that the use of 'all' here specifically includes women among those who are now compelled to fulfil their obligation to perform *'tefilah'* by the recitation of the Amidah.[17] This

---

[17] Loc. cit. p. 5.

certainly is the position of the central halachic code, the Shulchan Aruch:

> Women and slaves, although exempt from reading the Shema, **are obliged to pray the eighteen-blessing prayer**, because it is a positive mitzvah which does not relate to a specific time.
> *(OH 106:1)*

Note that this code does not use the general term of the Mishnah, namely *tefilah*, but rather the explicit term *shmoneh esrei*, which cannot be understood to mean anything other than the Amidah.

There is, however, one medieval writer who held that women might be exempt from the recitation of the Amidah. The Magen Avraham held that the Rambam only meant to oblige women in a once-daily turning towards God, 'in any form of words [*nusah*] that a person would want', and when the full Amidah was fixed as a specific prayer 'it is **possible** [emphasis mine] that the wise did not obligate them any further'.[18] The prevailing sense that women are exempt from the obligation to say the Amidah appears to be based on this 'possible'. However, this seems an errantly restrictive interpretation of the clear wording in the Shulchan Aruch and the Rambam, not only in Hilchot Tefilah, cited above, but also in his commentary on the Mishnah.

> All positive obligations that women are obligated in: eating matzah on the night of Pesach... and tefilah and reading the Megillah and lighting Shabbat candles and Kiddush... for each of them the **obligation for women is like the obligation for men.**
> *(Commentary on Mishnah Kiddushin 1:7 ed. Kafach)*

There is some discussion of whether the Amidah prayers recited in Musaf or Neilah are in the same category as the more regular prayers, but, following Golinkin,[19] I accept that the clear inclusive language of the Rambam – 'They fixed the eighteen blessings... and in this way they fixed **all** the blessings and prayers' – should be understood to include all the Amidah prayers.

In conclusion, on the issue of whether women are able to fulfil the obligation of men to say the Amidah, I hold that they are.

---

18 To OH 106:1.
19 Loc. cit. p. 10-11

In the course of this discussion we have raised a potential problem around the Shema. Recitation of the Shema is a positive time-bound obligation, a classification derived from the verse 'when you lie down and when you rise up' (Deut 6), and as the Mishnah teaches, 'Women, slaves and minors are exempt from the recitation of the Shema and from [wearing] tefillin' (Mishnah Brachot 3:3).

But this does not impact on our current discussion. The leader of prayer does not fulfil the obligation of a member of the community by reciting the Shema on their behalf. This is an obligation which, unlike saying the Amidah, cannot be fulfilled by another person, no matter their sex. Indeed, this is also true for the other exemption referred to in the Mishnah above. A leader of prayer cannot exempt a member of the community by their wearing of tefillin. If you are, as a male, obligated to wear tefillin, you must fulfil this obligation yourself, and no prayer leader, male or female, can exempt you from it by performing the obligation on your behalf.

The key question is not whether women are obligated to perform each and every mitzvah, but whether there are mitzvot – obligations – that a leader of prayer fulfils on behalf of a community that women are either not obligated to perform, or for which they have a partial or lesser obligation than men. I hold there are no such obligations. [20]

QUESTION 3.

Who can and should lead a prayer community consisting of both men and women?

As noted, the role of a leader in prayer extends beyond the technical responsibility of saying the Amidah on behalf of those who have failed to say it accurately themselves. As rabbinic Jews we hold that something special happens when a prayer community is constituted. God's presence can invoked in a community in ways an individual cannot achieve alone. This is reflected in the classification of several parts of the liturgy as *devarim shebikedushah* – 'words of [special] holiness' – which can only be said in a formally constituted community.

---

[20] I will return to the issue of *pores et shema* shortly.

Don't divide the Shema [*pores et shema*],[21] lead the prayers [*ovrin lifnei hatevah*][22] and don't do the priestly blessing and don't read from the Torah... and don't do the blessing for mourners or... the blessing for a groom... with less than ten. *(Mishnah Megillah 4:3)*

By the year 1000, the list of things that are only said in the presence of ten had developed to include the Kedushah and the various *kaddish* prayers (Mishneh Torah Hil. Tefilah 8:4), and by the sixteenth century the Barachu had joined the list (SA OH 55.1 quoted below).

SHOULD WOMEN BE COUNTED AMONG THE 'TEN'?

Before asking whether a woman can lead a constituted prayer community, or minyan, we need to investigate whether a woman can be counted among the 'ten'. While the mishnah cited above does specify the number that is required for a minyan, it is quiet on what, if any, required characteristics a member of the minyan should have. Should they, in particular, be men, or do women also count? The Talmud is also silent on the issue, being preoccupied instead with a struggle to explain the reason for the number ten. The explanation that is offered is a double *gezerah shavah*[23] – a tradition that comparing repeated words which appear in scripture in different contexts can have meaning.

Rav Hiya taught, we can learn this from the repeated mention of the word '**amongst**', the Bible states 'and I [God] will be made holy **amongst** the children of [*bnei*] Israel' (Lev 22) and elsewhere 'separate yourselves from **amongst** that **congregation**' (Numbers 16). And then from the repeated mention of the word '**congregation**', [firstly in the verse just mentioned and then] here 'How long will I [God] bear with this wicked **congregation**' (Numbers 14). Just as

---

[21] For Rashi this is a technical term for something not usually seen in contemporary prayer services. 'If a number of people come to the synagogue after the community have read the Shema, one of them stands up and says the Kaddish, Barachu and first blessing before the recitation of the *Shema* [thereby allowing latecomers to hear these parts of the service they might otherwise have missed]'; ad loc. Rambam considers pores et Shema to be 'One makes the blessings of the Shema and everyone who hears them answers amen' (MT Hil Tefilah 8:5).

[22] See Rashi, serve as *shaliach tzibur* – leader of the community.

[23] Though in Mishnah Sanhedrin 1.6 the same figure is derived from a straight application of the word 'congregation' in Numbers 14. See also Gen 42:5 and Psalm 82:1 for other congregationally minded verses.

this last verse refers to ten, so too the other ones. *(Megillah 23b)*

A verse that does indeed seem to discuss God's vesting of the Divine presence in some kind of community is connected first to a verse discussing Moses' reaction to the rebellion of Korach, and through this verse to one discussing God's reaction to the failures of the generation who left Egypt. Since God's disappointment is occasioned by the failure of the ten spies, so this verse is considered to define a congregation as ten.[24] This is tenuous, even by rabbinic standards. Golinkin argues that this tenuousness should incline us away from reading too much into the acceptance or exclusion of women from this 'ten'.[25]

Elsewhere (Sanhedrin 74b) we find exactly the same series of connections used in a discussion of whether the quorum of ten in front of whom misdeeds are considered committed *b'pharhesia* – in public – can include any people, or only Jews. The Rav Hiya passage from Megillah is used to prove that Jews only are meant. The discussion then checks whether Esther is considered to have sinned in public (by allowing herself to be married to a non-Jew – Ahashueros), only to conclude that she is exempt from sinning *b'pharhesia* because she was a passive agent in the sin: she was married, she didn't undertake any positive action. In other words, Esther – a woman – is, in theory, held to be capable of sinning *b'pharhesia*. Since she, as woman, is capable of shaming God in public by any misdeed, one might think she should be capable of proclaiming the holiness of God in public through any merit.

Also among those early sources silent on the need to count only men, we find the following extract from Rambam. There is more detail here than in the Mishnah, but again, no reference to a specific requirement of maleness.

> How do you do public prayer [*tefilah b'tzibur*]? One prays in a strong voice and everyone listens, and don't do it with less than ten free adults [*gedolim u'venei horin*], and the prayer leader is one of them. *(Mishneh Torah Hil. Tefilah 8:4)*[26]

---

24 As opposed to a congregation of feckless spies lacking in faith!
25 Golinkin, *Nashim B'Minyan*, p. 69.
26 See also Tur OH 55.1, which also leaves undefined any required gender for the 'ten'.

How are we to approach this silence as to any gender requirement? We are surely safe in assuming that, in ancient times, it was simply taken as given that women were not full members of the prayer community, and therefore there was no need to exclude them by name. But note that this is an assumption made NOT on the basis of any halachic norm or derived teaching (*midrash*), but rather as a reflection of prevailing sociological conditions at the time. Women in ancient and medieval times were simply not considered to have a role in 'proper' society and therefore frequently become invisible, not only in rabbinic texts, but in so many other ways both inside and beyond worlds of religious ritual.

It is in the context of this prevailing reality, I argue, that we should consider Joseph Caro's Shulchan Aruch, written in the sixteenth century. Here, for the first time, we see a shift in the language used to define the sort of person who can 'count'.

> Don't say the Kaddish with less than ten free adult **males** [*zecharim benei horin gedolim*] who have two hairs, and this is the law for the Kedushah and the Barachu, we don't say them with less than ten. (*Orach Haim 55:1*)

This is the text-based origin of the notion of not counting women in 'ten'. The Mishnah, Talmud and Rambam are silent. The androcentrism appears without explanation in the Shulchan Aruch. None of the classic commentators on this text explains the inclusion of this andocentric language, and Caro himself does not mention this new restriction in his commentary on the Tur. Again I hold that this represents not an explicit halachic stand, but merely the articulation of a fifteenth/sixteenth-century social reality in which women had no role in official communal life.

The question then becomes, how should we count 'ten' today? It makes a great deal of sense not to count minors, it is obvious that we should only count Jews, but is it a true reflection of the times in which we live only to count men? I argue no. In the world in which we live, a world where women play an equal role in all parts of communal life, from the Prime Minister down, it is most odd to consider that the precise legal quorum of 'ten' should preserve a social reality long since abandoned in other parts of our life. There can be no doubt that Judaism has always considered both 'male and female' to be created in the 'image of God' (Genesis 1). The time has come, indeed it came many years ago, to acknowledge this in terms of who counts, in our attempts to stand before God.

Of course, a more traditional perspective would scoff at the notion of using prevailing social norms to reinterpret a text once the text specifies a particular gender, and of course making the shift to count both men and women represents a major change in how we count 'ten'. Nonetheless, I believe it would be wrong to consider that women should not count when the ground for this claim is itself a societal norm and not a derived halachic stance. I do not make this claim for all Jewish communities. There clearly are Jewish communities in which women do not play any role in public life, and for these communities it is understandable that women should not count towards the 'ten'.

But St Albans Masorti Synagogue is not such a community. Rather, we are a community that values the public contributions of its women members in all parts of synagogal life. We recognise women as adult independent agents – *gedolot uvanot horot* – and for us to exclude women from the 'ten' on the basis of the unexplained mention in the Shulchan Aruch, rather than considering the Shulchan Aruch, Rambam and Talmud as presenting only a reflection of a long-since disappeared societal norm, is inappropriate.

We have therefore created the possibility of considering women as members of the prayer community. We now turn to consider who may lead such a community.

WHO MAY LEAD?

The major Talmudic discussion of how a leader is chosen from the members of the community is in Tractate Taanit, 16a. That discussion is specific to who should serve as leader at a time of great need, but, as we shall see, the teaching is accepted as normative practice.

> And who is considered appropriate [*regil*] to lead prayers [on a fast day]? Rabbi Yehudah said, 'one who is burdened [with a large family] and has no [means to support them], he works in the field and his home is empty. [Moreover] their youth is unblemished, they are

meek and they are wanted by the people, they are pleasant and their voice is sweet[27] and is expert at reading the Torah and other biblical works and is proficient in various fields of rabbinic learning and is expert in every one of the blessings.'
(Taanit 16a)

By the time of the Shulchan Aruch these requirements have been codified to apply to all prayer services:

The leader of the prayer community must be appropriate [*hagun*]. What is appropriate? They should be free from sin and never to have been the subject of gossip [*motzi shem ra*], not even in their childhood. They should be humble and desired by their community. They must look nice and have a pleasant voice and they must regularly read from the Torah, Prophets and Writings.
(OH 53:5)

To this list, the Mishnah Brurah adds:

Their clothes should be long, so you shouldn't be able to see their legs,[28] and they should be first into the synagogue and last out, nor should they be foolish or frivolous, rather they should be able to speak of the needs of the community.

These texts do more than set a high bar – they define the qualities needed to be an appropriate leader of prayers beyond any human reach. The insistence that a leader of prayer should be 'free from sin' is already enough to rule out the entire human race!

There is perhaps instruction to be gained from the Talmudic requirement that a prayer leader be 'one who is burdened [with a large family] and has no [means to support them]'. This is a powerful image; it speaks to the urgency and vital importance of congregational prayer. Leading a community is not about singing and it is not about sounding tuneful. It is about placing ourselves before God, taking our successes and failures, strengths and weaknesses and beseeching the Divine for mercy on behalf of the community.

---

[27] It is interesting to note the Hebrew term used here – *arev*, ayin-resh-vet. This is the same word used as proof that a woman's voice is *ervah*, ayin-resh-vav-heh (Song of Songs 2:14 and Brachot 24a; see discussion above). The man should be *arev*; the woman is, in traditional circles, banned from leading since she is *ervah*.

[28] This is based on Talmud Megillah 24b. See my responsum on Aliyot for Women at http://e-sams.org/standards_of_practice.htm.

But despite the clear wisdom and beauty in the requirement, it's gone by the time of the Shulchan Aruch. Indeed, the whole demand for perfection, clear in the Talmud and in the opening definition of what makes an appropriate leader of prayer in the Shulchan Aruch, is softened greatly by the very next comment: 'And if you can't find one who has all these qualities, choose the best of the community in matters of wisdom and good deeds' (OH 53:5).

The *shaliach tzibbur* must be desired by their community. And if, teaches the Shulchan Aruch, you can't find someone truly appropriate and entirely free of any failing, then you choose as best as you can.

The halachic system, with its myriad of caveats and nuances, is not designed for a perfect world, full of sinless, error-free humans. It is a very real and very realistic attempt to challenge us to do the right thing. Of course you cannot have a perfect leader of prayer. Rather, and this is critical, the key characteristic of the imperfect leader who ends up serving their community is that they are chosen by the community. We are the ones who decide whether a particular candidate to lead us in prayer is appropriate [*hagun*] or not good enough.

There are different ways to respond to this responsibility. One the one hand we can ratchet up the standards, thinning down the number of prospective candidates, excluding one for their failure to observe a certain rule of Shabbat observance, excluding another for their inability to distinguish between a *shva na* and a *shva nach*. Or alternatively we can lower the bar, welcoming in new prospective leaders of the community, tolerating occasional mispronunciation or personal failing in the hope that the honour of representing a community will inspire them and us to increase our learning and refine our behaviour. Different communities, at different times, will approach this decision in different ways.

So, how is this decision to be applied at St Albans Masorti Synagogue today? Certainly we wish to look up to our prayer leaders. Indeed, this is something that many members stressed in the consultations that preceded the writing of this paper. But we also see ourselves as an inclusive congregation, given to sharing honours broadly and encouraging those who wish to improve their skills to do so. We are, as a community, loath to label our members 'not good enough'. In the context of this broader approach, the lack of women prayer leaders felt awkward. Much as we might have wished to hide from the reality of what we were doing, we were claiming that women were not capable of being *hagun* – appropriate. More precisely, we made the claim that the inappropriateness of women was utterly connected to their gender. In other words, while we welcomed any male, provided they could recite the Hebrew, to lead the services, we permitted no woman, regardless of her level of knowledge, piety or commitment.

I know on a certain level it is possible to make the case that just because a particular community won't allow women to lead prayers doesn't necessarily mean that community thinks any less of its women. I know it is possible to think that women are perfectly good enough in all sorts of ways, other than leading services, without intending to demean 50 percent of the Jewish people. I know it is possible to feel that the unique nature of woman should keep her from leading a community in prayer before God, but not stop her in other enormously important ways from serving the Holy Blessed One. I know these things to be possible, but I don't accept them, either for myself, or the St Albans Masorti community.

Accordingly I conclude, on the question of a person's appropriateness to serve as prayer leader, that consideration of gender should not trump all other factors. Women and men are equally able to be considered *hagun* – appropriate – by the community.

AN ADDENDUM ON THE ANDROCENTRIC NATURE OF RABBINICS AND RABBINIC LANGUAGE

The approach of rabbis of antiquity towards women is complex. This passage from the early twentieth-century Rabbi J. H. Hertz (from his commentary to the Pentateuch) is a very good example of a traditional rabbinic voice:

> The Jewish sages recognized the wonderful spiritual influence [of the Jewish wife], and nothing could surpass the delicacy with which respect for her is inculcated. [As the Talmud states,] 'Love your wife as yourself and honour her more than yourself. Be care-

ful not to cause a woman to weep, for God counts her tears. Israel was redeemed from Egypt on account of the virtue of its women. He who weds a good woman, it is as if he had fulfilled all the precepts of the Torah.' *(J.H Hertz, Pentateuch)*

To a contemporary feminist there is something troubling about the very language used here, but, nonetheless, the intent is clear. Women are highly valued. More practically, the rabbis created many brave and creative legal structures to protect and strengthen the lot of women in ancient times, principally the institution of the *ketubah* to protect women with no means of economic self-sufficiency from being discarded by their husbands.[29]

There are also occasional glimpses, in the rabbinic canon, of what might be considered a gendered awareness of the relationship between men and women. In a discussion of what happens to inheritances a woman comes into once married, there is a consensus that these devolve to her husband, but there is disagreement about what happens to inheritances that an engaged woman comes into.

Bet Shammai says she can sell it and Bet Hillel says she can't...
Rabbi Yehuda said, the Rabbis said before Rabban Gamliel, 'Since [the husband] has acquired the woman, shouldn't he also acquire the property?'
[Rabban Gamliel] said to them, 'We are embarrassed [that a married woman who comes into an inheritance has no control of it],[30] and you [want us stretch such an embarrassment further]?!'[31]
(Mishnah Ketubot 8:1)

But even in a relatively aware text such as this, the woman is not considered an agent in her own right, deciding her own destiny; she is reliant on the man. Nowhere is this clearer than in the opening words in the rabbinic treatment of marriage:

'A women is acquired [*niknet*] in three ways... through money, a writ and sexual intercourse' *(Mishnah Kiddushin 1:1)*. The woman is passive. She is acquired, she is married; she does not acquire, she does not marry. The woman, in this and many other texts, is objectified. She is not the subject of her own marriage, just as women

---

[29] See generally Judith Hauptman, *Rereading the Rabbis: A Woman's Voice* (Westview Press, 1998), and particularly Section 3, pp. 60-74.
[30] Lit - regarding the new.
[31] Lit - impose on us the old.

were not, in ancient times, generally considered to be the subjects of their own lives.

While I would have been delighted to see a more 'enlightened' approach to these issues in texts over 1,500 years old, I am not distressed to find a somewhat old-fashioned and male-focussed or androcentric approach in texts written in an androcentric time and place. It would be unreasonable to expect anything else. More worrying, however, are moments of misogyny clearly visible in ancient texts. The rabbis lived in a homo-social world. In general they had no interaction with women, either socially or in their study. On occasion, it must be admitted, this lack of female socialisation is apparent to the point of creating offence.

A woman is as a pitcher full of excrement and her mouth is full of blood. (*Shabbat 152a*)

There is much to say about this statement. One can offer apologetics and explain context, but texts like this (and there are others) should not be saved. They should not be considered to reflect God's wish for humanity, the touchstone of all we consider holy. Tragically one can detect an impact, on contemporary and traditional forms of observance, of these moments of misogyny. Women tend not to be treated as pitchers of excrement, but, as a rabbi, I meet many women who complain they have been made to feel second-class Jews. It is surely impossible for anyone involved in traditional Jewish communities not to be struck by the words of Cynthia Ozick,[32] author and critic:

In the world at large I call myself, and am called, a Jew. But when, on the Sabbath, I sit among women in my traditional shul and the rabbi speaks the word 'Jew', I can be sure that he is not referring to me. For him, 'Jew' means 'male Jew'.

When the rabbi speaks of women, he uses the expression ... 'Jewish daughter'. He means it tenderly.

'Jew' speaks for itself. 'Jewish daughter' does not. A Jewish daughter is someone whose identity is linked to, and defined by, another's role.... 'Jew' signifies adult responsibility. 'Daughter' signifies im-

---

[32] In 'Notes Toward Finding the Right Question', 1979, originally published in *Forum*. Reprinted in Susannah Heschel (ed.), *On Being a Jewish Feminist: A Reader* (Schocken, New York, 1983), pp. 120-152, at p. 125.

maturity and a dependent and subordinate connection.

When my rabbi says, 'A Jew is called to the Torah', he never means me or any other living Jewish woman.

My own synagogue is the only place in the world where I, a middle-aged adult, am defined exclusively by my being the female child of my parents.

My own synagogue is the only place in the world where I am not named Jew.

Even when pre-modern rabbis strive to do well by women, there is something, quite literally, patronising in the way men put themselves forward as patrons – guardians and protectors – while simultaneously rejecting the notion that women could or should speak for themselves. We have, as Jews, existed for millennia with only half our voices being heard and recorded and we, now, need to open up our tradition to the unique contributions, challenges and inspiration that will come by welcoming women to make their contributions to Jewish life not only in the home, but also before the ark, in public, in synagogue.

This will not be an easy journey for many. Some men, and some women also, will find these new voices, contributions and challenges to be uncomfortable. But comfort is not the test of our religious quest to walk in God's ways. Rather we must always strive to do better, to recognise, ever more deeply, the divine image encoded in all humanity. It is in this context that I decide as follows.

CONCLUSION

1) There is nothing about women that distracts other worshippers or otherwise makes it impossible for them to 'conduct' prayers for a mixed, male and female, community.

2) There are no obligations a male leader of prayer can fulfil on behalf of the community that a woman cannot.

3) Women, at St Albans Masorti Synagogue, should be counted in the 'ten' that make up a minyan, and gender should not trump all other considerations when considering who should lead the community in prayer.

CHAPTER 9

Louis' Shul – My Shul

There are many for whom New London Synagogue will always be 'Louis' Shul,' actually I might even be among them. Rabbi Louis Jacobs CBE, voted 'Britain's Greatest Jew' in a poll held by the Jewish Chronicle to celebrate 350 years of British Jewry, was more than the founder Rabbi of New London Synagogue. He was its raison d'être. *I'm not going to retell the tale of the 'Jacobs Affair' here, but I am going to include the eulogy I gave at Rabbi Jacob's shiva and also the Quest Rabbi Louis Jacobs' Memorial Lecture I gave on the occasion of the 50th anniversary celebration of the foundation of New London Synagogue.*

A Eulogy for
Rabbi Jacobs z"tl
{2006}

The thirteen-year-old version of me would find my being a
rabbi strange. The forty-something version of me still finds
it strange that I am the rabbi of the very synagogue
I attended as a child. I don't know if I will ever grow out of
the strangeness of occupying a pulpit so comprehensively
dominated by the greatest scholar in Anglo-Jewish history.
For a while, especially as I was considering whether to
apply for the position at New London Synagogue, that
strangeness was terrifying. More recently it's become a
source of inspiration and tremendous pride. I love the
founding narrative of New London Synagogue – and the
celebration of our 50th Year was very special. As the shul
continues to grow and change I find myself one of a
declining number of members with direct memories of the
early glory days of New London, memories of Rabbi Jacobs
at his very best, and I will not let the memories of our
glorious inheritance fade.

This is the eulogy I delivered at the shiva held in
the New London Synagogue Hall in the days following
Rabbi Jacobs' death.

I was scheduled to give, this very evening, a lecture on the writings
of Rabbi Jacobs, and the notion that I instead find myself speaking at this shiva is an honour I far rather would have forgone.

Rabbi Dr Louis Jacobs was, and will always remain, my vision
of a rabbi. Learned, kind, and completely committed to the life of
Torah that inspires me and all my colleagues, in denominations and
countries across the world and through time.

As a small child I remember charging down the stairs at the end
of the children's services at New London to hear Louis' sermon.

Of course my friends and I weren't allowed to charge into the
sanctuary during the sermon, but we could slip unnoticed through

the doors at the back of the shul and crouch down, hidden, behind the thick green velvet curtains that stopped any of the adults from seeing us.

We would laugh at jokes we didn't fully understand and then, on the way home from shul, my father would tell me how wonderful the sermon had been, and I would smile, because I knew everything was well with the world.

As I grew up I began to understand for myself how wonderful the sermons always were and I would be in awe of the seeming effortless erudition, as Rabbi Jacobs took all of us on a journey through sources ancient and modern, always bringing us gently down to land at the end of his drosh. He was a master of that most difficult of sermonic arts – Rabbi Jacobs knew how to end a sermon perfectly.

As a bar mitzvah I stood, in this very synagogue, and I remember perfectly the words from my Haftarah that he singled out to share as a blessing. *Harchivi makom ohalech* – make wide the place of your tent, draw out the guide-ropes, he told me. It's the greatest *brachah* he could have given me, and it has stayed with me to this day.

There are others here who know, better than I, of Rabbi Jacobs' extraordinary gifts as a congregational rabbi. I want instead to speak as a religious seeker with a passion for the critical scholarship that Rabbi Jacobs made his own. I have spent seven years living and learning in Israel and America. Among my many teachers were theologians, Talmudists, legal scholars, teachers of *Chassidut* and mysticism, pedagogues. And I would always take enormous pleasure from the centrality of Rabbi Jacobs' teachings for all of them. Again and again, all these master teachers would refer, or assign, or discuss Rabbi Jacobs, my teacher, our teacher.

I don't think anything has been written on the nature of belief in the history of Jewish thought that matches *Principles of the Jewish Faith*. But I might be wrong.

It is possible, though far from clear, to argue that there are greater works of contemporary Jewish theology than *We Have Reason to Believe* or *A Jewish Theology*. But for me, both these books are utterly central in allowing me to explain my own relationship with God, revelation, and obligation.

It is possible there are more important works on the evolution of Halachah than *Tree of Life*, or more astounding collections of source material than are contained in *Theology in the Responsa*. For myself, I consider these the very best writings in the field of Jewish law.

One might suggest there are more important works on Hasidism than *Hasidic Prayer* or *Hasidic Thought*. But no-one can deny that these are masterful works.

Similarly, some would undoubtedly cite works on Talmud that surpass *Structure and Form in the Babylonian Talmud* and *Studies in Talmudic Logic and Methodology*. But these are still standard works, decades after their original publication.

Finally, you could say there are better guides to Jewish life than *The Book of Jewish Practice, The Book of Jewish Belief,* or *What does Judaism Say About...?*, but these are still the books I recommend to those wanting to know more about our faith and tradition.

One might quibble with any one of these claims, but there is one claim that is unarguable. There is no-one, no-one in the history of contemporary Jewish scholarship, who can match the quality of Rabbi Jacobs' extraordinary output across the utterly vast range of Jewish thought and practice over which he published.

We are all of us, surely, aware of Rabbi Jacobs' standing in Anglo-Jewry, but in truth he was world class. There is simply no-one to match him. There never has been, there probably never will be.

But the books alone are only part of it. There are also beautiful translations: *Tamar Devorah, Sur M'Ra,* the *Tract on Ecstasy,* the wonderfully well-edited Schocken Book of Jewish Mystical Testimonies, all of which sit on my shelves, and, at various points on my own journey, permitted me glimpses into a world of Jewish thought that language and esoteric technicalities were preventing me from gaining.

And the occasional articles on the Mussar Movement, Jewish ethics, liturgy, and even into the most recent of times, homiletics. The range is dizzying.

Not only was Rabbi Jacobs a walking encyclopaedia, he also wrote, single-handed, a one-volume Jewish encyclopaedia, published by the Oxford University Press.

These works are giant achievements. They appear again and again and again in bibliographies, footnotes, and acknowledgments of the contemporary academy. They have had an enormous influence on today's scholars and will continue to influence generations to come. The fact that this incredible achievement was fitted in around Rabbi Jacob's commitments as a very full-time congregational rabbi and loving husband and father is beyond inspiring. It is, certainly for this newly ordained rabbi, awesome – *nora* in the true sense of the word: a little terrifying.

But the real power of Rabbi Jacob's work is more than their breadth and quality. It is a certain tone, a quality of discourse, that makes him so beloved.

Academics can be dangerous. A spiritual person reads the work of the academy with a certain trepidation. All one's love and passion for a subject can be atomised and pulverised into nothingness by the withering critique of an academician. But that was never Rabbi Jacobs' way.

In books like *Hasidic Prayer* there is something about the gentleness of the tone that allows the spiritual seeker to come in. While Rabbi Jacobs was prepared to make explicit uncomfortable truths about Hasidic practice, or even the nature of revelation, reading the tradition through the eyes of Rabbi Jacobs it always remains beautiful, powerful, and warm. I'm not sure Rabbi Jacobs would ever have considered himself a mystic, but there is something about the way he brought scholarship to writing about the secrets and passions of the Jewish soul that leaves spiritual seekers undeflected by the scholarship, but rather feeling stronger in their beliefs, now grounded more accurately in historical reality.

Solomon Schechter, the first president of the Jewish Theological Seminary and an inspiration to all who try to fuse the academic and the spiritual quest, wrote about the midrash[1] in which Avraham Avinu, our patriarch Abraham, smashes the wares of his father, the seller of idols. It must have been tempting for Abraham, wrote Schechter, to continue the life of dishonesty of an idol salesman. He

---

[1] BR 38:13

could have sat quietly and waited until he entered into his due inheritance, the respectable family business.

But this dishonesty was not the way of our patriarch. Abraham felt the need to smash the idols of the house of his father, because they represented a lie. And dishonesty can never be squared with a true religious quest.

We might all look to religion for comfort, but truth, claimed Schechter, truth is more important. Abraham's great moment of spiritual bravery was the smashing of the idols of dishonesty, pledging himself to truth and the service of the one true God. *Adonai elochechim emet*. Even though telling these truths provoked discomfort. Even though Abraham himself had to henceforth strike out alone, without the comforts of the cosy religious life that he was born into.

Rabbi Jacobs was a tremendous disciple of Avraham Avinu.

When he saw deceit practiced in the name of religion he spoke out.

When there were uncomfortable truths that many a religious leader feared to utter, he stepped forward boldly, coolly, and always with tremendous scholarship.

Judaism, for Rabbi Jacobs, could never be dishonest.

Rabbi Jacobs was a great iconoclast in the most holy sense of the term.

This, I think, explains the gentle quality of his writing. He never broke idols for the sake of it, or to show how smart he was, but rather in pursuit of the deep religious quest for truth, a quest that is ultimately holy, even if idols need to be broken on the journey.

And, as was true for Avraham, Rabbi Jacob's iconoclasm came at a cost in this world. It provoked discomfort. It cost him his due inheritance – and one can only speculate how lonely the journey was for Rabbi Jacobs these past forty years.

But the rewards for the shattering of idols are not necessarily to be appreciated in this world. They are the rewards of the world to come: rewards Rabbi Jacobs is now freed to enjoy.

And what of the rest of us?

We are of course left with the books, but the spirit of Rabbi

Jacobs is not to be left on the bookshelf. It is to be lived, it is to be taken forward.

This space, this sacred place of prayer and study, must not be allowed to wither.

We have this week lost our *Moreh Derekh*, the one who led this community for over forty years, but we have not been left without signposts to illuminate the way ahead.

I want to conclude with an extract from one of Rabbi Jacobs' books. It seems appropriate. In *A Tree of Life*, Rabbi Jacobs wishes to suggest that a deep-rooted system of values, a spirit, informs the Halachah. This brief extract encapsulates many of the great virtues of Rabbi Jacobs' scholarship: a source that makes his point perfectly, the ability to prick the balloon of any suggestion of hyperbole, and always, underneath, the love of Torah and pursuit of truth.

The correct Jewish response to suffering seems to be expressed in the rule that when a mourner rends his garment in grief at the death of a near relative, he should do so while standing, not while sitting. As Dr Hertz puts it, 'According to ancient Jewish custom, the ceremony of rending our garments when our nearest and dearest on earth is lying dead before us, is to be performed standing up. This teaches, meet all sorrow standing upright. The future may be dark veiled through the eyes of mortals... but hard as life's terms may be life never dictates unrighteousness, unholiness, dishonour'. If this interpretation is considered too homiletical, the rule about standing upright might have been intended to denote a rising to the tragic occasion.

'A rising to the tragic occasion.'

Rabbi Jacobs never bowed, never folded in the face of idols. And neither can we, his friends, his disciples.

My charge is Rabbi Jacobs' charge – to rise to the tragic occasion. It is a charge I pledge myself to, and one I commend to us all.

Rabbi Dr Louis Jacobs – *Moreinu HaRav HaGaon Yehudah lev ben Tzvi.*

Zichrono l'vrachah.

Looking Back and Forward – The Louis Jacobs' Memorial Lecture

{2014}

I always look forward to our annual Memorial Lecture, organised by the Synagogue's Quest Committee. Some truly world class scholars have graced the pulpit and usually it's an easy evening for me to get some inspiration. On the occasion of the 50th year of New London Synagogue I wanted to be in charge of our founding narrative and its hero, our most precious inheritance, as a community, and I felt I wanted to be in charge of how this inheritance should shape us as a community moving forwards. I remember one Quest committee member querying if I were really the best booking; after all members could come and hear me any old week – thanks. Fortunately we had a terrific turn out and the evening was a centrepiece of the Synagogue's 50th year celebrations.

The story is told of a man who begins to commute on a railway carriage where every other occupant has long been commuting in just the same way. A woman calls out, 'seventeen.' Everyone laughs. A man says, 'thirty-two' and again everyone laughs. Eventually the man asks one of his fellow travellers what's going on. The fellow explains that since the jokes the commuters would tell were so well known they were given numbers, and instead of having to tell a whole story they could now simply say the number and laughter would result. The next day the man was ready. He opened with 'four,' nothing. 'Eighteen,' nothing. 'Twenty, twenty-one, twenty-two,' he's getting desperate. Still nothing. Eventually, close to despair he asks what is going wrong. 'The problem is,' the fellow traveller remarks, 'the way you tell them.'

I've heard the story of Rabbi Louis Jacobs many times, I've lived it. Many of us here today have also. I want to try it a little differently from the way I've ever heard it told before. Let me start this way.

I don't think Rabbi Louis Jacobs, of blessed memory – one of the greatest Jewish theologians of modern times - was really a theologian. His intellectual curiosity came from elsewhere, and his theology was driven by something other than theologising.

Let's go back 70 years to 1944, thirteen years before the publication of *We Have Reason to Believe*, twenty years before foundation of New London Synagogue. Louis was recently married and comes into contact with what is known as Wissenschaft des Judentums – the critical, academic study of Judaism – for the first time. There are two currents in Manchester Judaism at the time – one ultra-orthodox, typified by Rav Dubov, of the Manchester Yeshiva, and another more academically literate, though entirely observant, orthodoxy represented by Dr Alexander Altmann (notice, Dr, not Rabbi). We have the record of Louis' first meeting with Dr Altman preserved in his diary.

[Altmann] mentioned that certain writers in America write and advise a "Return to Ghetto Life" - they advocate isolation as far as humanly possible. [Altmann] said that a man like the Manchester Rosh Yeshiva agreed with this view and he admires him for it. He however thinks that for a man with a liberal education this attitude towards life is a sheer impossibility. He asked me to read a paper on *Toldot Halakha* by C. Chernovitz (sic).[1]

Toldot Halakha demonstrates – as its name suggests – how Jewish law passes down through the generations; how it changes over time. Louis goes home from this meeting, and shares the following in his diary.

I thought a lot about the theory of the development of halakha and have found one or two proofs. One in tosefot at the beginning of perek sheni "of [*kiddahin*]" about *ketana bizman hazeh* and also [in the] Rama [Rabbi Moses Isserles] about *daluka b'shabbat*.

---

[1] This extract is taken from Elliot Cosgrove's unpublished PhD Dissertation on Rabbi Jacobs, *Teyku: The Insoluble Contradistinctions in the Life and Thoughts of Louis Jacobs* (2008). Notice how Jacobs mis-spells the name of the author in his first encounter with Professor Tchernovitz – this is all very new.

Louis' first example is a reference to an ancient, no longer continued practice, of marrying minors – Jewish wedding rituals have
changed. His second is a reference to the notion that Ashkenazi
Jews are to be allowed not to place their Chanukiyah in the win-
dow if it's dangerous to so do. If the examples are technical, you can
nonetheless feel an excitement in the diary entries from the time.
Louis' world-view, his Jew-view is shifting, inspired by the developments of critical thought – Wissenschaft.

The notion that Judaism changes as it evolves to new understand-
ings and new challenges, as opposed to the notion that Judaism has
been unchanging and ever perfectly formed, is the key difference
between two schools of Jewish life and thought; one closed to the
enquires of science, the other not. And, for Louis, understanding,
documenting, embodying and teaching this evolutionary nature of
authentic Jewish practice became, more than his theological mus-
ing, the central driving force of his work. From this perspective of
Louis' intellectual engagement his most important work is probably *Tree of Life* with its self-explanatory sub-heading 'Diversity,
Flexibility and Creativity in Jewish Law.'

The chapter headings make clear the approach of the book;

The Influence of Philosophy on Halakhah
The Influence of Mysticism and Kabbalah on Halakhah
Responses to the Gentile World Halakhic Responses to Social
Changes: General Principles
Halakhic Responses to Social Changes: Further Examples

This is Louis doing Wissenschaft des Judentums, the critical
study of Judaism,

This is Louis doing history.

History, of course, is a never-ending education into the notion
that 'things change', adapt and shift. This is what history does to
one. It takes neat convenient labels and anatomises them. It messes
up neat lines and complicates simple stories.

You can't be a fundamentalist and a historian. Louis, the non-fun-
damentalist, chose history and history inured, yet further, Louis
from fundamentalism.

And all of this history is working against a backdrop of an extraordinary range of personal characteristics. Louis was insatiably curious. He had a voracious entirely un-bordered fascination with everything. He had courage, the courage to speak truths, even if they made some uncomfortable. And he believed in carrying things through to their inevitable conclusions. Where some felt nervous applying the rigour of critical academic study to theology, Louis felt he had to face these challenges. There is a touch of arrogance too, a belief that he could make a contribution, and a refusal to back down before the bullying of others.

So Louis couldn't, wouldn't and didn't do the thing so many orthodox scholars of historical development in Judaism do; namely stop being historically curious when it comes to the question of the Torah itself. When Louis was at Jews College, he reports in *Beyond Reasonable Doubt*, his teachers used critical methodology, but only for history and grammar, Talmud and codes. Never for Torah itself.

But Louis was led inexorably towards not only the classic problems of theology- choseness, evil, the end of time – but also the radioactive question of who wrote the Torah.

But even when writing theology, Louis was really writing as a historian. You can see this most clearly in his greatest theological work – *Principles of the Jewish Faith* (1964). It's a work of history, it tells how different eras, different environments, different external influences lead to different theologies.

I want to share an extract from Louis' last major work, *Beyond Reasonable Doubt* (published two years before death in 2004). It comes from a chapter on the purpose of the creation of the world and the human. Louis surveys both Talmuds, the great legal codes, mussar, and mystical literature on the subject with usual brilliance, and concludes;

> I have tried to show that Judaism is not monolithic and that when Jewish thinkers speak of normative Judaism they tend to affix the label to those aspects of the tradition to which they are personally attracted. There is liberation in the thought that there is no alternative for a religious Jew, in his quest for the transcendent, than to try, guided by the tradition, to think some things through for himself.

Louis becomes aware not just of differences over time and space, but also between people. He has become unable to mono-ise (it's a word I'm inventing, please excuse me) - to mono-ise is to demand that all people should be the same. Louis was deeply allergic to mono-isation. He chose as a title for his personal theological reflection *A Jewish Theology* –not 'The Jewish Theology.'

I want to suggest something that perhaps drove this allergy to mono-isation, something beyond an understanding of historical development and unbounded curiosity. It's something to do with the most remarkable aspect of Louis' academic achievement. All the books were written, all the lectures were given, and all the academic plaudits were earned while Louis served as a congregational Rabbi – a congregational Rabbi of this very congregation.

Let me digress for a few moments. I read recently of a survey that said that 81% of mothers felt that their being a mother had impacted on their professional success. And the thought that struck me was this - what on earth were the other 19% possibly thinking?! Let me assume they hadn't all just checked their children into 24 hour daycare. How could a person, juggling professional and personal responsibilities not feel the limitations of this impossible balancing act?

I came to this conclusion. There is something about being a parent that helps, professionally. There is something about being a parent which helps you realise you are not going to be able to control the life of others by imperious dictats. There is something about having to rehearse arguments, again and again, in a myriad of different ways before you can, for example, persuade a small child to put on their shoes in the morning. And sometimes you have to go along with your small child just not putting on their shoes – and these are all important things to know if you want to be a successful professional. Certainly they are things you find out pretty quickly in the congregational rabbinate. Certainly this is something you find out as Rabbi of this community.

Louis knew he couldn't stand up here and insist that the congregants of New London should keep Shabbat because it said so in the good book. Not only did he need to marshal other arguments, ultimately he needed to realise that people are just not going all fall neatly in line, because people are... people. They are going to behave differently.

In the idiom of a very different kind of a ghetto, being a Rabbi to real people, ensured Louis always 'kept it real.'

Indeed the writing of *We Have Reason to Believe* came as a result of a study group with real congregants, held at the New West End Synagogue. It's a book that owes its origins to the real questions, real concerns and the real beliefs of real people.

Louis' theology was not forged – as Rambam or Rebbe Nachman, thought theologies should be forged – in intellectual or spiritual retreat,[1] transcending finite human concerns and emotions. On the contrary it was forged in the rigmarole of competing congregational needs, in living alongside members as they journey through Rabbinic rituals of hatch, match and dispatch that I recognise so well. I believe that this grounding in congregational life shaped Louis' aversion towards a monopolistic approach to theology – the sort of one-size-should-fit-all approach he loathed.

So what do we have? What is the inheritance of Louis' Torah in this community, the community he served with such distinction, for over four decades?

● The way in which history anatomises and breaks up simple narratives replacing grand sweeps with rigorous analysis. Replacing a sense that 'this is the way it has always been' with an understanding of how things have always been in flux.

● A combination of curiosity, a breadth of engagement, courage, maybe even the arrogance to believe he could make a contribution.

● And a grounding in the individual experience of individuals, a grounding that dissipates any possibility of creating a one-size-fits-all approach to Jewish life.

So where are we now, New London, as a community, in this 50th Jubilee Year?

---

[1] Noting Rambam's desire for intellectual retreat was not, practically, matched in his own life.

Some things remain vital parts of who we have always been. There is still a certain pride, a refusal to back down, a certain arrogance, maybe, that we have something special to offer. Certainly there is still a remarkable breadth of levels of engagement and commitment that makes serving as this community's rabbi such a joyous challenge.

But, as we face our next 50 years I want to share two insights. One based on numbers, the other based on the relationship between theology and change.

When Louis passed away – eight years ago – this was an aging community in decline; leaking members and finances at terrifying rates. When I arrived here, as Rabbi, I brought the average age of Shabbat morning congregants down – sharply.

We were at 330 member units. The Cheder was 15 students and Carmi was the only the child in the non-functioning children's service. We are now some 570 member units. The Cheder is bursting with 100 students and growing. This Rosh Hashanah season we are going to have to erect a tent in the courtyard outside to accommodate the burgeoning children's service. I now bring the average age of Shabbat morning congregants up. That's pretty remarkable.

Or is it? As some of you will know I have a much-loved brother who is Ultra-Orthodox – he lives in Har Nof – and he and I do, as you do, get involved in conversations about Jewish stuff from time to time. Usually our arguments go something like this.

He asks about some element of Masorti practice. And we get in an argument about its textual basis and we trade blows, text against text.

Then we move to the sociological realm. My brother puts this sort of question, 'How many people in your community actually keep Shabbat, or actually come to synagogue three times a day, or actually immerse themselves in Rabbinic study on a daily basis?' And there I run out of blows.

When New London Synagogue gets aggrieved by something – maybe I've given a particularly inflammatory sermon, or God forbid there has been some terrible atrocity perpetrated against our people – I get two or three emails.

When Har Nof gets aggrieved by something – 400,000 turn out

to protest on the streets and the entire capital of Israel can be shut down.

I tweet. I've 400-and-something followers, which sounds OK. Lord, Rabbi Sacks, has some 16,000. Rick Warren, the evangelical American Pastor who gave a blessing to President Obama when he took office, has 1.42million twitter followers. Now that's a twitter presence.

I fight to gain every new member, every child, every soul, I get upset when members have the temerity to leave the country. In the meantime 10,000 turn up weekly at the Belzer Synagogue in Jerusalem. Gevalt, 20,000 turn up weekly at the Church Rick Warren serves in Southern California. This is the greatest weakness of what we have, or haven't accomplished, as a community these past 50 years, when viewed critically, through the lens of Wissenschaft. There just aren't very many of us, at all. Even across the movement. We are a blink of an eye. A good story to tell, but no more than a footnote.

If you are going to be historically rigorous and academically grounded in your analysis of the most important developments in the last 50 years of Anglo-Jewry, the story isn't about us. It's about them. The answer, from a perspective of cool indifference to emotion, is that the ultra-orthodox were right to crank up the drawbridge and leave anyone with a scintilla of heresy in them on the outside.

Evangelism and theological purity, from the perspective of numbers, looks like the right way to go. So much for numbers.

What about the intersection of theology and change? It was my teacher, Rabbi Gordon Tucker, who noted that all theologies come with a price-tag. You pick what you believe – or maybe what you believe picks you – and you have to pay the price.

It's a testament to his integrity and intellectual honesty, that Rabbi Jacobs was prepared to pay the cost of his theology; a theology that couldn't hide from the reality of history and the lived experience of real people. He did that throughout his life, but perhaps the way he paid the price of his theology in his last years is less well known.

In his last significant work, *Beyond Reasonable Doubt*, published in 2004. Rabbi Jacobs gives up on calling himself orthodox. 'It would be ridiculous for someone with my views to lay claim to Othodoxy,' he admits, 'Honesty compels me,' he writes, 'to define my position as Masorti.' In part he claims this is because orthodoxy had shifted radically to behind the drawbridge, and that is certainly true, but I think there is something else.

Over 50 years, I believe, Louis has been contaminated by his engagement in history, and the interaction with real people with their real problems and honestly held heresies. It's seeped into him. In 2004, Rabbi Jacobs admits something he denied in *We Have Reason to Believe*, written almost half a century earlier.

In 2004 Louis writes, 'It is undeniable that a clear recognition of the human development of Jewish practice and observance is bound to produce a somewhat weaker sense of allegiance to the minutiae of Jewish law.' I would agree, in part; weaker allegiance to the minutiae, but not necessarily weaker in terms of meeting God's will for us, God's people.

Here's a story. I was speaking to Rabbi Jackie Tabick, the first woman ordained as Rabbi in the United Kingdom. She was at Leo Baek College doing courses without a view towards ordination, when it was Rabbi Louis Jacobs who, she said, encouraged her to become ordained. I don't mean to make the claim that Louis wanted to be part of a religious community where female Rabbis worked personally, but he believed in the possibility, in the potential, the 'kashrut,' of female Rabbis. On the one hand one can say, 'how terrible that he was contaminated by his experiences of modernity to that extent.' On the other hand one can say, and I do, 'how wonderful, that Louis' sensitivity to humanity in its enormous breadth and in the way the narrative of the human story unfolds from one generation to another, opened his eyes to possibilities not known in the books he knew so well.' I think, there is a place in the evolution of Louis' thought and that of the community he led for so many years, that finds its justification in the lives of its people, not the edict of its books.

And that has always been the case.

There are many new challenges that face us, the issue of egalitarianism principally. Same-sex marriages is another example. We need to face them with a courage to hold both a fidelity to God's will and an understanding of the lived realities of this community.

One last point.

I want to return to the way in which a cool, scientific analysis of the major trend of the last 50 years in world Jewry, and certainly in this country, suggests that the right way to go is to draw up the drawbridge, exclude the heretics, and propagate a pure more fundamentalist approach to religion. The point is that we must never give up.

Rabbi Jacobs never gave up. He never stopped teaching what he believed to be true; even as he apologises in the 5th version of the preface to *We Have Reason to Believe*, for running through this all, one more time. Even as, especially towards the end of his life, he came to believe that British Jewry just was not going to get the sort of nuanced perspective on Jewish life he offered. We also need to refuse to give up.

We need to keep banging the drum, today, perhaps more than ever. We live, increasingly, in a world that likes simple truths and clear distinctions. We live, increasingly, in a world that finds nuance disreputable and contradiction unnerving. We represent a different approach to the nature of truth; one that understands that extremes are, almost by their very nature, to be untrusted, one that understands that truth lies in a tension between tugs between different polarities. We dare not yield ground to those who suggest that the way to truth lies by pursuing extremes. That's horrifyingly dangerous.

As we celebrate our fiftieth year, we remain a community committed to understanding nuance, celebrating the individuality of its members. We remain allergic to oversimplification and a sense that all of us should line up, somehow, in identical columns. These are commitments that are important not only for the future of our own community, but of this poor beaten and bedraggled world. And in this commitment we remain inspired, motivated and enormously grateful for the work of our founder, our Rabbi, my Rabbi, Louis Jacobs, may his memory always be for a blessing.

CHAPTER TEN

Sermons on the Front Page

Rabbi Marshall Meyer, the inspiration behind
Bnei Jeshurun, a community that had a huge
influence on me during my time in New York,
is quoted as saying rabbis should preach with
a Torah in one hand and the New York Times
in the other. That's a bit too newsy for me.
Sometimes, however, there is no choice to be
made about the subject for a sermon – the
front pages demand a rabbinic response.
But on those occasions the challenge is finding
a distinctly Jewish way to engage with
the issue that is being processed 24/7 across
more 'platforms' than there are books in the
Hebrew Bible.

On Politics
{2010}

This is the sermon I gave on the Shabbat before the
2010 General Election.

I'm nervous, whenever I trespass on overtly political
territory. I have some sympathy for those who feel that
synagogues should be places of escape from the cut and
thrust of politics, and party politics most especially. But
Judaism deems nothing foreign from its capacious
interests, and so I do politics.

Shmuly Cohen has passed away and appears before the Ministering Angel in the heavenly court. The Angel checks his paperwork and informs Shmuly that his is an unusual situation. He is to be given a choice between Heaven and Hell.

That's easy, says Shmuly, slightly confused. "I take Heaven."

"Well, says the Angel, "it does say here I have to take you on a tour of both Heaven and Hell before you make your decision.

"Really," says Shmuly, "that's not necessary. I choose Heaven. Of course I choose Heaven."

"I'm sorry", says the Angel, "the tour is compulsory. Hell first."

So Shmuly takes a tour of Hell with a glamourous, charismatic Devil. The music is fabulous. The food is fabulous. There's raucous laughter, scandalous gossip... who knew Hell could be such fun?!!

Goodness, thinks Shmuly, if this is Hell just think how wonderful Heaven will be!

But, frankly, Heaven is a bit dull.

The angelic tour guide is a bit worthy, and too interested in the historic nature of some of the marble carvings.

Shmuly is spotted by the Levins from Stanmore, who want to know if Shmuly would like to make up a foursome for bridge.

Shmuly had never really liked the Levins.

The food is all very ambrosia and nectar – and Shmuly is trying to cut down on sugars.

Shmuly finds himself back at the gates, and the Angel with the clipboard is ready for a decision.

"You know", says Shmuly, "I can hardly believe I'm saying this, but I think I'm going to go for Hell. Yes, Hell. That's my decision."

There is a crack of thunder and Shmuly finds himself chained around the ankle, carrying a sledgehammer and facing a mountain of medium-sized stones which he will have to smash into small stones until the end of time.

Eventually Shmuly gets the attention of one of the supervising Devils and asks what happened to the raucous laughter and fabulous music of the day before.

Oh, says the Devil, yesterday we were campaigning – then you voted.

POLITICS AND RELIGION.

I want a more political religious engagement from this community.

I mean politics in the true sense of term – politics as matters 'of the state and its citizens'. I'm not talking party politics.

We have, of course, just prayed for the welfare of the Government. This is a prayer some 700 years old, and the sentiment is even older. In the second century we have the recorded command of Rabbi Hananya, the Deputy High Priest, who insisted we should 'Pray for the welfare of the Kingdom [=Rome], for were it not for the fear of it, a person would swallow his neighbour alive.' [1]

It is an extraordinary blessing to live in a democracy. And the simple gift of a vote must not be taken for granted. After all, suffrage was only extended to Jewish men in 1867, and it's been a mere 82 years since women in this country were able to vote on the same basis as men.

It's trendy to say religion has no place in politics. But that's nonsense and unfair.

It's nonsense because politics needs to find a rooting in ultimate values somewhere. Without a reference to an ultimate authority, how does one deal with problems raised by the Australian philosopher Peter Singer? Singer believes animals should have the same

---

[1] Mishnah Avot 3:2.

rights as human beings, with all the implications that principled position has for our diet, medical developments and more. Any suggestion of our essential difference from animals is, for Singer, specist – a sort of anti-species brand of racism.

On the radio recently, some professor of media studies suggested that making nature documentaries was an invasion of animal privacy. That's the sort of place you can get into if you don't have a sense of the value of the human as qualitatively different from the animal kingdom. *Sof ma'aseh, b'machshevah techilah*, as the Lecha Dodi puts it – human beings, in the religious imagination, are the pinnacle and purpose of creation. It's not that I don't feel animals have rights and should be protected, but religiously I believe that human beings are different. If you are going to rely on logic alone, I defy you to find a point on which to disagree with Peter Singer – and that's a strange place to be.

It's also unfair to suggest religion should have nothing to do with politics because it refuses to acknowledge the role religions have played in every suffrage movement since the time of the Exodus.

'And God made *adam* – humanity – in God's image, male and female God created them.' *(Genesis 1:26)*

To me this verse contains within its extraordinary depths, the foundation of our conceptions of human rights, democracy and the equality of all people. It was at the heart of the work of René Cassin, the Jew who drafted the UN Declaration on Human Rights. It was at the heart of the work of the suffragists in this country. And it was at the heart of the work of the American Civil Rights movements of the 1960s.

So, what would religion say, if let into the debate? What would happen if we allowed our faith to impact on our politics?

Let me share two ideas, relating to two of the most pressing issues.

IMMIGRATION

I am, of course, a descendant of immigrants to this country – I suspect we all are. My ancestors were economic migrants.

From our own experience we know that it is possible to come to this country, not speaking the language, with no capital, no skills, and become productive members of society. We are or were not looking for handouts, just the possibility of normalising as part of a host society while still remaining distinct in terms of our own identity.

At a recent training I attended with the campaigning organisation London Citizens, I got into a conversation with a 19-year-old Somali Muslim living in London's East End – just round the corner from where my grandparents lived. He wanted to know if I would answer a question he had, and I said, of course. So he asked me why there were so many Jews at the top of media organizations in this country. My hackles rose, of course they did, but I decided not to answer him with an accusation of anti-Semitism. Instead I suggested that the parents of these media titans lived in the very same crummy housing that he now lived in. That they suffered similar levels of hostility, abuse, but they found – through education, family values, the love of storytelling: all factors I believed he shared as a new immigrant to Britain – the ability to develop and grow. We ended up having a conversation about what it means to sit on the edge of a society, and how to use those insights to make a contribution that no more settled viewer can offer.

ECONOMICS

There is a little known mishnah in Kritut that offers a great deal of insight into the rabbinic attitude to economics.[2] In Temple times, for a certain kind of emission women needed to bring a sacrifice of up to five birds. When Rabban Shimon ben Gamliel realised the dealers in birds were running up the prices so each bird cost a whole gold dinar, he swears off sleep until he has solved the problem. He decreed each person can bring one sacrifice only, and the price drops.

This is a mishnah about a centralised governing organisation's response to price-gouging.

Judaism has a moral-based approach to economics, one which recognizes inequalities of production and takes the side of the have-nots.

We have, in Judaism, no rights over the resources we have.

---

[2] 1:7

L'adonai ha'aretz umelo'ah, teaches the book of Psalms – 'God's is the earth and all its fullness.' We are custodians and guardians over that which we possess, placed on earth *l'ovdah ul'shomrah* – 'to work it and to protect it'. Not to exploit it.

Judaism is not a Shabbat-morning-only faith.

Everywhere, our faith looks to force us to consider more carefully our engagement with the *polis*, the society we live in and the resources that are placed in our possession.

Of course, it's not a rabbi's job to be party-specific in how we should vote, but let me try this.

Cast your vote through this lens – the lens of the most important verse in the Bible. 'And God made *adam* in God's image, male and female God created them.'

Which candidate will most protect the notion of the divine image enfolded into each human being?

Which candidate will most advocate that the divine image of each human being is celebrated and vouchsafed?

And we should indeed pray –

Pray for the welfare of the Kingdom, for were it not for the fear of it, a person would swallow his neighbour alive.

Vote well.

Shabbat shalom.

Mandela

{2013}

The death of Nelson Mandela had to be the subject for the sermon on 'that' Shabbat, but with so much being shared, by veteran commentators and those who knew the great man personally, I remember being confused as to what to say until I reread that week's parasha – one part of the Joseph story. The advice of Marshall Meyer, that one should preach from both newspaper and Torah, shouldn't be forsaken, perhaps most especially, when the newspaper is dictating the subject matter.

I want to give a sermon in honour of the passing of a giant in my life, and that of the world. And I'll have a word or two to share about Joseph, another leader who knew darkness and imprisonment and came through that experience of oppression to provide great leadership.

Mandela was in a category of one, an elder to the world, and his life touched mine. I want to share three insights into his life and death.

FAITH

Mandela had great faith.

When I say faith, it's not the classic relationship with God I have in mind. Mandela's faith was complex. Clearly he had great love for Desmond Tutu in particular, but I'm not talking about religious dogma and belief in a particular kind of deity.

True faith is that which exists when the physical corporeal environment gives one nothing to rely on. When all that goes, what is left? What inspires a person to believe in the possibility of a future, in human possibility, when left to rot in a prison cell for more than 20 years?

The thing that is left in the face of utter physical depravity is faith. Faith is the thing that cannot be taken away by oppressors, whether the oppression comes dressed as prison wardens or cancer cells or P45s or anything else.

Faith is that thing we should all pray never to have tested. But it's the thing that keeps us believing even in the darkest of times.

I mentioned Joseph – in the darkness of the pit, in the experience of being sold into slavery, in the experience of being imprisoned because of the false accusation of Potifar's wife, Joseph demonstrated faith. And through his experiences on Robben Island, even through the death of his own son, it's clear that Mandela also demonstrated faith. And that faith is the source of hope and of love, and that faith is the source of what makes us human.

And the greater the faith, the greater the human.

And Mandela's faith was great.

HOW TO LOOK AT A HUMAN BEING

Mandela worked out how to look at a human being and see a creation in the image of God.

Again, I don't want to co-opt Mandela religiously. He had his own way of explaining his life and work. But this is the way I have to talk about the outstanding moral contribution of his life.

Exactly what he did and believed as a young man, I make no claim. But from the time he walked out of those prison gates, he looked at the face of the hated Afrikaner opponents to everything he, Mandela, believed in, and saw humanity.

Maybe that's a little over-romantic. In his autobiography Mandela records how he and those who followed him even in prison worked to befriend the prison wardens. 'Hostility', wrote Mandela, 'was self-defeating. There was no point in having a permanent enemy among the warders.'

But he goes on to say, 'It was ANC policy to try to educate all people, even our enemies; we believed that all men, even prison service warders, were capable of change.'

It's this commitment to the possibility of 'all men, even prison warders' that, surely, explains some of the great acts of leadership in Mandela's earliest days as President of a truly democratic South Africa, wearing the Springbok jersey to the World Rugby Finals, inviting to his inauguration his jailors, his prosecutors and his interrogators.

That's his remarkable moral strength. The strength to live through oppression and refuse to come out hating. The strength to live through the experience of having your humanity stripped from you, and still to believe in the inherent decency and goodness of all humanity.

It takes great strength to fight violence not with violence, but with love. And were it not for that strength, God help us, God help Africa.

There is, perhaps, an equivalence in the story of Joseph.

Joseph has, of course, had a difficult relationship with his brothers, who were prepared to leave him to die, only to decide to sell him into slavery.

In this week's parashah we get the moment Joseph reveals himself to his long-lost family as his brother. And in his first words he seeks to reassure his brothers – don't think I am angry that you sold me into this, for this is all God's doing.

He's able to open his heart and not carry the hate.

This is an extraordinary achievement. And one that, thank goodness, we read of from any number of people who have experienced oppression and rise beyond it.

So many of these moral giants talk of not wanting to carry the hatred as an additional burden. I'm sure that's right. But I don't know how you open a person's heart to see that there is another way beyond the playground battles of he 'hit me, so I'll hit him back'.

Or rather, I know of only one way. It takes a witness.

It takes someone you trust and respect who finds a way to respond to hatred with an open heart. And all of a sudden a different way opens up.

When a person has experience of oppression, their standing and witnessing can change – well, in the case of Mandela it changed a country. It might even have changed a world.

WHERE NOW?

Mandela was no saint. His own life was – just like any other life – sprinkled with foibles and failures. And South Africa remains a country still struggling with its share of strife, inequity and violence.

But maybe that is the point.

Jonathan Freedland, writing earlier in the year, warned of seeing Mandela as a saint, in a way that suggests something 'beyond' what he achieved. Freedland's point was that Mandela's achievements were human achievements, achieved by a human being, just like you or me.

There is no saint coming to make the changes needed in our own post-Mandela world. There is only us, simple human beings, just as Mandela was ultimately human.

Mandela himself, I suspect, understood this perfectly. Tony Blair eulogised Mandela as someone who came to a Labour Party conference after his retirement and introduced himself as an 'out-of-work pensioner with a criminal record.'

I understand that when asked what he wanted his tombstone to read, Mandela replied, 'I would like it to be said, "Here lies a man who has done his duty on Earth". That is all.'

I suspect he said it with a smile on his lips, but he said it knowing his own humanity.

There are rabbinic teachings that make the same point. From Pirkei Avot we learn *Lo alecha hamlecha ligmor, aval lo atah ben horin l'hivatel mimena*: 'You are not required to finish the work, but neither are you free to desist from it.' Mandela certainly did that, and much much more.

Uv'makom she'ain anashim, hishtadel lihiyot ish. 'In a place where there is no humanity, be a human being, an *ish*' – a mentsch. Mandela was certainly a man in a world desperately bereft of men of true faith, morality and courage.

This is the conclusion of Mandela's massive autobiography, *Long Walk to Freedom*. I took my well-thumbed copy of the book back off the shelf this morning.

> When I walked out of prison, that was my mission, to liberate the oppressed and oppressor both. Some say that has now been achieved, but I know that is not the case. The truth is that we are not yet free. We have merely achieved the freedom to be free, the right not to be oppressed. We have not taken the final step of our journey. For to be free is not merely to cast off one's chains, but to live in a way that respects and enhances the freedom of others. The true test of our devotion to freedom is just beginning.

I have walked that long road to freedom. I have tried not to falter. I have made missteps along the way. But I have discovered the secret that after climbing a great hill, one only finds that there are many more hills to climb. I have taken a moment here to rest, to steal a view of the glorious vista that surrounds me, to look back on the distance I have come. But I can rest only for a moment, for with freedom come responsibilities and I dare not linger, for my long walk is not yet ended.

Mandela's death should remind us of the importance of faith, as the source of hope and the source of humanity.

His death should remind us of the importance of seeing every human being as a creation in the image of God, even our enemies. It should serve as a witness to the power of fighting hatred with an open heart and an embrace.

And Mandela's death should remind us that he was only a man, just like you and I, and in his absence, the responsibility to complete his legacy now falls on us all.

May he rest in peace. His memory will always be for a blessing.

Acknowledgements

The cover photograph of unsorted manuscripts from the Jacques Mosseri Genizah Collection at Cambridge University Library is used with the permission of the Syndics of Cambridge University Library. My thanks to Ben Outhwaite of the Genizah Research Unit.

Author photograph by Gary Perlmutter.

Jewish Reflections on War & Peace originally appeared in Arches Quarterly (Vol. 3 Edition 5, 2010) and appears here by permission of The Cordoba Foundation.

Israel – A Case Study in Jewish Discourse and *On Cohanim and Converts* originally appeared in Quest Journal volume 4 & 5 respectively and appear here by permission.

More Theos, Less Ology originally appeared in Jewish Theology In Our Time – A New Generation Explores the Foundations and Future of Jewish Belief (2010) ed. Elliot J. Cosgrove. Permission granted by Jewish Lights Publishing, P.O. Box 237, Woodstock, VT 05091 www.jewishlights.com.

Playing Dice with Einstein, God, and Suffering originally appeared in Conservative Judaism 64.1 (2012) and appears here with the permission of the Rabbinical Assembly.

The Jews of England originally appeared in the Jewish Chronicle, 30th March 2006 and appears here by permission.

What Should a Gay Jew Do? originally appeared in *My Beloved, My Friend: Masorti Conversations on Marriage and Relationships* and appears here by permission.